WORLD MISSION:

An Analysis of the World Christian Movement

The Strategic Dimension

Part Two of a Manual in Three Parts

GENERAL EDITOR: **JONATHAN LEWIS**
Assistant Editors: **John Dubler, Susan Peterson & Pat Roseman**
Illustrators: **John Devine & Dawn Lewis**
Technical Assistants: **Lois Dubler, Ken Hoornbeek & Dick Miller**

WILLIAM CAREY LIBRARY
1705 N. Sierra Bonita Ave.
Pasadena, California 91104
and
THE INSTITUTE OF INTERNATIONAL STUDIES
1605 Elizabeth St.
Pasadena, California 91104

ACKNOWLEDGEMENTS

All of the articles and excerpts in this manual are found in *Perspectives on the World Christian Movement,* (Steven Hawthorne and Ralph Winter, editors, William Carey Library, P.O. Box 40129, Pasadena, CA 91104). We are heavily indebted to the editors of this mission anthology for their encouragement in the production of this course. We would especially like to thank Dr. Ralph Winter for his inspiration and genius in the organization of much of this material, and recognize his tireless work on behalf of the unreached peoples.

All the articles in this manual have been used by permission of the current copyright holders.

PART II - THE STRATEGIC DIMENSION

	Page
CHAPTER 6 HISTORY AND STRUCTURE	1
I. The Strategic Dimension	2
II. History of Mission Strategy	8
III. Two Structures of Expansion	24
CHAPTER 7 THE TASK REMAINING	39
I. The Nations and Cross-Cultural Evangelization	39
II. Unreached People: Five Megaspheres	50
III. Hindu, Muslim, and Tribal Megaspheres	57
CHAPTER 8 TO REACH THE UNREACHED	73
I. The Four Strategies of Missions	74
II. People Movements	82
III. The Unique Solution Strategy	90
CHAPTER 9 EVANGELISM, DEVELOPMENT, AND CHURCH PLANTING	107
I. Evangelism	108
II. Development	119
III. Church Planting	129
CHAPTER 10 WORLD CHRISTIAN TEAMWORK	149
I. Teaming Up With God	150
II. Teaming Up With God's People	162
III. Worldwide Christian Teamwork	175

ORGANIZATION AND USE OF THIS MANUAL

WORLD MISSION: An Analysis of the World Christian Movement, is a manual that can be used by study groups in a formal or informal educational setting. The manual is in three parts; each being a separate unit. **Part One,** *The Biblical/Historical Foundation,* examines the roots of world mission, its origin and its development throughout the ages. **Part Two,** *The Strategic Dimension,* defines the remaining mission task and the strategies necessary to reach the unreached. **Part Three,** *Cross-Cultural Considerations,* explores the challenge of cross-cultural communication of the gospel.

Each one of the fifteen chapters of the manual is divided into three study units. Each unit develops a distinct concept and relates it to the material studied in preceding units. Questions interspersed throughout the text direct the reader's attention to key points and stimulate reflection on the readings.

Each chapter ends with two sections of questions. The first section, *Integrative Assignment,* is designed to help the reader assimilate the material studied. The questions invite the student to further research and encourage the development of his abilities to communicate what is learned. Study groups should use these questions for group discussion. In Part Two of the manual, an "Unreached Peoples" research project is incorporated into the *Integrative Assignment.* This fascinating project will require extra time and effort from the student. The second section, *Questions for Reflection,* asks for a response to personal and spiritual issues raised by the readings. We recommend that each student enter his thoughts in a personal diary and that a devotional time be provided during each group session to share these comments.

CHAPTER 6

History and Structures

INTRODUCTION

Seen from a mission perspective, history reveals itself in a unique and refreshing way. The kingdom of our Lord plays the major role in history's unfolding drama, rather than the kingdoms of this world. God's purpose to redeem a people and reestablish His rule upon the earth is the central plot, as revealed in the Bible. In unfolding this plot, the Bible details the exciting story of how God defeated His enemies by raising Jesus Christ from the dead, and it provides an outline for what is to come. The disciples of Jesus Christ are to act as God's agents in establishing His kingdom throughout the earth. They are to carry the liberating good news of Christ's victory over sin, Satan, and death to the ends of the earth.

As noted in the preceding chapter, the "ten epochs" of mission history reveal that God's people have seldom been willing agents of the kingdom. God frequently has had to carry out His purposes through exile, dispersion, persecution, and invasion. Yet, from time to time, movements and structures have appeared which have motivated believers to carry out God's mission purpose voluntarily as well. When God's people willingly have set out to fulfill their obligation to share the gospel with the nations, God has greatly blessed those efforts.

Such has been Protestant involvement in world mission. Although only in the last two centuries have Protestants taken their responsibility for world evangelization seriously, phenomenal growth and expansion have taken place. This growth has been categorized into three distinct "eras" of expansion. The first era was marked by an awakening of Protestants to the task, and the sending of missionaries to the coastal areas of the unreached continents. The second era saw a movement towards the unreached interiors of Asia and Africa. The third era, which has just begun, is characterized by a movement towards unreached people groups. Most of these groups are no longer isolated geographically from the gospel but are isolated instead by social, cultural, and linguistic barriers. These barriers have effectively prevented these "hidden peoples" from hearing and receiving the gospel even though geographically another cultural expression of the church may exist nearby.

This third era of expansion will require tens of thousands of new cross-cultural missionaries with a clear understanding of the missionary task. Nothing short of a massive Spirit-filled movement of God will see the penetration of the gospel among the estimated 16,750 culturally distinct groups left to be evangelized. Although traditionally the vast majority of missionaries have been sent from North America and Europe, the rise of nationalism in the developing countries, along with a false assumption that the missionary task is now complete, has led to a decline of mission personnel from the traditional sending bases.

God can reverse this trend. But in the meantime, a vital new force in world mission is emerging. The vigorous young churches of the developing countries are beginning to send out hundreds of missionaries to other cultural groups both within and beyond their own borders. Some missiologists are predicting that these new cross-cultural missionaries will play the most significant part in meeting the challenge of the third and final era of mission history. This is an exciting prospect, but one which can only be realized if the lessons from mission history can be learned and serious mistakes avoided.

This dynamic new force for world evangelization cannot afford to ignore the past in its present zeal for mission. A naive urge to "reinvent the wheel" will only lead to repeating the mistakes of the past out of ignorance or simplistic optimism. Existing mission structures need to be evaluated on the basis of their strategic worth to world evangelization, not on negative biases that may be held toward them. In addition, the many valuable lessons in mission strategy which have been learned over the centuries cannot be ignored. Let us hope that in our enthusiasm we do not "toss out the rice with the chaff."

I. THE STRATEGIC DIMENSION

In this second part of this manual, we will examine the strategic dimension of mission. Because strategy is not always defined uniformly, it is important that we arrive at a comfortable working definition before we go any further.

When relating strategy to God's work, Christians tend to think of the former as conflicting with the spontaneous leading of God's Spirit. If this were true, a discussion of strategy would be useless. But we are convinced that strategy, when properly understood and implemented, can work in perfect harmony with God's leading. We are aware of the dangers of merely applying human intelligence to the mission task, for "unless the Lord builds the house, they labor in vain that build it" (Ps. 127:1). But to deny the intelligent application of biblical mission principles which have emerged during the course of history is to deny the use of one of man's greatest assets, that is, the use of his intelligence for God's glory and the expansion of His kingdom.

Consider again the parable of the talents in Matthew 25:14-30. Each servant was entrusted with a certain amount of money, and each one was expected to invest that money for the master's gain. The unfaithful servant was not condemned for squandering his talent, but for failing to develop even the simplest investment strategy (such as putting the money in the bank), so that he could see growth for his master. The other two servants used their investment skill, doubled their money, and were received "into the joy of [their] master" (Matt. 25:21, 23). It is this very matter of "investment skill" with which mission strategy deals.

Peter Wagner, Professor of Church Growth at Fuller School of World Mission, defines strategy as follows: "Strategy is the means agreed on to reach a certain goal. Missionary strategy is the way the body of Christ goes about obeying the Lord and accomplishing the objectives He lays down."[1]

Wagner goes on to challenge the reader regarding the use of strategy:

> I contend that every Christian every day uses strategy of some kind or other in the attempt to do God's will. I also contend that some strategies are demonstrably superior to others, and that we do poorly if we do not examine them all and choose the best.[2]

---

[1]C. Peter Wagner, *Stop the World, I Want to Get On* (Glendale, CA: Regal Books, 1974), p. 76.

[2]Wagner, p.76.

He then gives three criteria by which strategy can be evaluated:

> The best strategy is, first of all, biblical because God's work must be done in God's way. Secondly, it is efficient. Since our personnel, money, and time are all limited, we need to make decisions sooner or later as to what priorities to assign in their use. We can't do everything we would like to do, so we must on the basis of efficiency--do what will best accomplish God's objective. Third, strategy must be relevant. Missions is such a fast-moving field that strategy useful five years ago might well be obsolete today. It needs constant updating.[3]

1. If Wagner is right in what he says, what should every Christian who attempts a work for Christ do?

_____

_____

Others who have written extensively on mission strategy are Edward R. Dayton and David A. Fraser. In the following article,[4] they define the term, present a rationale for the use of strategy, and evaluate some approaches to mission strategy.

Strategy

Edward R. Dayton and David A. Fraser[5]

In one sense everyone and every organization has a strategy or strategies, a way of approaching a problem or achieving a goal. Most organizations do this quite unconsciously, others have developed their strategies into almost standard approaches. The apostle Paul had a strategy. We read in Acts 17:2 that on the Sabbath Paul went into the synagogue *as was his custom*. Paul's strategy was to move to a major city, visit the synagogue if there was one, proclaim Jesus, and then let events take their natural course.

A strategy is an overall approach, plan, or way of describing how we will go about reaching our goal or solving our problem. It is not concerned with details. Paul's ultimate goal was that Christ should be preached throughout the world. His day-to-day plans would differ, but at least in the beginning of his missionary journeys, his strategy remained the same.

Unfortunately, strategy means different things to different people. It was originally used as a military term meaning an overall approach, unlike the detailed approach of "tactics." In a military sense, both strategy and tactics mean "how one goes about

---

[3]Wagner, pp. 76-77.

[4]Edward R. Dayton and David A. Fraser, *Planning Strategies for World Evangelization* (Grand Rapids: Wm. B. Eerdmans Publishing Co., 1980), pp. 15-19. Used by permission.

[5]Edward R. Dayton is Vice-President for Missions and Evangelism with World Vision International. He is the founder of World Vision's Missions and Advance Research and Communications Center (MARC) and has written extensively on management and mission strategy. David A. Fraser is a research associate for the Mission Training and Resource Center in Pasadena, California, and has taught at Columbia Bible College in Columbia, South Carolina.

things" rather than the idea of plans. This should not surprise us since the military strategist always has to assume that there is another military strategist trying to imagine his opponent's strategy. In other words, the military strategist has to take into account the many possible moves of his opponent. Thus his strategy has to include many options. However, although strategy can include a wide range of "means and methods," "contingency plans," and various "operations," it can also exclude a wide range of options. It has a great deal to say about what will *not be done*.

Strategy is a way to reach an objective, a time and place when things will be different than they are now. For the military it might be capturing a key town or city. For the businessperson it might mean achieving a desired volume in a particular market. For a Christian organization it may mean everything from deciding what country to serve in to the overall approach to reaching a particular group of people.

Strategy, then, has a much broader scope than long-range or major plans.

2. Define and contrast the terms "strategy" and "tactics".

_____

_____

_____

WHY HAVE A STRATEGY?

As Christians, a strategy forces us to seek the mind of God and the will of the Holy Spirit. What does God desire? How can we conform to the future that He desires?

Strategy is an attempt to anticipate the future. Strategy, like plans and goals, is our *statement of faith* as to what we believe the future should be like and how we should go about reaching that future.

Strategy is a way of communicating our intention to others. It helps us to communicate with one another within our own organization as well as with other Christians, organizations, and churches.

Strategy gives us an overall sense of direction and cohesiveness. It also helps us in deciding what we will *not* do, for it excludes certain ways of doing things. For example, on a worldwide basis, we might decide to work primarily with people who are very receptive. This excludes for the moment all non-receptive people.

3. According to the authors, why is planning strategy a spiritual exercise?

_____

_____

4. Why is strategy important to communication with others?

_____

_____

5. Why does strategy give us an overall sense of direction?

_____

_____

_____

TYPES OF STRATEGIES

There are many different approaches to strategies. We will discuss four: the Standard Solution Strategy, the Being-in-the-Way Strategy, the Plan-So-Far Strategy, and the Unique Solution Strategy.

The Standard Solution Strategy works out a particular way of doing things, then uses this same approach in every situation. An example would be the approach of World Literature Crusade (also known as the Every Home Crusade), which attempts to put a piece of Christian literature in the hands of people in every home in every city in the world. Members of this crusade assume that everyone can read and that everyone can make a decision for Christ if they are exposed to the right kind of literature.

Evangelism-in-Depth, which was first begun in Latin America, is an example of a standard country-wide strategy which was used in a number of different countries in Latin America. It was eventually adapted for Africa as New Life for All.

The problem with the Standard Solution Strategy is, first, that there is a tendency not to take into account what others are doing. Because this strategy has a standard solution, it assumes that the problems are standard. Second, a standard strategy usually assumes that everyone will participate and understand what the strategy is. Obviously this does not always work. Third, a standard strategy usually grows out of one culture and has more and more difficulty as it moves into new contexts.

The Being-in-the-Way Strategy at first appears to be no strategy at all. People who adopt this strategy believe that it is not necessary to plan. They have no specific intentions about the future. They assume that God will lead. The implications of this strategy are that long-range planning is not very important because this is God's job. This strategy also eliminates failure because that is God's problem. Many times it labels everything it accomplishes as "success." It also runs into the problem of consensus; if two or more people or organizations are each using a Being-in-the-Way Strategy, they may be in *each other's way*. This strategy is usually adopted when emphasis is placed on the basic need for a deeper personal spirituality. It is assumed that if this deeper spirituality occurs, evangelism will take care of itself.

There is much to be said for this strategy. One could point to the evangelist Philip in the book of Acts, who was certainly led by the Lord into new situations. In the early days of the faith missions, particularly the inland missions, such as the China Inland Mission, the Africa Inland Mission, and the Sudan Interior Mission, missionaries courageously took the gospel into unknown continents. They knew that they had a goal. They often did not know what they were going to encounter.

Often it was disease and death. We need to honor these earlier missionaries who laid the foundations for modern-day missionary journeys.

A third strategy is the Plan-So-Far Strategy. This assumes that we will plan to begin the work, and God will do the rest. This strategy does not focus on outcomes, but on beginnings. It assumes that "once we're there," God will do the rest. An example would be the agency that after negotiations with a local government received permission to begin a craft industry in a country. However, the agency made no specific plans as to how it would relate to the Christian churches that were already in the country, churches that in their view were a mixture of Christianity and animism.

At first glance it would appear that the Plan-So-Far Strategy, as well as the Being-in-the-Way Strategy, requires greater faith. Deeper reflection will reveal, however, that it takes considerably more faith to understand what God wants to happen in a particular situation and to make a commitment to bring about what one believes God intends.

The Unique Solution Strategy assumes that every situation we face is different, that each one requires its own special strategy. It assumes that we can find a way, that there is an answer. It assumes that we should make statements of faith (set goals) about the future. It assumes that standard solutions probably will not work. We believe that there are some approaches that can be used to discover God's strategy for each unique situation.

As Christians we have a tremendous advantage in considering strategy. Because we have the Word of God, a source of ultimate values and absolutes, we can most appropriately develop grand strategies. God has ordained the means as well as those who will be saved. We can rest in the confidence that God's will will be done. Our role is to cooperate with Him in bringing His kingdom to fruition.

6. The authors have pointed out the weaknesses in some approaches to strategy. List four major weaknesses of the first three strategies and suggest how you might counter those weaknesses in your own approach to strategy.

Strategy Weakness	Counter to Weakness

1._____

2._____

3._____

4._____

In the preceding excerpts Wagner, Dayton, and Fraser have helped clarify the concept of mission strategy. They have pointed out that all Christians have a strategy by which they operate, whether they are conscious of it or not. Strategy was defined as the way we approach the task that God has given us to do. Since some strategies are better than others, it is wise to examine the strategies of others in determining how best to approach the task God has given each of us.

We have seen that setting forth a strategy is not an "unspiritual" activity but rather one which has a sincere seeking of the will of God as its foundation. Much of God's will is already revealed to us in His Word. How to fulfill that will within a specific framework will require the use of our intelligence. It will also drive us to our knees. Prayer and strategy are inseparably linked in effective mission.

We must pray as if we could not plan, and plan as if we could not pray.

II. HISTORY OF MISSION STRATEGY

"Therefore every scribe who has become a disciple of the kingdom of heaven is like a head of a household, who brings forth out of his treasure things new and old" (Matt. 13:52).

In formulating our own strategy, it is important to see how mission strategy has developed and to note success factors as well as actions which have led to failure. This evaluation should help us to determine what to attempt as well as what to avoid in our mission strategy.

In the following article,[6] Professor R. Pierce Beaver outlines a history of mission strategy. As you read each section, note the distinctives which mark the strategy of each period.

The History of Mission Strategy

R. Pierce Beaver[7]

Fifteen centuries of missionary action preceded the rise of Protestant world mission. Therefore, Protestant missionary action did not begin *de novo* , and with modern Roman Catholic theory makes up only the last chapter of a long story. These pages will present a capsule history of mission strategy before the rise of Protestant efforts, briefly trace the course of Protestant strategy, and unfortunately for lack of space, completely omit reference to modern Roman Catholic missions.

---

[6]R. Pierce Beaver, "The History of Mission Strategy," *Southwestern Journal of Theology 12* (Spring 1970), pp. 7-28. Used by permission.

[7]R. Pierce Beaver is Professor Emeritus from the University of Chicago. He has specialized in the history of missions in America and was for 15 years a formative director of the Missionary Research Library in New York City. Beaver is the author of, among other books, *All Loves Excelling*, a description of the initiatives of American women in world evangelization.

BONIFACE

The first instance of a well-developed mission strategy in the 20th century understanding of the term, is that employed in the English mission to the continent of Europe by Boniface in the eighth century. Boniface preached to Germanic pagans in a language so akin to their own that they could understand. He did use aggression: he defied their gods, demolished their shrines, cut down the sacred trees, and built churches on holy sites. But he made converts and educated and civilized them. He founded monasteries which not only had academic schools but programs which taught people agriculture, grazing, and domestic arts. This made possible a settled society, a well-grounded church, and good Christian nurture. Into a second line of educational and domestic science institutions Boniface brought nuns from England. This is the first time that women were formally and actively enlisted in mission work. Clergy and monks were recruited from the people. All of this activity was supported by the church back "home" in England. Boniface sent reports and requests. He discussed strategy with people back home. The bishops, monks, and sisters in turn sent Boniface personnel, money, and supplies. They also undergirded the mission with intercessory prayer.

Unhappily such a true sending mission ceased to exist because of the ravages which invaders wreaked on the people of England. Mission on the Continent became too much an instrument of imperial expansion, both political and ecclesiastical, for it was employed by the Frankish kings, their German successors, the Byzantine emperor, and the Pope. Consequently the Scandinavian kings kept out missionaries from the Continent and in the evangelization of their countries used English missionaries who were their own subjects or had no political connections.

THE CRUSADES

The series of European wars against the Muslims, called the Crusades, can hardly be considered a form of true mission. They made mission to Muslims almost impossible down to the present because they left an abiding heritage of hatred in Islamic lands. Yet even before the Crusades had ended, Francis of Assisi had gone in love to preach to the sultan and had created a missionary force which would preach in love and in peace. Ramon Lull, the great Franciscan tertiary, gave up his status as a noble high in the court of Aragon and devoted his life to mission to Muslims as "the Fool of Love." He would convince and convert by reason, using the instrument of debate. To this end he wrote his *Ars Magna*, which was intended to answer convincingly any question or objection which could be put by Muslim or pagan, and devised a kind of intellectual computer into which the various factors could be registered and the right answer would come forth. Lull for many decades before his martyrdom ceaselessly begged popes and kings to establish colleges for the teaching of Arabic and other languages and for the training of missionaries and urged upon them many schemes for sending missionaries abroad.

1. What were the prominent features of Boniface's strategy?

_____

_____

_____

2. What is the main lesson in strategy to be learned from the Crusades?

_____

_____

COLONIAL EXPANSION

It was in the period of the 16th to 18th centuries that Christianity actually became a worldwide religion in connection with the expansion of the Portuguese, Spanish, and French empires. When the Pope divided the non-Christian lands of the earth already discovered or yet to be discovered between the crowns of Portugal and Spain, he laid upon the monarchs the obligation to evangelize the peoples of those lands, to establish the church, and to maintain it. Mission was thus made a function of government.

The Portuguese built a trade empire and, except in Brazil, held only small territories under direct rule. There they suppressed the ethnic religions, drove out the upper class who resisted, and created a Christian community composed of their mixed-blood descendants and converts from the lower strata of society.

Spain, on the other hand, endeavored to transplant Christianity and civilization, both according to the Spanish model. Ruthless exploitation killed off the Carib Indians and stimulated the heroic struggle for the rights of the remaining Indians by Bartholome de las Casas and other missionaries. Since then protection of primitive people against exploitation by whites and by colonial governments has been an important function of missions. After that mighty effort abolished slavery and forced baptism, the missionaries were made both the civilizers and protectors of the Indians. A mission would be established on a frontier with a central station about which a town was gathered and Indians brought into permanent residence. There was usually a small garrison of soldiers to protect both missionaries and Christian Indians. Satellite stations, smaller towns, were connected with the central one. The Indians were taught by catechists and supervised by priests in the cultic life of the church. They were actively enlisted in participation, serving as acolytes, singers, and musicians. Folk festivals were Christianized, and the Christian feasts and fasts were introduced. Indian civil officers performed a wide range of supervisory functions under the careful oversight of the missionaries. Farms and ranches were developed, and the Indians were taught all aspects of grazing and agriculture. Thus the Indians were preserved, civilized, and Christianized, not killed off or displaced as would later be the case in the United States. Unfortunately, when the government decided that the missions had civilized the Indians, the missions were "secularized;" the missionaries were replaced by diocesan clergy usually of low quality and too few in number; regular government officers came in as rulers in place of the missionaries and lacking their love for the people; the lands were parceled out among Spanish settlers; and the Indians were gradually reduced to peonage.

French policy in Canada was the opposite of the Spanish. Only a small colony was settled to be a base for trade and a bulwark against the English. The French wanted the furs and other products of the forests and consequently disturbed Indian civilization as little as possible. The missionaries had to develop a strategy consonant with this policy. Therefore, they lived with the Indians in their villages, adapting to conditions as well as they could, preaching, teaching, baptizing individuals, performing the rites of the church, allowing the converts still to be Indians. Some permanent towns with church and school were founded on the borders of French settlements, but most of the inhabitants were transients.

On the other side of the globe in what was to become French Indochina, now Vietnam, where the region came under French rule only much later, a radical new evangelistic strategy was devised by Alexander de Rhodes. This was necessary because the French missionaries were persecuted and expelled from the region for long periods. Evangelization could only be achieved by native agents. Rhodes created an order of native lay evangelists living under rule who won converts by the thousands. Stimulated by this experience, Rhodes and his associates founded the Foreign Mission Society of Paris, dedicated to the policy of recruiting and training a diocesan clergy, who would be the chief agents in the evangelization of the country and the pastoral care of the churches, rather than missionaries. It was a policy marked by outstanding success.

3. How did Spanish and French strategies in the New World differ?

_____

_____

_____

4. What radical new evangelistic strategy was devised by the French in Indochina?

_____

_____

MISSION STRATEGISTS OF THE 17TH CENTURY

The first modern mission theorists appeared in the 17th century in connection with this great expansion of the faith, including Jose de Acosta, Brancati, and Thomas a Jesu. They wrote manuals of missionary principles and practice, described the qualifications of missionaries, and told them how to work with the people. In 1622 there was created in Rome the Sacred Congregation for the Propagation of the Faith which henceforth gave central direction to Roman Catholic missions and established colleges or institutes for the training of missionaries.

The great and courageous innovators in this period were the Jesuits who went to the Orient through Portuguese channels but defied Portuguese restrictions. They were of many nationalities. These were the modern pioneers in accommodation, acculturation, adaptation, or indigenization, whatever one may wish to call it. The first venture was in Japan where the missionaries adopted Japanese houses, costume, most customs, and the etiquette of social intercourse. They did not, however, make use of Shinto and Buddhist terms and concepts, forms, or rites in presentation of the gospel and establishing the church. They did make great use of the Japanese language in production of Christian literature printed on the mission press by Japanese converts. The heaviest burden in evangelism and teaching was borne by native deacons and catechists. A few were admitted to the priesthood. A large Christian community soon came into being. When the Shogun, fearing foreign aggression, closed Japan to all outsiders and persecuted Christianity in the 17th century, many thousands suffered martyrdom. Christianity went underground and endured until Japan was opened to Western intercourse two centuries later.

A second experiment at Madurai in South India went much farther. Robert de Nobili believed that the Brahmin caste must be won if Christianity were to succeed in India. Consequently he became a Christian Brahmin. He dressed like a *guru* or religious teacher, observed the caste laws and customs, and learned Sanskrit. De Nobili studied the major schools of Hindu philosophy and presented Christian doctrine as much as possible in Hindu terms. He is one of the very few evangelists who won many Brahmin converts.

The most noted attempt at accommodation was in China, where the strategy was set by Matteo Ricci and developed by his successors as head of the mission, Schall and Verbiest. Just as in Japan, the missionaries adopted the national way of life and fundamentals of Chinese civilization, but they went much farther and gradually introduced Christian principles and doctrine through the use of Confucian concepts. They permitted converts to engage in ancestral and state rites, regarding these as social and civil rather than religious in character. The missionaries gained tremendous influence as mathematicians, astronomers, cartographers, and masters of various sciences, thus introducing Western learning to the Chinese, making friendships with influential persons, and finding opportunities personally to present the faith. They served the emperor in many capacities. All of this had one purpose--to open the way for the gospel. Success crowned the strategy, and a large Christian community developed, including influential persons in high places.

Other missionaries, however, were unable to appreciate anything that was not European and were absolutely wedded to traditional Roman Catholic terminology and practices. Motivated by nationalistic and party jealousies, they attacked the Jesuits and laid charges against them in Rome. Ultimately Rome pronounced against the Jesuits' principles, banned their practices, and required that all missionaries going to the Orient take an oath to abide by that ruling. Christians were forbidden to practice family and state rites. It was henceforth impossible for any Christian to be a genuine Chinese and a Christian simultaneously. The profession of the Christian faith appeared to strike at the root of filial piety, which was the very foundation of Chinese society. Two centuries later the oath was abolished and modified rites permitted. The Jesuits lost the battle but ultimately won the war. Today almost all missionaries of all churches acknowledge the necessity of accommodation or indigenization.

5. What were the main innovations the Jesuits brought to mission strategy?

_____

_____

_____

NEW ENGLAND PURITANS: MISSIONS TO THE AMERICAN INDIANS

The participation of Protestants in world mission began early in the 17th century simultaneously with the evangelistic work of the chaplains of the Dutch East Indies Company and the New England missions to the American Indians. Mission was a function of the commercial company, but many of its chaplains were genuine missionaries. They had little influence on later mission strategy, but it was the Puritan missions to the red men that would provide the missions of a later day with inspiration and models. The aim of the missionaries was so effectively to preach the gospel that the Indians would be converted, individually receive salvation, and be gathered into churches where they would be nurtured in the faith under strict discipline. The intention was to make of the Indian a Christian man of the same type and character as the English Puritan member of a gathered Congregationalist church. This involved civilizing the Indian according to the British model.

Evangelism was the first item in the strategy. Preaching was the "grand means," supplemented by teaching. Most missionaries followed John Eliot in beginning with public preaching, although Thomas Mayhew, Jr., was very successful at Martha's Vineyard in beginning with a slow, individual, personal approach. Heavily doctrinal sermons stressing the wrath of God and the pains of hell, just like those given an English congregation, were addressed to the Indians. But David Brainerd, who like the Moravians preached the love of God rather than His wrath, was extremely effective in moving men and women to repentance.

The second point of the strategy was to gather the converts into churches, but the new Christians were at first put through long years of probation before the first churches were organized. On the contrary, when the second phase of the Indian mission opened in the 1730's, this delay was no longer required, and the churches were speedily gathered and organized. Both before and after the organization of the churches, the converts were being instructed and disciplined in the faith.

A third strategic emphasis was the establishment of Christian towns. John Eliot and his colleagues in the mission believed that segregation and isolation were necessary to the converts' growth in grace. They must be removed from the baneful influence of their pagan brethren and of bad white men. It was thought that in purely Christian towns of "Praying Indians" the new members could live together under the strict discipline and careful nurture of the white missionaries and Indian pastors and teachers. This would insure what Cotton Mather called "a more decent and English way of living." Christianization and civilization would be simultaneous and indistinguishable. Eliot put his towns under a biblical form of government based on Exodus 18, but the General Court of Massachusetts, which gave the land and built the church and school, appointed English commissioners over the towns in 1658. Within the towns the Indians did live together under a covenant between them and the Lord, and both personal and community life were regulated by laws of a biblical flavor.

Most of the towns of the Praying Indians did not survive the devastation of King Philip's War in 1674, but the strategy of the special Christian town was again followed when John Sergeant established the Stockbridge mission in 1734. Stockbridge was not so closed a place as those earlier towns. There was constant movement between town and forest, even to great distances. Stockbridge Christians could, therefore, be evangelistic agents in their natural relationships.

Whatever may have been achieved in the development of Christian character in the early towns, no evangelistic influence could be exerted by the inhabitants, cut off as they were from other Indians. Throughout the 19th and early 20th centuries missionaries to primitive people in Africa and the isles would continue to be enamored of the idea of guaranteeing the purity of the converts' faith and conduct by segregating them in separate Christian villages or wards. The usual effect was to alienate the Christians from their people, to create a "mongrel" kind of society, neither native nor European, and to prevent any evangelistic impact on others. A separated people cannot pass on the contagion of personal faith.

At the center of each town or mission station was a church flanked by a school house. Sermons on Sunday and in prayer meetings, catechization, and general elementary education all tended to nurture the convert in faith and civilization.

John Eliot's *Indian Catechism* was the first book ever to be published in an American Indian language. Both the vernacular and the English language were used. The English would enable the Indian better to adjust to white society, but his own tongue was more effective in imparting an understanding of Christian truth. Eliot produced textbooks in both languages. Reading, writing, and simple arithmetic were taught along with Bible study and religious instruction. Agricultural and domestic crafts were also introduced so that support in a settled and civilized way of life might be possible. In the second century of the mission, strategic considerations led John Sergeant to introduce the boarding school, so that youths could be entirely separated from the old life and brought up in the new. This institution, too, would become a primary strategic resource of the missions in the 19th century.

It is to the credit of the New England Puritans that they never doubted the transforming power of the gospel nor the potential ability of the Indians. They expected that some of them at least could attain the same standard as Englishmen. Therefore, more than the rudimentary schooling of the towns was required. Some promising youths were sent to the Boston Latin Grammar School, and a few were placed in the Indian College at Harvard College. Sergeant's boarding school at Stockbridge and Eleazer Wheelock's school at Lebanon, Connecticut, were better conceived efforts at a higher degree of education.

Worship, spiritual nurture, and education all demanded a vernacular literature of rather broad dimensions. Eliot produced the Massachusetts Bible and a library of other literature, to which a few of his colleagues added.

Absolutely fundamental to the entire plan of New England mission strategy was the recruiting and training of native pastors and teachers. Both the missionaries and their supporters realized that only native agents could effectively evangelize and give pastoral care to their people. In 1700 there were 37 Indian preachers in Massachusetts. Unfortunately, the old Christian Indian towns declined under continuing white pressure, and with them the supply of ministers and teachers also declined to the vanishing point.

Perhaps the most lasting effects of the Indian missions of the 17th and 18th centuries were two: first, they inspired numerous missionary vocations in a later day as men read the lives of Eliot and Brainerd; and second, they endowed the great overseas Protestant enterprise with its initial strategic program. This included evangelism through preaching, organization of churches, education aimed at Christian nurture and the attainment of civilization in European terms, Bible translation, literature production, use of the vernacular language, and the recruitment and training of native pastors and teachers.

6. What were the three main points of strategy developed by the Puritans?

_____

_____

_____

7. What was the primary strategic weakness of the Indian Christian towns?

_____

_____

THE DANISH-HALLE MISSION

The American missions to the indigenous population had been supported by missionary societies organized in England and Scotland, but missionaries had not been sent from Britain. The first sending mission from Europe was the Danish-Halle Mission. Beginning in 1705 the King of Denmark sent German Lutheran missionaries to his colony of Tranquebar on the southeast coast of India. The pioneer leader, Bartholomew Ziegenbalg, developed a strategy which was bequeathed to later generations of missionaries, although in some respects he was far ahead of his time. He stressed worship, preaching, catechization, education, translation work, and the production of vernacular literature. He blazed a trail in the study of Hindu philosophy and religion, discerning the great importance of such knowledge for evangelization and church growth, but the authorities in Germany decried such activity. This mission early added medical work to its program. It also pioneered in the use of Tamil lyrics in worship.

The most famous of the Halle missionaries after Ziegenbalg was one of the last, Christian Frederick Schwartz, who spent his life in ministry in the British-controlled portion of south India. He had a remarkable influence with Indians of all religions and with Europeans of several nationalities, both troops and civilians. His strategy was unique and unplanned. Although still a European to all appearances, Schwartz actually became in effect a *guru* or spiritual teacher, loved and trusted by all. Persons of all religions and castes could gather around him as his disciples regardless of the difference in their status. His ministry was essentially a remarkable kind of adaptation or accommodation to the culture.

MORAVIAN MISSIONS

The most distinctive strategy developed in the 18th century was that of the Moravian Church developed under the direction of Count Zinzendorf and Bishop Spangenberg. The Moravian missionaries, beginning in 1734, were purposely sent to the most despised and neglected people. These missionaries were to be self-supporting. That emphasis led to the creation of industries and business concerns which not only supported the work but brought the missionaries into intimate contact with the people. Such self-support could not be undertaken among the American Indians, however, and consequently communal settlements, such as Bethlehem in Pennsylvania and Salem in North Carolina, were founded with a wide range of crafts and industries, the profits of which supported the mission.

Moravian missionaries were told not to apply "the Herrnhut yardstick" (i.e., German home base standards) to other peoples and to be alert to the recognition of the God-given distinctive traits, characteristics, and strong points of those people. Furthermore, the missionaries were to regard themselves as assistants to the Holy Spirit. They were to be primarily messengers, evangelists, preachers, who were not to stress heavy theological doctrines but rather tell the simple gospel story of God's loving act of reconciliation of men to Himself in Christ our Savior, who lived and died for all men. In God's providence the time would come when the Holy Spirit would bring converts into the church in large numbers. Meanwhile the missionary messengers would gather the first fruits. If there should be no response they were to go elsewhere. Actually the missionaries left only when persecuted and driven out. They were remarkably patient and did not give up readily.

8. What distinctive did Ziegenbalg bring to mission strategy which was deployed so well by Schwartz?

    _____

    _____

    _____

9. What strategic emphasis led the Moravians to create businesses and industries, and what two advantages were gained through this practice?

    _____

    _____

    _____

THE GREAT CENTURY OF PROTESTANT MISSIONS

Out of all these earlier beginnings there came the great Protestant missionary overseas enterprise of the 19th century. It took initial form in Britain with the founding of the Baptist Missionary Society by William Carey in 1792. Organization had begun in the United States in 1787, and a score of societies came into being, all having a worldwide objective. However, the frontier settlements and the Indians absorbed all their resources. At length a student movement in 1810 broke the deadlock and launched the overseas mission through the formation of the American Board of Commissioners for Foreign Missions. The Triennial Convention of the Baptist Denomination for Foreign Missions was next organized in 1814, followed in 1816 by the United Foreign Mission Society.

The new societies and boards began their work with the strategic presuppositions and methods inherited from the American Indian missions and the Danish-Halle Mission. For many years the directors at home thought that they understood fully how the mission was to be carried out, and detailed instructions were handed each missionary when he sailed. After half a century or so it was discovered that the experienced missionaries on the field could best formulate strategy and policy, which might then be ratified by the board back home. There was in 1795 a conflict over strategy in the London Missionary Society between two strong personalities. One man wanted well-educated, ordained missionaries sent to countries of high civilization and high religions. The other wanted artisan missionaries under an ordained superintendent to be sent to primitive peoples in the South Seas to Christianize and civilize them. Both objectives were accepted.

Even in countries with a high culture, such as India and China, European missionaries stressed the "civilizing" objective as much as their brethren in primitive regions because they regarded the local culture as degenerate and superstitious--a barrier to Christianization. During the early decades there was never debate about the legitimacy of the stress on the civilizing function of missions. Debate was only about priority; which came first, Christianization or civilization? Some held that a certain degree of civilization was first necessary to enable a people to understand and accept the faith. Others argued that one should begin with Christianization since the gospel inevitably produced a hunger for civilization. Most persons believed that the two mutually interacted and should be stressed equally and simultaneously.

India was soon receiving the greatest degree of attention from mission boards and societies, and the strategy and tactics developed there were copied and applied in other regions. The Baptist "Serampore Trio" of Carey, Marshman, and Ward was especially influential in the early period. Although Carey sought individual conversions, he wanted to foster the growth of a church that would be independent, well sustained by a literate and Bible-reading laity, and administered and shepherded by an educated native ministry. This self-educated genius was not content with establishing elementary schools but founded a college. The King of Denmark (Serampore was a Danish colony) gave him a college charter which permitted the giving of even theological degrees. At Serampore there were schools for Indians and for foreign children. The vast program of Bible translation and printing, ranging beyond the Indian vernaculars even to the Chinese, established the high priority of such work among all Protestants. Other literature was produced for the churches. The Trio also demonstrated the importance of scholarly research for mission strategy and action, producing linguistic materials needed by all and taking the leadership in the study of Hinduism.

Furthermore, this famous Trio worked for the transformation of society under the impact of the gospel, and they became a mighty force for social reform, bringing pressure on the colonial government and leading Hindus to enlightened views on old wrongs and their elimination. These men were influential in causing the abolition of *suttee* or widow-burning, temple prostitution, and other dehumanizing customs. Carey also introduced modern journalism, publishing both vernacular Bengali and English newspapers and magazines. He stimulated a renaissance of Bengali literature. It was a very comprehensive mission which was based at Serampore.

Much like Robert de Nobili before him, the Scotsman Alexander Duff believed that the Indian populace could be won for Christ only if the Brahmin caste were first brought to our Lord. He sought to win Brahmin youths through a program of higher education in the English language. Where he succeeded in large measure, others failed; but his venture led to tremendous emphasis being put on English language schools and colleges. They produced few converts, but they did give economic advancement which made for the welfare of the churches, and to the pleasure of the colonial establishment they produced English-speaking staff for the civil service and commercial houses. Such education soon consumed a large part of the resources of all the missions.

At the same time without any strategic planning there developed huge concentrated central mission stations where the converts clustered in economic and social dependence on the missionaries. Unless a convert came to Christianity with an entire social group, he was cast out of his family and lost his livelihood. Simply to keep such persons alive they were given jobs as servants, teachers, and evangelists. The church became over-professionalized, laymen being paid to do what they should have done voluntarily. This bad practice passed on to missions in other regions. In such a main station there were the central church, the schools, the hospital, and often the printing press. A missionary was pastor and ruler of the community. Such a system had little place for a native pastor as William Carey had planned, and there were only preaching points, no organized churches, in the villages for 50 miles and more in the hinterland. Then in 1854-55 Rufus Anderson went on deputation to India and Ceylon. He caused the American Board missionaries to break up the huge central stations, to organize village churches, and to ordain native pastors over them. He decreed that education in the vernacular should be the general rule and education in English the exception.

10. What strategic mistake did the new mission boards of the early 19th century make?

_____

11. How did the central mission stations develop, and what was their general impact on evangelization?

_____

_____

MISSION STRATEGISTS OF THE 19TH CENTURY

The two greatest mission theoreticians and strategists of the 19th century were also the executive officers of the largest mission agencies. Henry Venn was general secretary of the Church Missionary Society in London. Rufus Anderson was foreign secretary of the American Board of Commissioners for Foreign Missions. Anderson's mission strategy dominated American mission work for more than a century as did that of Venn in the British scene. The two men arrived independently at practically the same basic principles and in late years mutually influenced each other. Together they established as the recognized strategic aim of Protestant mission the famous "three self" formula to which British and American missions gave assent from the middle of the 19th century until World War II: the goal of mission is to plan and foster the development of churches which will be self-governing, self-supporting, and self-propagating.

Rufus Anderson was a Congregationalist and Venn an Anglican Episcopalian, but both would build the regional church from the bottom upward. Venn wanted a bishop appointed as the crowning of the process of development when there was an adequate native clergy and a church supported by the people. Anderson protested the great stress on "civilization" and the attempt to reform society overnight, holding that such change would eventually result from the leaven of the gospel in the life of a nation. He based his strategy on that of Paul as he found it recorded in the New Testament.

According to Anderson, the task of the missionary was to preach the gospel and gather the converts into churches. He was always to be an evangelist and never a pastor or ruler. Churches were to be organized at once out of converts who showed a change of life towards Christ without waiting for them to reach the standard expected of American Christians with 2,000 years of Christian history behind them. These churches were to be put under their own pastors and were to develop their own local and regional polity. The missionaries would be advisers, elder brothers in the faith to the pastors and people.

Both Anderson and Venn taught that when the churches were functioning well the missionaries should leave and go to "regions beyond," where they would begin the evangelistic process once again. The whole point of church planting was to be evangelism and mission. The churches would engage spontaneously in local evangelism and in a sending mission to other peoples. Mission would beget mission. In Anderson's view education in the vernacular would be for the sole purpose of serving the church or raising up a laity of high quality and an adequately trained ministry. All ancillary forms of work were to be solely for evangelism and for the edification of the church.

The British missions resisted Anderson's views on vernacular education. American missions adopted his strategy officially and unofficially and in theory held to his system for more than a century. However, after his day they stressed secondary and higher education in English to an ever greater extent. This was partly due to the fact that social Darwinism had converted Americans to the doctrine of inevitable progress. This led to the replacement of the old eschatology with the idea that the kingdom of God was coming through the influence of Christian institutions such as schools. Also by the end of the 19th century a second great strategic objective had been more or less explicitly added to the three-self formula, that is, the leavening and transformation of society through the effect of Christian principles and the Christian spirit of service infused into the common life. High schools and colleges were essential to this aim.

John L. Nevius, Presbyterian missionary in Shantung, devised a strategy which somewhat modified that of Anderson, placing more responsibility on the layman. He advocated leaving the layman in his own craft or business and in his usual place in society. He was to be encouraged to be a voluntary, unpaid evangelist. Nevius advocated also constant Bible study and rigorous stewardship in combination with voluntary service and proposed a simple and flexible church government. His brethren in China did not adopt his system, but the missionaries in Korea did so with amazing success.

12. What were the elements of the "three-self" formula?

_____

_____

13. Briefly describe Rufus Anderson's strategy.

_____

_____

14. What influence did social Darwinism have on missions of the late 19th century?

_____

_____

A COLONIALIST MENTALITY

Despite the avowed continued adherence to the Anderson-Venn formula, there was a great change in missionary mentality and consequently in strategy in the last quarter of the 19th century. Under Venn British missions in West Africa, for example, had aimed at (1) the creation of an independent church under its own clergy which would evangelize the interior of the continent, and (2) the creation of an African elite, i.e., an intelligentsia and middle class, which would produce the society and economy which could support such a church and its mission. Almost immediately after Venn's termination of leadership, mission executives and field missionaries took the view that the African was of inferior quality and could not provide ministerial leadership, which consequently would be furnished indefinitely by Europeans. The African middle-class businessman and intellectual was despised. This imperialist viewpoint was an ecclesiastical variant of the growing devotion to the theory of "the white man's burden," and it reduced the native church to a colony of the foreign planting church.

A very similar development occurred in India in the 1880's. Americans and others caught this colonialist mentality by contagion from the British. German missions, under the guidance of their leading strategist, Professor Gustav Warneck, were simultaneously aiming at the creation of *Volkskirchen*, national churches, but until their full development had been reached the churches were kept in bondage to the missionaries. Paternalism thwarted development. Thus all missions were paternalist and colonialist at the turn of the century. This unhappy state of affairs lasted until the studies and surveys made for the World Missionary Conference at Edinburgh in 1910 suddenly destroyed complacency and inertia. They revealed that the native church was really a fact and was restive under paternal domination. Consequently, following the conference, there was a tremendous drive for "devolution" of authority from the mission organization to the church, and practically all boards and societies gave lip service, at least, to this ideal.

EVANGELISM, EDUCATION, AND MEDICINE

Missionary strategy of the 19th century (down to Edinburgh 1910), in summary, aimed at individual conversions, church planting, and social transformation through three main types of actions, which became known as evangelism, education, and medicine. Evangelism included preaching in all its forms, the organizing and fostering of churches, Bible translation, literature production, and the distribution of Bibles and literature.

In the realm of education, industrial schools were stressed in earlier times but generally abandoned because of the desire for an academic education. By the end of the century a vast educational system was in existence in Asian countries, ranging from kindergarten to college and including medical and theological schools. Africa, however, was neglected with respect to secondary and collegiate education.

The first doctors sent abroad were sent primarily to take care of the families of other missionaries, but it was soon discovered that medical service to the general populace brought good will and provided an evangelistic opportunity. Thereupon, it was made a major branch of mission work. It was not until the middle of the 20th century that it came to be realized that health services in the name and spirit of the Great Physician are in themselves a dramatic form of the preaching of the gospel. But at a very early date even the rural evangelistic missionary had taken to carrying a medicine bag with him on his travels.

It was the same spirit of general helpfulness and cultivation of good will, as well as out of a desire to improve the economic base of the church, that missionaries introduced improved poultry and livestock and better seeds along with new crops. The great orchard industry and the big peanut industry in Shantung were introduced in this manner.

With regard to the other religions, mission strategy was aggressive, seeking their displacement and total conversion of the peoples. This aggressive spirit declined towards the end of the century, and something of an appreciation of the work of God in the other faiths grew slowly until by 1910 many regarded them as "broken lights" which were to be made whole in Christ and as bridges to the gospel.

The customs of the Oriental peoples made it almost impossible for male missionaries to reach women and with them children in large numbers. Missionary wives endeavored to set up schools for girls and to penetrate the homes, zenanas, and harems, but they did not have enough freedom from home-making and child care and they could not itinerate. Realistic strategy demanded that adequate provision be made for women and children, but the boards and societies were stubbornly resistant to sending single women abroad for such work. Finally in desperation the women in the 1860's began organizing their own societies and sent forth single women. A whole new dimension was thus added to mission strategy: the vast enterprise to reach women and children with the gospel, to educate girls, and to bring adequate medical care to women.

When women came into the church, their children followed them. Female education proved to be the most effective force for the liberation and social uplift of women. The emphasis which the women placed on medical service led the general boards to upgrade the medical work, and greater stress was put on medical education. Out of these two great endeavors of American women, followed by the British and Europeans, there opened to women of the Orient what are today their most prestigious professions, medical service both as physicians and nurses, and teaching.

COMITY

One more feature of 19th century missionary strategy must be listed. This was the practice of comity [mutual courtesy]. Southern Baptists were among the founders and practitioners of comity. Good stewardship of men and money held a high priority among boards and societies. Waste was abhorred, and there was a strong desire to stretch resources as far as possible. The practice of comity was intended to make some agency responsible for the evangelism of every last piece of territory and every people. It was further intended to prevent double occupancy of a region (excepting big cities) and overlapping of mission programs, so that competition might be eliminated along with denominational differences which would confuse the inhabitants and thus hamper evangelism. Prior occupation of territory was recognized; the newcoming missions went to unoccupied areas. This custom produced "denominationalism by geography," but the general expectation was that when the missionaries left for the "regions beyond," the nationals would put the several pieces together into a national church which might be different from any of the planting churches.

Missions agreed on recognizing each other as valid branches of the one church of Christ, on baptism and transfer of membership, on discipline, on salaries, and on transfer of national workers. These agreements led to further cooperation in the establishment of regional and national boards for the arbitration of conflicts between missions and to union Bible translation projects, publication agencies, secondary schools and colleges, teacher training schools, and medical schools. Effective strategy called more and more for doing together all things which could be better achieved through a united effort. City, regional, and national missionary conferences in almost every country provided occasions for common discussion and planning.

15. What bred the "imperialistic" and "paternalistic" mentalities of missions in the late 19th century?

_____

_____

16. What trend in mission strategy was the outcome of the 19th century emphasis on education and medicine?

_____

_____

17. What was the aim of comity?

_____

_____

CONSULTATIONS AND CONFERENCES

Such cooperation on the mission fields led to increasing home base consultation and planning. The World Missionary Conference at Edinburgh in 1910 inaugurated the series of great conferences: Jerusalem 1928, Madras 1938, Whitby 1947, Willingen 1952, and Ghana 1957-58. In these the directions of strategy were largely determined and then applied locally through further study and discussion in national and regional bodies. The International Missionary Council was organized in 1921, bringing together national missionary conferences (such as the Foreign Missions Conference of North America, 1892), and national Christian councils (such as the NCC of China), and thus there was established a universal system at various levels for the voluntary study of problems and planning of strategy in common by a host of sovereign mission boards. In 1961 the IMC became the Division of World Mission and Evangelism of the World Council of Churches.

From 1910 to World War II the most notable development of strategy was increasingly putting the national church in the central place, giving it full independence and authority, and developing partnership between the Western churches and the young churches. "The indigenous church" and "partnership in obedience" were watchwords which expressed the thrust of prevailing strategy. The participants in the Jerusalem Conference in 1928 defined the indigenous church, underscoring cultural accommodation. The Madras Conference of 1938 restated the definition, emphasizing witness to Christ in "a direct, clear, and close relationship with the cultural and religious heritage of [the] country." Whitby 1947 held up the ideal of "partnership in obedience."

SINCE WORLD WAR II

A radically different mission strategy, based on Paul, was expounded by Roland Allen in his books *Missionary Methods: St. Paul's or Ours ?* and *The Spontaneous Expansion of the Church,* but he gathered no following until after World War II, when the missionaries of the faith missions especially rallied to his standard. In barest essentials this is his strategy: The missionary communicates the gospel and transmits to the new community of converts the simplest statement of the faith, the Bible, the sacraments, and the principle of ministry. He then stands by as a counseling elder brother while the Holy Spirit leads the new church, self-governing and self-supporting, to develop its own forms of polity, ministry, worship, and life. Such a church is spontaneously missionary. Allen's theory applied to new pioneer beginnings. The old boards and societies were dealing with churches already old and set in their ways; they seldom sought untouched fields.

One after another the mission organizations on the fields were dissolved. Resources were placed at the disposal of the churches and missionary personnel assigned to their direction.

The Western boards and societies initiated very little that was new in the way of strategy, but much to develop new methods: agricultural missions or rural development, some urban industrial work, mass media communications, more effective literature. This was the final stage of a mission which had been in progress for 300 years. Now the world was no longer divided into Christendom and heathendom. There could no longer be a one-way mission from the West to the remainder of the world. The base for a mission was established in almost every land, for a Christian church and community with an obligation to give the gospel to the whole world existed there. The moment for a new world mission with a radical new strategy had arrived. The revolution which swept the non-Western portions of the world during and after World War II unmistakably put an end to the old order of Protestant missions.

A new age of world mission has arrived, one in which other religions are now engaged in world mission also. A new understanding of mission, a new strategy, new organization, new ways, means, and methods are the demand of this hour in the central task of the church which shall never end until the kingdom of God has come in all its glory. It will help as we pray, study, plan, and experiment if we know the past history of mission strategy.

18. What are the principal tenets of Roland Allen's mission strategy?

_____

_____

19. What is the author's conclusion regarding current developments in world mission?

_____

_____

The following timeline provides an historical overview of mission strategy as described by Beaver:

Figure 6.1 HISTORY OF MISSION STRATEGY

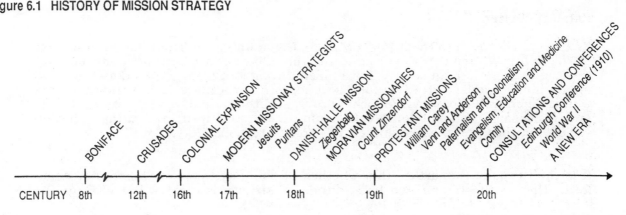

23

Since this article was written, several major consultations on world evangelization have taken place in acknowledgement of "a new age of world mission." Three of the most notable ones are Lausanne (1974), Pattaya (1980), and Edinburgh (1980). These consultations have opened dialogue on the new "ways, means, and methods" to which Beaver alludes in his conclusion.

III. TWO STRUCTURES OF EXPANSION

The preceding study has made it evident that mission structures have played an indispensable role in the spread of the gospel. The widespread use of mission agencies in the ongoing work of world evangelization continues today. Most Christians accept this phenomenon without a thought. Others are troubled by it. They question whether mission agencies are truly biblical. Do they perhaps usurp a role which rightfully belongs to the church? Shouldn't the church exercise its God-given authority in controlling the mission effort?

Occasionally questions arise challenging the existence of mission structures and raising doubts about the legitimacy of any Christian organizations other than the church. When such doubts become a prevailing sentiment, they greatly influence further development of mission structures. We will consider some of these questions which are of special significance to our discussion of mission strategy.

As we enter the "third era" of world evangelization, many missiologists believe that mission societies will continue to play an indispensable part, as they have in the past. In the following excerpt[8] Ralph Winter looks at the past in presenting a convincing argument for the continued development and use of mission structures for world evangelization.

The Two Structures of God's Redemptive Mission

Ralph D. Winter

[In an address given to the All-Asia Mission Consultation in Seoul, Korea in August 1973, Ralph Winter describes the forms that God's two "redemptive structures," existing in every human society, have taken throughout history. His thesis has two major implications: (1) We must accept *both* structures, represented in the Christian church today by the local church and the mission society, as legitimate and necessary; and (2) non-Western churches must form and utilize mission societies if they are to exercise their missionary responsibility.]

It is the thesis of this article that whether Christianity takes on Western or Asian form, there will still be two basic kinds of structures that will make up the

---

[8]Ralph D. Winter, "The Two Structures of God's Redemptive Mission," in *Crucial Dimensions in World Evangelization*, ed. Arthur F. Glasser et al. (Pasadena, CA: William Carey Library, 1976), pp. 326-341. Used by permission.

movement. Most of the emphasis will be placed on pointing out the existence of these two structures as they have continuously appeared across the centuries. This will serve to define, illustrate, and compare their nature and importance. The writer will also endeavor to explain why he believes our efforts today in any part of the world will be most effective only if both of these two structures are fully and properly involved.

REDEMPTIVE STRUCTURES IN NEW TESTAMENT TIMES

First of all, let us recognize the structure so fondly called "the New Testament church" as basically a Christian synagogue.[10] Paul's missionary work consisted primarily of going to synagogues scattered across the Roman Empire, beginning in Asia Minor, and making clear to the Jewish and Gentile believers in those synagogues that the Messiah had come in Jesus Christ, the Son of God; that in Christ a final authority even greater than Moses existed; and that this made possible the winning of the Gentiles without forcing upon them any literal cultural adaptation to the ritual provisions of the Mosaic Law. An outward novelty of Paul's work was the development eventually of wholly new synagogues that were not only Christian, but Greek.

Very few Christians, casually reading the New Testament and with only the New Testament available to them, would surmise the degree to which there had been Jewish evangelists who went before Paul all over the Empire, people whom Jesus Himself described as "traversing land and sea to make a single proselyte." Paul followed their path; he built on their efforts and went beyond them with the new gospel he preached, which allowed the Greeks to remain Greeks and not be circumcised and culturally assimilated into the Jewish way of life.

Yet not only did Paul apparently go to every existing synagogue of Asia,[11] after which he declared, ". . . all Asia has heard the gospel," but, when occasion demanded, he established brand new synagogue-type fellowships of believers as the basic unit of his missionary activity. The first structure in the New Testament scene is thus what is often called the *New Testament church*. It was essentially built along Jewish synagogue lines,[12] embracing the community of the faithful in any given place. The defining characteristic of this structure is that it included old and young, male and female. Note, too, that Paul was willing to build such fellowships out of former Jews as well as non-Jewish Greeks.

There is a second, quite different structure in the New Testament context. While we know very little about the structure of the evangelistic outreach within which pre-Pauline Jewish proselytizers worked, we do know, as already mentioned, that they operated all over the Roman Empire. It would be surprising if Paul didn't follow

---

[10]"One can hardly conceive of more providentially supplied means for the Christian mission to reach the Gentile community. Wherever the community of Christ went, it found at hand the tools needed to reach the nations: a people living under covenant promise and a responsible election, and the Scriptures, God's revelation to all men. The open synagogue was the place where all these things converged. In the synagogue, the Christians were offered an inviting door of access to every Jewish community. It was in the synagogue that the first Gentile converts declared their faith in Jesus." Richard R. DeRidder, *The Dispersion of the People of God* (Netherlands: J. H. Kok N. V. Kampen, 1971), p. 87.

[11]In Paul's day Asia meant what we today call Asia Minor, or present-day Turkey. In those days no one dreamed how far the term would later be extended.

[12]That Christians in Jerusalem organized themselves for worship on the synagogue pattern is evident from the appointment of elders and the adoption of the service of prayer. The provision of a daily dole for widows and needy reflects the current synagogue practice (Acts 2:42; 6:1). It is possible that the epistle of James reflects the coming "into your assembly." The term translated "assembly" is literally "synagogue." J. Ramsey Michaels, *The New Testament Speaks* (New York: Harper & Row, 1969), pp. 126-127.

somewhat the same procedures. And we know a great deal more about the way Paul operated. He was, true enough, sent out by the church in Antioch. But once away from Antioch he seemed very much on his own. The little team he formed was economically self-sufficient when occasion demanded. It was also dependent, from time to time, not alone upon the Antioch church, but upon other churches that had risen as a result of evangelistic labors. Paul's team may certainly be considered a structure. While its design and form are not made concrete for us on the basis of remaining documents, neither, of course, is the New Testament church so defined concretely for us in the pages of the New Testament. In both cases, the absence of any such definition implies the pre-existence of a commonly understood pattern of relationship, whether in the case of the church or the missionary band which Paul formed.

Thus, on the one hand, the structure we call the *New Testament church* is a prototype of all subsequent Christian fellowships where old and young, male and female are gathered together as normal biological families in aggregate. On the other hand, Paul's *missionary band* can be considered a prototype of all subsequent missionary endeavors organized out of committed, experienced workers who affiliated themselves as a second decision beyond membership in the first structure.

Note well the *additional* commitment. Note also that the structure that resulted was something definitely more than the extended outreach of the Antioch church. No matter what we think the structure was, we know that it was not simply the Antioch church operating at a distance from its home base. It was something else, something different. We will consider the missionary band the second of the two redemptive structures in New Testament times.

In conclusion, it is very important to note that neither of these two structures was, as it were, "let down from heaven" in a special way. It may be shocking at first to think that God made use of either a *Jewish* synagogue pattern or a *Jewish* evangelistic pattern. But this must not be more surprising than the fact that God employed the use of the pagan Greek language, the Holy Spirit guiding the biblical writers to lay hold of such terms as *kurios* (originally a pagan term), and pound them into shape to carry the Christian revelation. The New Testament refers to a synagogue dedicated to Satan, but this did not mean that Christians, to avoid such a pattern, could not fellowship together in the synagogue pattern. These considerations prepare us for what comes next in the history of the expansion of the gospel, because we see other patterns chosen by Christians at a later date whose origins are just as clearly "borrowed patterns" as were those in the New Testament period.

In fact, the profound missiological implication of all this is that the New Testament is trying to show us *how to borrow effective patterns*; it is trying to free all future missionaries from the need to follow the precise *forms* of the Jewish synagogue and Jewish missionary band, and yet to allow them to choose comparable indigenous structures in the countless new situations across history and around the world-- structures which will correspond faithfully to the *function* of patterns Paul employed, if not their *form!* It is no wonder that a considerable body of literature in the field of missiology today underlies the fact that world Christianity has generally employed the various existing languages and cultures of the world-human community--more so than any other religion--and in so doing, has cast into a shadow all efforts to canonize as universal any kind of mechanically formal extension of the New Testament church. As Kraft has said earlier, we seek *dynamic equivalence* , not formal replication.[13]

---

[13]Charles H. Kraft, "Dynamic Equivalence Churches,"*Missiology: An International Review* (1973), pp. 39ff.

1. According to Winter, what two Jewish structures did the early Christian movement borrow?

   _____

   _____

2. What conclusion does Winter draw concerning the adaptability of Christianity to pre-existing cultural forms and structures?

   _____

   _____

   _____

THE EARLY DEVELOPMENT OF CHRISTIAN STRUCTURES WITHIN ROMAN CULTURE

We have seen how the Christian movement built itself upon two different kinds of structures that had pre-existed in the Jewish cultural tradition. It is now our task to see if the *functional* equivalents of these same two structures were to appear in the Roman cultural tradition as the gospel invaded that larger world.

Of course, the original synagogue pattern persisted as a Christian structure for some time. Rivalry between Christians and Jews, however, tended to defeat this as a Christian pattern, and in some cases to force it out of existence, especially where it was possible for Jewish congregations of the dispersion to arouse public persecution of the apparently deviant Christian synagogues. Unlike the Jews, Christians had no official license for their alternative to the Roman Imperial cult.[14] Thus, whereas each synagogue was considerably independent of the others, the Christian pattern was soon assimilated to the Roman context, and bishops became invested with authority over more than one congregation with a territorial jurisdiction not altogether different from the pattern of Roman civil government. This tendency is well confirmed by the time the official recognition of Christianity had its full impact: the very Latin word for Roman magisterial territories was appropriated--the *diocese*---within which parishes are to be found on the local level.

In any case, while the more "congregational" pattern of the independent synagogue became pervasively replaced by a "connectional" Roman pattern, the new Christian *parish church* still preserved the basic constituency of the synagogue, namely, the combination of old and young, male and female--that is, a biologically perpetuating organism.

Meanwhile, the monastic tradition in various early forms developed as a second structure. This new, widely proliferating structure undoubtedly had no connection at all with the missionary band in which Paul was involved. Indeed, it more substantially drew from Roman military structure than from any other single source. Pachomius, a former military man, gained 3,000 followers and attracted the attention of people like Basil of Caesarea, and then through Basil, John Cassian, who labored in southern Gaul at a later date.[15] These men thus carried

[14]Christians, it is said, resorted to the formation of "burial clubs," which were legal, as one vehicle of fellowship and worship.

[15]Kenneth Scott Latourette, *A History of Christianity* (New York: Harper & Brothers, 1953), pp. 181, 221-234.

forward a disciplined structure, borrowed primarily from the military, which allowed nominal Christians to make a second-level choice--an additional specific commitment.

Perhaps it would be well to pause here for a moment. Any reference to the monasteries gives Protestants culture shock. The Protestant Reformation fought desperately against certain degraded conditions at the very end of the 1,000-year medieval period. We have no desire to deny the fact that conditions in monasteries were not always ideal; what the average Protestant knows about monasteries may be correct for certain situations, but the popular Protestant stereotype surely cannot describe correctly all that happened during the 1,000 years! During those centuries there were many different eras and epochs and a wide variety of monastic movements, radically different from each other, as we shall see in a minute; and any generalization about so vast a phenomenon is bound to be simply an unreliable and no doubt prejudiced caricature.

Let me give just one example of how far wrong our Protestant stereotypes can be. We often hear that the monks "fled the world." Compare that idea with this description by a Baptist missionary scholar:

> The Benedictine rule and the many derived from it probably helped to give dignity to labour, including manual labour in the fields. This was in striking contrast with the aristocratic conviction of the servile status of manual work which prevailed in much of ancient society and which was also the attitude of the warriors and non-monastic ecclesiastics who constituted the upper middle classes of the Middle Ages. . . . To the monasteries . . . was obviously due much clearing of land and improvement in methods of agriculture. In the midst of barbarism, the monasteries were centres of orderly and settled life and monks were assigned the duty of road-building and road repair. Until the rise of the towns in the eleventh century, they were pioneers in industry and commerce. The shops of the monasteries preserved the industries of Roman times. . . . The earliest use of marl in improving the soil is attributed to them. The great French monastic orders led in the agricultural colonization of Western Europe. Especially did the Cistercians make their houses centres of agriculture and contribute to improvements in that occupation. With their lay brothers and their hired labourers, they became great landed proprietors. In Hungary and on the German frontier the Cistercians were particularly important in reducing the soil to cultivation and in furthering colonization. In Poland, too, the German monasteries set advanced standards in agriculture and introduced artisans and craftsmen.[16]

For mission leaders the shattering of the "monks fled the world" stereotype is even more dramatically and decisively reinforced by the magnificent record of the Irish *peregrini*, who were Celtic monks who did more to reach out to convert Anglo-Saxons than did Augustine's mission, and who contributed more to the evangelization of Western Europe, even Central Europe, than any other force.

From its very inception this second kind of structure was highly significant to the growth and development of the Christian movement. Even though Protestants have an inbuilt prejudice against it for various reasons, as we have seen, there is no denying the fact that apart from this structure it would be hard even to imagine the vital continuity of the Christian tradition across the centuries. Protestants are equally dismayed by the other structure--the parish and diocesan structure. It is, in

---

[16]Kenneth Scott Latourette, *A History of the Expansion of Christianity*, vol. 2: *The Thousand Years of Uncertainty* (New York: Harper & Brothers, 1938), pp. 379-380.

fact, the relative weakness and nominality of the diocesan structure that makes the monastic structure so significant. Men like Jerome and Augustine, for example, are thought of by Protestants not as monks but as great scholars; and people like John Calvin lean very heavily upon writings that derive from such monks. But Protestants do not usually give any credit to the specific structure within which Jerome and Augustine and many other monastic scholars worked, a structure without which Protestant labors would have had very little to build on, not even a Bible.

We must now follow these threads into the next period, where we will see the formal emergence of the major monastic structures. It is sufficient at this point merely to note that there are already by the fourth century two very different kinds of structures--the diocese and the monastery--both of them significant in the transmission and expansion of Christianity. They are each patterns borrowed from the cultural context of their time, just as were the earlier Christian synagogue and missionary band.

It is even more important for our purpose here to note that while these two structures are *formally* different from--and historically unrelated to--the two in New Testament times, they are nevertheless *functionally* the same. In order to speak conveniently about the continuing similarities in function, let us now call the synagogue and diocese *modalities*, and the missionary band and monastery, *sodalities*. Elsewhere I have developed these terms in detail, but briefly, a modality is a structured fellowship in which there is no distinction of sex or age, while a sodality is a structured fellowship in which membership involves an adult second decision beyond modality membership and is limited by either age or sex or marital status. In this use of these terms, both the *denomination* and the *local congregation* are modalities, while a mission agency or a local men's club are sodalities.[17]

In this early post-biblical period there was little relation between modality and sodality, while in Paul's time his missionary band specifically nourished the churches--a most significant symbiosis. We shall now see how the medieval period essentially recovered the healthy New Testament relationship between modality and sodality.

3. What two new forms emerged through the assimilation of the Christian pattern to the Roman context?

_____

_____

4. Why does Winter stress that the forms which developed in Roman times were *functionally* the same as the two in the New Testament, although they were "formally different from and historically unrelated" to them?

_____

_____

_____

---

[17]Ralph D. Winter and R. Pierce Beaver, "The Warp and the Woof of the Christian Movement", *The Warp and Woof: Organizing for Christian Mission* (Pasadena, CA: William Carey Library, 1970), pp. 52-62.

Winter traces the development of two functionally distinct structures. To distinguish between the two, he introduces two terms, modality and sodality. Modality refers to a structured fellowship in which no distinction of sex or age is made for membership. This fellowship is composed of the "modal" or conventional fabric of a given society. Its primary growth is usually biological. The synagogue, diocese, and the local church congregation are all examples of modalities.

A second term, sodality, has been coined to designate a structured fellowship involving an adult, second decision beyond the modality structures. A sodality is composed of those who make a voluntary commitment to a particular group or agency and agree to abide by its regulations in the pursuit of a common objective. Paul's missionary band, monasteries, and mission agencies are all examples of Christian sodalities.

Figure 6.3 THE TWO STRUCTURES

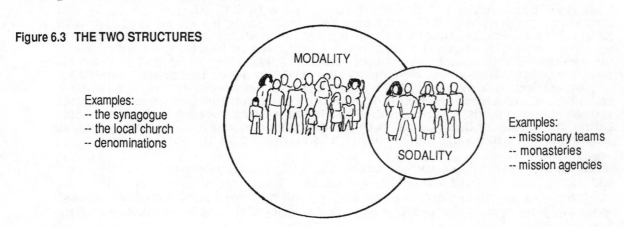

Examples:
-- the synagogue
-- the local church
-- denominations

Examples:
-- missionary teams
-- monasteries
-- mission agencies

5. Using the concept of modality and sodality, explain why the China Inland Mission was more like a football team than a local church.

_____

_____

_____

THE MEDIEVAL SYNTHESIS OF MODALITY AND SODALITY

We can say that the medieval period began when the Roman Empire in the West started to break down. To some extent the diocesan pattern, following as it did the Roman civil-governmental pattern, tended to break down at the same time. The monastic (or sodality) pattern turned out to be much more durable and as a result gained greater importance in the early medieval period than it might have otherwise. The survival of the modality (diocesan Christianity) was further compromised by the fact that the invaders of this early medieval period generally belonged to a different brand of Christian belief--they were Arians. As a result, in many places there were both "Arian" and "Catholic" Christian churches on opposite corners of a main street--something like today, where we have Methodist and Presbyterian churches across the street from each other.

Again, however, it is not our purpose to downplay the significance of the parish or diocesan form of Christianity, but simply to point out that during this early period of the medieval epoch the specialized house called the *monastery*, or its equivalent, became ever so much more important in the perpetuation of the Christian movement than was the organized system of parishes, which we often call the church *as if there were no other structure making up the church.*

Perhaps the most outstanding illustration in the early medieval period of the importance of the relationship between modality and sodality is the collaboration between Gregory the Great and a man later called Augustine of Canterbury. While Gregory, as the bishop of the diocese of Rome, was the head of a modality, both he and Augustine were the products of monastic houses--a fact which reflects the dominance even then of the sodality pattern of Christian structure. In any case, Gregory called upon his friend Augustine to undertake a major mission to England in order to try to plant diocesan structure there, where Celtic Christianity had been deeply wounded by the invasion of Saxon warriors from the Continent.

As strong as Gregory was in his own diocese, he simply had no structure to call upon to reach out in this intended mission other than the sodality, which at this point was a Benedictine monastery. This is why he ended up asking Augustine and a group of other members of the same monastery to undertake this rather dangerous journey and important mission on his behalf. The purpose of the mission, curiously, was not to extend the Benedictine form of monasticism. The remnant of the Celtic "church" in England was itself a network of sodalities since there was no parish system in the Celtic area. No, Augustine went to England to establish diocesan Christianity, though he himself was not a diocesan priest.

This is quite characteristic. During a lengthy period of time, perhaps a thousand years, the building and rebuilding of the modalities was mainly the work of the sodalities. That is to say, the monasteries were uniformly the source and the real focus point of new energy and vitality which flowed into the diocesan side of the Christian movement. We think of the momentous Cluny reform, then the Cistercians, then the Friars, and finally the Jesuits--all of them strictly sodalities, but sodalities which contributed massively to the building and the rebuilding of the *Corpus Cristianum*, the network of dioceses, which Protestants often identify as "the" Christian movement.

At many points there was rivalry between these two structures, between bishop and abbot, diocese and monastery, modality and sodality, but the great achievement of the medieval period is the ultimate synthesis, delicately achieved, whereby Catholic orders were able to function along with Catholic parishes and dioceses without the two structures conflicting with each other to the point of a setback to the movement. The harmony between the modality and the sodality achieved by the Roman Church is perhaps the most significant characteristic of this phase of the world Christian movement and continues to be Rome's greatest organizational advantage to this day.

Note, however, that it is not our intention to claim that any one organization of either the modality or sodality variety was continuously the champion of vitality and vigor throughout the thousands of years of the medieval epoch. As a matter of actual fact, there really is no very impressive organizational continuity in the Christian movement, either in the form of modality or sodality. (The list of bishops at Rome is at many points a most shaky construct and unfortunately does not even provide a focus for the entire Christian movement.) On the other hand, it is clear that the sodality, as it was recreated again and again by different leaders, was almost always the prime mover, the source of inspiration and renewal which overflowed into the papacy and created the reform movements which blessed diocesan Christianity from time to time. The most significant instance of this is the accession to the papal throne of Hildebrand (Gregory VII), who brought the ideals, commitment, and discipline of the monastic movement right into the Vatican itself. In this sense are not then the papacy, the College of Cardinals, the diocese, and the parish structure of the Roman Church in some respects a secondary element, a derivation from the monastic tradition rather than vice versa? In any case it seems appropriate that the priests of the monastic tradition are called *regular priests*, while the priests of the diocese and parish are called *secular priests*. The former are voluntarily bound by a *regula*, while the latter as a group were other than, outside of ("cut off"), or somehow less than the second-decision communities bound by regula. Whenever a house or project or parish run by the regular clergy is brought under the domination of the secular clergy, this is a form of the "secularization" of that entity. In the lengthy "Investiture Controversy," the regular clergy finally gained clear authority for at least semi-autonomous operation, and the secularization of the orders was averted.

We may note that the same structural danger of *secularization* exists today whenever the special concerns of an elite mission sodality fall under the complete domination of an ecclesiastical government, since the Christian modalities (churches) inevitably represent the much broader and, no doubt, mainly inward concerns of a large body of all kinds of Christians, who, as "first decision" members, are generally less select.

We cannot leave the medieval period without referring to the many unofficial and often persecuted movements which also mark the era. In all of this, the Bible itself is perhaps the ultimate prime mover, as we see in the case of Peter Waldo. His work stands as a powerful demonstration of the simple power of a vernacular translation of the Bible, where the people were unable to appreciate either Jerome's classical translation or the celebration of the Mass in Latin. A large number of groups referred to as "Anabaptists" are to be found in many parts of Europe. One of the chief characteristics of these renewal movements is that they did not attempt to elicit merely celibate participation, although this was one of their traits on occasion, but often simply developed whole "new communities" of believers and their families, attempting by biological and cultural transmission to preserve a high and enlightened form of Christianity. These groups usually faced such strong opposition and grave limitations that it would be very unfair to judge their virility by their progress. It is important to note, however, that the average Mennonite or Salvation Army community, where whole families are members, typified the desire for a "pure" church, or what is often called a "believers" church, and constitutes a most significant experiment in Christian structure. Such a structure stands, in a certain sense, midway between a modality and a sodality, since it has the constituency of the modality (involving full families) and yet, in its earlier years, may have the vitality and selectivity of a sodality. We will return to this phenomenon in the next section.

We have space here only to point out that in terms of the durability and quality of the Christian faith, the 1,000-year medieval period is virtually impossible to account for apart from the role of the sodalities. What happened in Rome is merely the tip of the iceberg at best and represents a rather superficial and political level. It is quite a contrast to the foundational well-springs of biblical study and radical obedience represented by the various sodalities of this momentous millennium.

6. What major role in the development of Christianity did sodalities play during the medieval period?

_____

_____

THE PROTESTANT RECOVERY OF THE SODALITY

The Protestant movement started out by attempting to do without any kind of sodality structure. Martin Luther had been discontented with the apparent polarization between the vitality he eventually discovered in his own order and the very nominal parish life of his time. Being dissatisfied with this cleavage, he abandoned the sodality in which he finally found faith and took advantage of the political forces of his time to launch a full-scale renewal movement on the general level of church life. At first, he even tried to do without the characteristically Roman diocesan structure, but eventually the Lutheran movement produced a Lutheran diocesan structure which to a considerable extent represented the readoption of the Roman diocesan tradition. The Lutheran movement did not in a comparable sense readopt the sodalities, the Catholic orders, that had been so prominent in the Roman tradition.

This omission, in my evaluation, represents the greatest error of the Reformation and the greatest weakness of the resulting Protestant tradition. Had it not been for the so-called Pietist movement, the Protestants would have been totally devoid of any organized renewing structures within their tradition. The Pietist tradition, in every new emergence of its force, was very definitely a sodality, inasmuch as it was a case of adults meeting together and committing themselves to new beginnings and higher goals as Christians without conflicting with the stated meetings of the existing church. This phenomenon of sodality nourishing modality is prominent in the case of the early work of John Wesley. He absolutely prohibited any abandonment of the parish churches. A contemporary example is the widely influential so-called East African Revival, which has now involved a million people but has very carefully avoided any clash with functioning of local churches. The churches that have not fought against this movement have been greatly blessed by it.

However, the Pietist movement, along with the Anabaptist new communities, eventually dropped back to the level of the biological growth; it reverted to the ordinary pattern of congregational life. It reverted from the level of the sodality to the level of the modality and, in most cases, rather soon became ineffective either as a mission structure or as a renewing force.

What interests us most is the fact that in failing to exploit the power of the sodality, the Protestants had no mechanism for missions for almost 300 years, until William Carey proposed "the use of means for the conversion of the heathen." His key word _means_ refers specifically to the need for a sodality, for the organized but non-ecclesiastical initiative of the warm-hearted. Thus, the resulting Baptist Missionary Society is one of the most significant organizational developments in the Protestant tradition. It set off a rush to the use of this kind of "means" for the conversion of the heathen, and we find in the next few years a number of societies forming along similar lines: the LMS and NMS in 1795, the CMS in 1799, the CFBS in 1804, the BCFM in 1810, the ABMB in 1814, the GMS in 1815, the DMS in 1821, the FEM in 1822, and the BM in 1824--12 societies in 32 years. Once this method of operation was clearly understood by the Protestants, 300 years of latent energies burst forth in what became, in Latourette's phrase, "The Great Century."

The 19th century is thus the first century in which Protestants were actively engaged in missions. For reasons which we have not space here to explain, it was also the century of the lowest ebb of Catholic mission energy. Amazingly, in this one century Protestants, building on the unprecedented world expansion of the West, caught up with 18 centuries of earlier mission efforts. There is simply no question that what was done in this century moved the Protestant stream from a self-contained, impotent European backwater into a world force in Christianity. Looking back from where we stand today, of course, it is hard to believe how recently the Protestant movement has become prominent.

Organizationally speaking, however, the vehicle that allowed the Protestant movement to become vital was the structural development of the sodality, which harvested the vital "voluntarism" latent in Protestantism, and surfaced in new mission agencies of all kinds, both at home and overseas. Wave after wave of evangelical initiatives transformed the entire map of Christianity, especially in the United States, but also in England, and to a lesser degree in Scandinavia and on the Continent. By 1840, the phenomenon of mission sodalities was so prominent in the United States that the phrase "the Evangelical Empire" and other equivalent phrases were used to refer to it, and now began a trickle of ecclesiastical opposition to this bright new emergence of the second structure. This brings us to our next point.

7. Why does Winter consider the early Protestant omission of sodalities to be "the greatest error of the Reformation"?

_____

_____

8. Describe what happened once Protestants began using the sodality structure for missions.

_____

_____

_____

THE CONTEMPORARY MISUNDERSTANDING OF THE MISSION SODALITY

Almost all mission efforts in the 19th century, whether sponsored by interdenominational boards or denominational boards, were substantially the work of initiatives that were mainly independent of the ecclesiastical structures to which they were related. Toward the latter half of the 19th century, there seemed increasingly to be two separate structural traditions.

On the one hand, there were men like Henry Venn and Rufus Anderson, who were the strategic thinkers at the helm of older societies--the Church Missionary Society (CMS) in England and American Board of Commissioners for Foreign Missions (ABCFM), respectively. These men championed the semi-autonomous mission sodality, and they voiced an attitude which was not at first contradicted by any significant part of the leaders of the ecclesiastical structures. On the other hand, there was the centralizing perspective of denominational leaders, principally the Presbyterians, which gained ground almost without any reversal throughout the latter two-thirds of the 19th century, so that by the early part of the 20th century the once-independent structures which had been merely *related* to the denominations gradually became *dominated* by the churches. Partially as a result, toward the end of the 19th century, there was a new burst of totally separate mission sodalities called the *faith missions*, with Hudson Taylor's CIM taking the lead. It is not widely recognized that this pattern was mainly a recrudescence of the pattern that had been established earlier in the century, prior to the trend toward denominational boards.

All of these changes took place very gradually. Attitudes at any point are hard to pin down, but it does seem clear that Protestants were always a bit unsure about the legitimacy of the second structure, the sodality. The Anabaptist tradition consistently emphasized the concept of a pure community of believers and thus was uninterested in a voluntarism that would involve only part of the believing community. U.S. denominations for their part, lacking tax support as on the Continent, were generally a more selective and vital fellowship than the European state churches, and at least in their youthful exuberance, felt quite capable as denominations of providing all of the necessary initiative for overseas mission. It is for this latter reason that the many new denominations of the U.S. have tended to act as though centralized church control of mission efforts is the only proper pattern.

As a result, by the Second World War, a very nearly complete transmutation had taken place in the case of almost all mission efforts related to denominational structures. That is, almost all older denominational boards, though once semi-autonomous or very nearly independent, had by this time become part of unified budget provisions and so forth. At the same time, and partially as a result, a whole new host of independent mission structures burst forth again, especially after the Second World War. As in the case of the earlier emergence of the faith missions, these tended to pay little attention to denominational leaders and their aspirations for church-centered mission. The Anglican church with its CMS, USPG, etc., displays the medieval synthesis, and so, almost unconsciously, does the American CBA with its associated CBFMS, CBHMS structures. Thus, to this day, among Protestants, there continues to be deep confusion about the legitimacy and proper relationship of the two structures that have manifested themselves throughout the history of the Christian movement.

To make matters worse, Protestant blindness about the need for mission sodalities has had a very tragic influence on mission fields. Protestant missions, being modality-minded, have tended to assume that merely modalities, e.g., churches, need to be established. Even in the case where mission work is being pursued by what are essentially semi-autonomous mission sodalities, it is modalities, not sodalities, that are the only goal. That is to say, the mission agencies (even those that have most independent from themselves been denominations back home) have tended in their mission work very simply to set up churches and not to plant, in addition, mission sodalities in the so-called mission lands.[18]

As we look back on it today, it is surprising that most Protestant missionaries, working with (mission) structures that did not exist in the Protestant tradition for hundreds of years and without whose existence there would have been no mission initiative, have nevertheless been blind to the significance of the very structure within which they have worked. In this blindness they have merely planted churches and have not effectively concerned themselves to make sure that the kind of mission structure within which they operate also be set up on the field. As a matter of fact, many of the mission agencies founded after World War II, out of

[18]Ralph D. Winter, "The Planting of Younger Missions," in *Church/Mission Tensions Today*, ed. C. Peter Wagner (Chicago: Moody Press, 1972), pp. 129-145.

extreme deference to existing church movements already established in foreign lands, have not even tried to set up *churches* and have worked for many years merely as auxiliary agencies in various service capacities trying to help the churches that were already there. . . .

The question we must ask is how long it will be before the younger churches of the so-called mission territories of the non-Western world come to that epochal conclusion (to which the Protestant movement in Europe only tardily came), namely, that there need to be sodality structures, such as William Carey's "use of means," in order for church people to reach out in vital initiatives in mission, especially cross-cultural mission. There are already some hopeful signs that this tragic delay will not continue. We see, for example, the outstanding work of the Melanesian Brotherhood in the Solomon Islands.

CONCLUSION

This article has been in no sense an attempt to decry or to criticize the organized church. It has assumed both the necessity and the importance of the parish structure, the diocesan structure, the denominational structure, the ecclesiastical structure. The modality structure in the view of this article is a significant and absolutely essential structure. All that is attempted here is to explore some of the historical patterns which make clear that God, through His Holy Spirit, has clearly and consistently used another structure other than (and sometimes instead of) the modality structure. It is our attempt here to help church leaders and others to understand the legitimacy of *both* structures and the necessity for both structures not only to exist but to work together harmoniously for the fulfillment of the Great Commission and for the fulfillment of all that God desires for our time.

9. What "transmutation" of denominational mission boards had taken place by World War II, and what resulted from this change?

   _____

   _____

   _____

10. To what "tragic influence on mission fields" has Protestant blindness regarding sodality structures led?

    _____

    _____

    _____

11. Based on the concluding statements of the preceding article, what do you think the author would like to see happening today?

    _____

    _____

    _____

Two Structures, Two Functions

Most of us are members of a Christian modality--a local church. From our own experience, we can affirm that this structure is dedicated primarily to worship, fellowship, and teaching. Because of the churches open nature, within any local body of believers there are usually various levels of spiritual maturity. While all members make some acknowledgement of Christ's sovereignty in their lives, not all exhibit the same level of commitment to conforming to the image of Christ through personal sanctity and service. Much of the pastor's time is dedicated to exhortation, counseling, and teaching to encourage the brethren in their personal growth.

Because of this preoccupation with nurturing activities, local churches seldom focus on wider church ministry. Rare is the church which is consistently evangelizing its own community. Rarer still is the church which has a clear focus on the "regions beyond." Although sodality structures which serve the church's internal needs (such as deacon boards and women's leagues) are common, few local churches have thought of forming sodalities from their own ranks for world evangelization.

Often as not, within a local congregation individuals are found who have high ideals of service for the Lord. Many are young people who face a lifetime and want to make it count for Christ. They may look to the local church for a means of expressing this desire, but the church may not offer channels for service commensurate with their ideals. They are looking for a cause bigger than themselves, a higher commitment level than that found in the local modality structure.

It is the sodality structure which has filled this need. Whether it has been St. Francis' calling of those who would embrace poverty and a simple lifestyle as a purifying influence in a materialistic church, or Hudson Taylor's pleading for the millions of lost souls in the vast interior of China, sodalities have provided the means by which tens of thousands of Christians have been able to express their desire to commit themselves wholly to the service of Christ and His cause.

12. Why have sodalities played such an important part in world evangelization?

_____

_____

_____

SUMMARY

Simply stated, strategy is the means agreed on to reach a certain goal. All Christians operate with a strategy, whether they are conscious of it or not. But some strategies are better than others, and it is worthwhile to look at them all in formulating our own. We don't have to think of this activity as unspiritual.

Good mission strategy causes us to make a statement of faith regarding the establishment of God's kingdom among a particular people who are yet unreached. It forces us to depend on the Holy Spirit to meet the challenges of each unique situation.

A look at the historical development of mission strategy reveals that strategy is not static. Strategy builds on strategy and is molded by the circumstances in which it finds itself. Principles for effective mission have emerged through trial and error and have been refined by time. As disciples of the kingdom, we do well to take from our treasure the old and the new in formulating strategy to meet the challenge of the present era of mission.

Historically, it is undeniable that God has used two structures with distinct functions in carrying out His redemptive plan. Modalities have functioned as the primary nurture structure; sodalities, as the primary mission structure. Both are needed to fulfill Christ's global mandate. Sodalities will continue to be needed as primary channels for those desiring to commit their lives wholly for evangelization.

INTEGRATIVE ASSIGNMENT

1. Using the principles of mission strategy you gleaned from your reading, write down *Ten Commandments of Mission Strategy*. Use negative as well as positive commandments: "Thou shalt not . . .," as well as "Thou shalt . . . ."

2. Outline a short talk entitled, *The Need for Mission Structures in World Evangelization.* Give three reasons for such structures, and support your statements from Scripture or historical evidence.

3. If a local church in a city wanted to become involved in missions beyond their geographical and cultural boundaries, what would they have to do? Outline in a logical sequence the steps they would have to take.

QUESTIONS FOR REFLECTION

It is true that all of us who are attempting to do God's will use some kind of strategy. Even the lack of a conscious strategy is a strategy in itself-- the "no strategy" strategy. But this lack of method in what we do often results in ineffectiveness for the Lord. What can you do to improve your personal strategy for doing God's will? Towards what goals are you working? What disciplines will help you to achieve those goals? Reflect on these matters and enter your thoughts in your journal.

CHAPTER 7

THE TASK REMAINING

INTRODUCTION

It is important to know how far we've come in missions. To plan an effective strategy, however, it is also essential that we understand what's left to be done. What is the task remaining?

In 1974, Christians from all over the world met in Lausanne, Switzerland, for an International Congress on World Evangelization. This Congress, like its historic predecessor in Edinburgh (1910), attempted to analyze the current progress of world evangelization and to define the remaining task. Perhaps the most significant address of the Congress was delivered by Dr. Ralph Winter. In this address, Winter convincingly demonstrated that there were 2.4 billion people still beyond the current reach of the gospel message. He defined the task remaining in terms of the biblical definition of "nations," labeling those yet to be reached as "unreached" or "hidden" peoples. He proved conclusively that the "crucial need" in world evangelization today is for missions which will cross cultural frontiers with the gospel.

In this chapter, we will look at Winter's thesis, define his terminology, and examine the rationale behind his conclusions. We will also take a brief survey of the major blocks of unreached peoples. An overview of these blocks or "megaspheres" will show us where we should focus the major thrust of future evangelism.

I. THE NATIONS AND CROSS-CULTURAL EVANGELIZATION

In the following excerpt,[1] Winter defines the biblical concept of "nation" and graphically illustrates how this term applies today.

---

[1]Ralph D. Winter, "The Task Remaining: All Humanity in Mission Perspective," in *Perspectives on the World Christian Movement*, ed. Ralph D. Winter and Steven C. Hawthorne (Pasadena, CA: William Carey Library, 1981), pp. 312-317. Used by permission.

The Task Remaining: All Humanity in Mission Perspective

Ralph D. Winter

No perspective on the entire human race can be brief without tending to be simplistic. When God chose Abraham and his lineage both for special blessing and for special responsibility to share that blessing to "all the families of the earth" (Gen. 12:3; 18:18, etc.), Abraham mercifully did not understand how big and complex the task was.

Now however, 4,000 years later, over half of "all the families of the earth" are at least superficially what Toynbee calls "Judaic" in religion and have certainly received at least some direct blessing through people with faith like Abraham's and through the redemptive work of the One to whom Abraham looked (John 8:56). If we take into account indirect influences, it would be possible to estimate that nine-tenths of all humanity has by now received some of that blessing, even if mixed with other elements.

NATIONS AND COUNTRIES

In today's world we tend to think "political entity" or "country" when we see the word "nation." Unfortunately, this is not the concept expressed in the Bible. A closer translation comes directly from the Greek word *ethnos*, which has not only been translated "nation" but also "ethnic unit," "people," or (as in the New Testament) "heathen" or "Gentiles." In no case does it refer to a country as we think of a political unit today. A more correct usage would be as in the phrase "the Cherokee nation," referring to the tribe of American Indians known as the Cherokee. Even in the Old Testament this same concept holds true. Two words are used in the Old Testament. *Gam*, which occurs 1,821 times, refers to a people, a single race or tribe, or to a specific family of mankind, as in Deuteronomy 4:6 and 28:37. The other word, *mishpahgheh*, occurs only 267 times and is mainly used to refer to family, kindred, or relatives. This is the word used in Genesis 12:3, "In thee shall all the families of the earth be blessed." The concept of "country" or a politically defined nation is totally absent in both of these cases. The fact that not countries, but rather ethnic units or people groups is what is implied is made even more pointed when in a number of places (e.g., Rev. 5:9; 10:11, etc.) not only is the word "nation" used, but it is further spelled out as peoples, tribes, tongues, and kindred.

Figure 7.1 **THE BIBLICAL "NATION"**

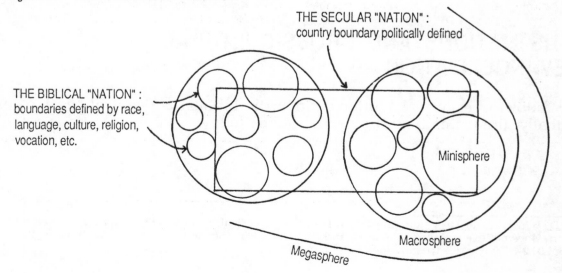

Paul knew himself as the apostle to the Gentiles (read "peoples" or "nations"). He was one of the first of the new church to conclude that God wanted to use the marvelous diversity of the cultural mosaic of mankind. He came to see that God did not require a Gentile to commit cultural suicide to become a believer. Paul spoke of this as a mystery long hidden, but now made plain (Eph. 3:4). There was nothing new about a Gentile becoming a Jew and joining the community of faith of the people of God. A few hardy proselytes in Paul's day did this, though they had a hard time. Most Gentiles would not have gone that far. (Did they sense instinctively that such a shift could not in itself be salvific?) They needed a Paul to establish a synagogue of, by, and for their own people, that is, a Gentile synagogue. The new thing was unity without uniformity. Gentiles could follow Jesus without becoming culturally Jewish.

Many Americans in particular tend to assume that all who live in China are racially Chinese, by which they probably mean "Han" Chinese. Or they may assume all the peoples of Russia are ethnically the same. However, even the unity-seeking government of the People's Republic of China recognizes a number of ethnic minorities, that is, distinctly non-Han groups of people who were born and have lived in China for hundreds of years. Furthermore, there are a great many varieties of Han Chinese. There are at least 100 mutually unintelligible varieties of the Chinese family of languages! India is a country of 3,000 nations, only 100 of which have any Christians at all. The Soviet Union also has widely diverse peoples with practically nothing in common except the political glue that binds them together.

For example, one major mission organization states its purpose as "multiplying laborers in every nation," yet it only keeps track of how many *countries* it works in, not how many biblical *nations* it is touching, nor whether such nations already have a well established work or not. Another outstanding mission agency has produced a book entitled *The Discipling of a Nation*, which speaks of needing one church for every thousand people in a "nation." The thinking of the leaders of that mission is clear, but the book title is ambiguous since most people would understand it to mean countries, not biblical nations. Yet, strange as it may at first sound, it is perfectly possible to reach the goal of having planted one church per thousand people in, say, the *country* of India and not have touched even half of the 3,000 different biblically-defined nations in that country.

Thus to look at the world from the "peoples" concept is not only biblical, it is also highly strategic, for there is one kind of cross-cultural evangelism and church planting that is far more strategic than all the others. Moreover, the "peoples" concept stresses the need to look at people as part of their own culture, not merely as individuals, and to see them, when converted as individuals, as strategic, natural bridges to the rest of their society. To give a diagrammatic example of the significance of the "peoples" concept for mission strategy, let us look at one small sector of the world.

1. What is the difference between a "country" and the biblical concept of "nation"?

   _____

   _____

2. What is the importance of this distinction?

   _____

   _____

The term "people group" has been coined to refer to the biblical concept of nation. People groups are sociological groupings of people, not political groupings. As defined, a people group is "a significantly large sociological grouping of individuals who perceive themselves to have a common affinity for one another because of their shared language, religion, ethnicity, residence, occupation, class or caste, situation, etc., or combinations of these."[2]

MEGASPHERES, MACROSPHERES, AND MINISPHERES

Figure 7.2 shows some people groups within two large cultural blocs or "megaspheres"--the Muslim megasphere and the Han Chinese megasphere. Within these megaspheres we find three large circles filled with a number of smaller circles. Each large circle represents a "cultural macrosphere"--a group of societies that have certain cultural similarities both within and between them. The middle macrosphere consists of Cantonese-speaking people, most of whom are found in a single country, the People's Republic of China, and they number in the millions of people. The smaller circles, which I will call "minispheres," represent groups of people which speak divergent dialects of Cantonese mutually unintelligible to each other. People from two such subgroups can be understood by each other only if they learn a "trade language" variety of Cantonese. Either the macrosphere or the minisphere could be considered a *nation* in biblical terms, but note that neither is a *country*. (Still smaller "microspheres" could be defined by clan or family or vocational differences too small to require separate churches for maximally effective outreach.)

Figure 7.2   **REGULAR MISSIONS / FRONTIER MISSIONS**

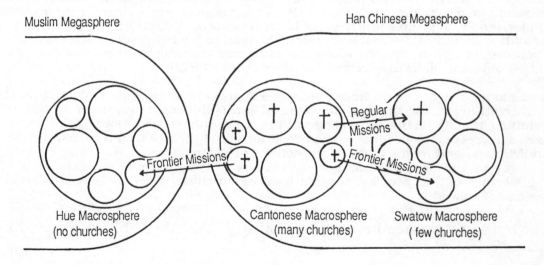

3. In Figure 7.2, which are the "megaspheres"?

_____

[2]Edward R. Dayton, "To Reach the Unreached," in *Unreached Peoples '79,* ed. C. Peter Wagner and Edward R. Dayton (Elgin, IL: David C. Cook Publishing Co., 1978), p. 23.

4. Which are the "macrospheres"?

_____

5. Which are the "minispheres"?

_____

E-1, E-2, AND E-3 EVANGELISM

Note further that in some of the minispheres--the smaller circles--there is a cross, representing an indigenous church that has been planted within that culture sometime in the past. These churches, if they are vital and witnessing, are readily able to win the remaining non-Christians in that dialect group by normal, near-neighbor evangelism. We call this E-1 evangelism. There is only one barrier to be crossed in near-neighbor evangelism, the "stained glass barrier." Should that barrier get too thick, the believing community then becomes an enclave that is essentially a different minisphere and must be treated as such.

Some of the smaller circles, however, have no cross. Those minispheres obviously need someone from somewhere else to do that initial evangelizing and to plant the first church. That kind of evangelism from the outside is much more difficult than near-neighbor evangelism, for it requires the evangelist from the outside to learn another language, or at least another dialect of Cantonese. Also, he will find out that some of the cultural assumptions will be different. In other words, ordinary evangelism will not do the task that is required to pioneer in this frontier area. This type of evangelism we call E-2 or E-3. The evangelist must penetrate significant cultural barriers.

Looking again at Figure 7.2, you will notice that schematically we show only six of the many minispheres in the Cantonese macrosphere, and that five have a cross, meaning an indigenous church. The Swatow macrosphere, by contrast, has only one minisphere with an indigenous church, and the Muslim Hue macrosphere, which pertains to an entirely different Muslim megasphere, has no Christian church at all in any of its minispheres. Each of these macrospheres numbers millions of people; indeed, even some of the minispheres may number over a million people. The job of the ordinary evangelist is to plant churches in his own minisphere. That we call E-1, near-neighbor evangelism.

But where there is no church--no indigenous community of believers--there is not the evangelism potential to reach the entire minisphere. In fact, there may be a number of individual believers who (like the New Testament "God fearers") worship outside their culture. There may even be some believers from that group who have left their minisphere and become "proselytized" to another. But there is still no viable, indigenous church. By viable church we mean a minimum, yet sufficiently developed indigenous Christian tradition, capable of evangelizing its own people without cross-cultural help. This implies that there would be a cluster of indigenous evangelizing congregations and a significant part of the Bible translated by the people themselves. Minispheres which do not have that cluster of indigenous, growing, evangelizing congregations can be considered "unreached." These people groups require cross-cultural evangelism.

A people group can be considered "reached" if there is a body of Christians with the potential to evangelize its own people such that outside, cross-cultural efforts can be "safely" terminated. This potential may be roughly predicted by measuring the percentage of practicing Christians. The figure of 20 percent has been established by the Lausanne Committee for World Evangelization, to be on the "safe side," but this figure is not absolutely crucial if in a given case it is known that the indigenous church shows every indication that it can and will evangelize its entire minisphere. Where there is no viable church it takes a Paul, or someone from outside that language group and culture, to go to that people and plant a church there. Or it takes a Luther within the culture to wake up and go indigenous. In any case, the Cantonese evangelist in Figure 7.2 who goes to a Swatow dialect where there is no church, is doing a missionary type of evangelism. In Paul's words, he is "going where Christ is not named."

Figure 7.3   **E-1, E-2 AND E-3 EVANGELISM**

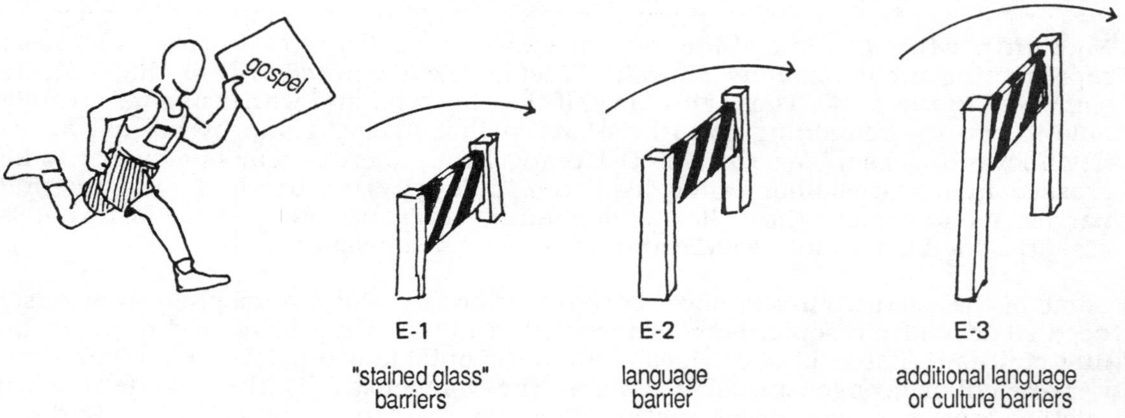

E-1	E-2	E-3
"stained glass" barriers	language barrier	additional language or culture barriers

6. What is the main barrier to be crossed in E-1 evangelism?

_____

7. What is the difference between E-1 evangelism and E-2 and E-3 evangelism?

_____

8. How do we know when a people group has a *viable* church?

_____

_____

EVANGELISM AND MISSIONS

If, however, a Cantonese evangelist goes from his Cantonese-speaking church to a Swatow minisphere where there already is an indigenous church, to help those believers to evangelize their own non-Christian Swatows, remaining in the same minisphere, he may very well be making a "missionary trip," but he is doing evangelism, not missions. We have defined as evangelism the activity of reaching out from an existing church within the same minisphere, working to its fringes. The people back home in his Cantonese minisphere may very likely call such a person their "missionary," but technically speaking, even in the biblical and classical sense, he is an evangelist who happens to be working at a cultural distance from his own background. The main point is that winning people into a church that is already within their own minisphere is the work of an evangelist, even if the "missionary" comes from a great distance. We must admit that this is the usual pattern of so-called "missions" today. Most "missionaries," whether from the U.S.A., Europe, Asia, or Africa, go from their own cultures to work in another culture where a church is already established. We may have to concede the term "regular missions" to such activity, just because of social pressure; in that case we fall back to the term "frontier missions" for the other activity. Some workers are incorrectly called "missionaries" even when they go to work with Christians from their own culture who have moved to a foreign country. In that case, such people are not even evangelists but rather "transplanted pastors."

9. What is the difference between "regular" and "frontier" missions?

_____

_____

Cultural Barriers

Linguistic Barriers

When the biblical definition of "nation" is applied, Christ's words, "Go ye into all the world and make disciples of all *nations*" (Matt. 28:19), may take on new significance. Most of the world's politically defined nations have a viable church. But thousands of the world's culturally defined nations still don't have a viable Christian witness in their midst. These nations, or people groups, are isolated from the gospel by cultural barriers.

The most obvious cultural barrier which distinguishes one people from another is language. People who speak a language different from one's own are obviously foreign. To a slightly lesser degree, the same is true of those who speak a different dialect of one's own language. Dialects, or regional variations of a language, are distinguishable because of differences in accent, vocabulary, or grammar. Often these differences are so marked that it is difficult or impossible for people who belong to different dialect groups of the same language to understand each other. More than 7,000 different languages and dialects are spoken in the world today.

Dialects reflect geographical, economic, or social distance of members of the same tribe or ethnic grouping. Because of this distance, significant cultural differences beyond language usually exist. For example, most people think of the United States as a single nation, bound by a common language, English, which only has some slight regional differences. But a study by Joel Garreau entitled *The Nine Nations of North America*,[3] demonstrates that there are nine distinct regions in North America, whose economies and value systems are so different that they defy political boundaries and could well be considered culturally and economically as separate nations. Even though most North Americans speak the same language, their value systems are sufficiently different that the gospel must be communicated to each region in a distinct and culturally relevant way.

---

[3]Joel Garreau, *The Nine Nations of North America* (New York: Avon Books, 1981).

10. What is your first language? Which of its dialects do you speak?   Name some other dialects of your own language.

_____

_____

In many countries, a national language is spoken for the purpose of trade, education, and government, but many local languages and dialects are spoken in the homes and in the localities where the languages originate. For example, in Cameroon, West Africa, English and French are spoken as national languages, but 183 distinct languages and dialects are spoken regionally. Cameroon must not be thought of as evangelized simply because French and English speaking congregations are established throughout the country. We can consider Cameroon a reached country only when its 183 linguistically defined "nations" have viable churches ministering to them.

11. What is the "official" language of your country? What other languages are spoken regionally or by major groups within your country?

_____

_____

Social Barriers

The cultural barriers to spontaneous evangelization are not simply linguistic. Some of the most significant barriers are social. Within most societies there are social classes which are defined along racial, occupational, educational, economic, hereditary, or religious lines. We give these classes designations such as "upper" and "lower" class, working class, professional class, ruling class, etc. In India, an intricate class or "caste" system has developed with hundreds of distinct classifications.

Perhaps because of a greater awareness of their own need and dependence on God, the poor "lower" classes have often been the most responsive to the gospel. But it is improbable, and in some cases nearly impossible, for upper class members or castes to become Christians if it means forsaking their own social position to become members of a "lower" class or caste church. For example, millions of Hindus in Southern India speak the same language. The church is well established there, but its membership is drawn from approximately five percent of the castes. We could not consider Southern India to be reached until "viable" churches are established which can minister effectively to the other 95 percent of the castes that are still unevangelized.

12. Name some classes which stratify the society in which you live.

_____

_____

Rivalries and Prejudices

The barriers preventing the gospel from spreading spontaneously from one culture to the next are many and complex. Linguistic and sociological factors are the most significant, but there are also other factors which bar Christian neighbors from evangelizing peoples who are geographically, linguistically, and even sociologically similar. For example, herdsmen and farmers in the same region may speak a common language and may be considered on the same social level. A viable church may exist among the farmers, but age-old rivalries over land use will probably prevent the farmers from evangelizing the herdsmen. It may well require E-2 or E-3 evangelism from the outside to reach the herdsmen successfully.

In many countries, racial or class discrimination is widely practiced. Black/white tensions in the United States and the practice of apartheid in South Africa are perhaps the best known examples. But each part of the globe has its own racial prejudices. Native American populations of North and South America, Russian Jews, pygmies in Africa, Palestinians in Israel, tenant farmers, religious minorities in India, and powerless majorities elsewhere have all suffered tyranny and exploitation. The net result is that such mistrust and hate have built up over the years that it is highly unlikely that the dominant group will ever find a hearing among those who have been oppressed. Only E-2 or E-3 evangelists from the outside are likely to receive an open hearing.

13. What rivalries and prejudices are you most aware of in your society?

_____

_____

Crossing Cultural Barriers

In Acts 1:8 Christ emphasizes the importance of cross-cultural evangelism. At first glance, it may seem that He is speaking simply of a geographical progression of the gospel from Jerusalem, throughout Judea, to Samaria, and from there to the uttermost part of the earth. Although geographic distance does figure into this expansion, the fact remains that this sequence reflects a cultural progression from the center of Jewish culture, Jerusalem, throughout the Jewish fringes of Judea, to the part-Jewish, part-Gentile Samaritans, and on to the Gentiles of the "uttermost parts."

Although the book of Acts reveals that the gospel did spread in just this manner, the progression was not as neat and simple as it might first appear. The message of Christ did not simply flow from Jew to Samaritan to Greek. The Jews and the Samaritans, though culturally near, had no dealings with each other. The Jews despised the Samaritans for having defiled the Jewish race through intermarriage with Gentiles. Thus, although the Samaritans were only at E-2 distance from the Jews culturally, long-standing prejudicial hatred was a difficult barrier to cross with the gospel. Indeed, when the Samaritans were reached, the contact was made not by an ethnic Jew, but by Philip, a Hellenistic Jew of Greek ethnicity (Acts 8). In this case, Philip was culturally more distant from the Samaritans than were the Jews, but it was this very distance which may well have given him a hearing among the Samaritans.

Paul himself, though ethnically a Jew, was raised in a Gentile culture. This heritage put him closer culturally to the Gentiles than the disciples were, thus explaining in part why he was chosen to go to these people. Using Winter's terminology, we could say that Paul was at an E-2 distance from the Greeks, while Peter was at E-3 distance from them. Luke, who himself was Greek, was at E-1 distance. Likewise, Barnabas was probably sent to Antioch by the elders in Jerusalem, because, being a native of those parts, he could minister on an E-1 basis.

Although analyzing the cultural distance of evangelists to specific peoples in the book of Acts is an interesting exercise, the point is, there are *many* factors that determine cultural distance and the possible effectiveness of an evangelist. In the great cultural mosaic of societies, it will not always be those who are culturally closest who will be able to evangelize a given people. As noted above, it took a man such as Philip to evangelize the Samaritans. On the other hand, when prejudice is not a factor, it makes sense to send evangelists who are culturally near, as in the case of Barnabas going to Antioch.

In today's complex world, there are many "Jerusalems," "Judeas," "Samarias," and "uttermost parts." One man's "Samaria" is another's "Judea" and a third person's "uttermost part." The following diagram illustrates these relationships:

Figure 7.4

CULTURAL DISTANCES

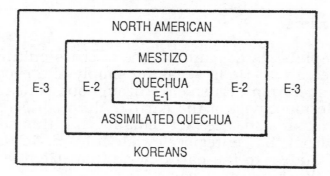

The above diagram (Figure 7.4) is a schematic of the cultural distance between the Highland Quechuas of Peru and several other groups. The peoples farthest away culturally are the North Americans and the Koreans. These groups are clearly at E-3 distance because they must cross two linguistic barriers to get to the Quechuas (Spanish and a dialect of Quechua), and they must also deal with many major cultural changes.

48

Mestizos, the descendants of marriages between the Spanish conquerors and the Quechuas, are culturally closer, at an E-2 distance. But age-old dominance of the Quechuas by the Mestizos has produced a "Jew/Samaritan" situation. Walls of prejudice in most cases inhibit effective evangelization of the Quechuas by the Mestizos.

Also at E-2 distance are first and second generation Quechuas who, through urbanization and opportunities offered by education, have moved into cities and are being assimilated into Mestizo culture. Although the lifestyle and professions of these assimilated Quechuas have now distanced them from their Quechua heritage, these people are barely beyond E-1 distance. Many understand at least one Quechua dialect and perhaps speak it also.

14. Based on the preceding discussion, which people group is least likely to be able to evangelize one of the many distinct Highland Quechua groups?

_____

15. Which groups could possibly evangelize the Quechuas but, because of cultural distance, would be limited in their effectiveness and would find the task very difficult?

_____

16. Which group would seem best suited to evangelize the Highland Quechuas? Why?

_____

_____

The Priority

There is no way of arriving at an exact figure, but missiologists estimate the total number of people groups in the world at nearly 22,000. Of these, just over 5,000 are considered to have a viable church. This leaves us with approximately *16,750 unreached people groups*. It will take E-2 and E-3 evangelism to reach these groups. Christians must be willing to forsake security and familiarity in the interest of crossing cultural barriers with the gospel. "Frontier" or "cross-cultural" mission is the crucial priority in the completion of the Great Commission.

When setting goals for evangelism, it is helpful to understand the biblical concept of nation or people group. If a particular people does not have a viable church, then we can consider that group "unreached" and in need of having a specific effort launched to reach them. Any strategy to reach such a people must take into consideration what kind of evangelism will be needed, whether E-1, E-2, or E-3. Unless an insurmountable wall of prejudice exists, E-2 is easier than E-3 evangelism. Moreover, where a viable church exists at E-1 or

E-2 distance from unreached groups, it is logical that evangelism be attempted from that church rather than from one at E-3 distance.

II. UNREACHED PEOPLE: BUDDHIST AND CHINESE MEGASPHERES

There are unreached peoples all around us; in ethnic and social enclaves of cities and isolated countryside pockets. These people have been "hidden" from the gospel because the church has not known about them or perhaps has not wanted to look for them. The church has often assumed that, as long as she keeps her doors open, it is the unreached who are at fault if they don't choose to walk through those doors. But very real cultural barriers will continue to prevent the evangelization of these peoples unless the church removes her blinders and takes the initiative to cross those barriers with the gospel. In addition, beyond the hidden peoples which surround the church everywhere, there are entire blocks of people that have so few Christians in them that a massive thrust of E-2 and E-3 evangelism is required to reach them.

Study Figure 7.5. Darkened areas represent people who lie totally beyond the current reach of church or mission efforts, needing E-2 and E-3 evangelism. The two shaded areas represent nominal Christians needing revival and non-Christians needing E-1 evangelism. White areas represent committed Christians who could be mobilized to reach the unreached.

Figure 7.5   THE GLOBE AT A GLANCE

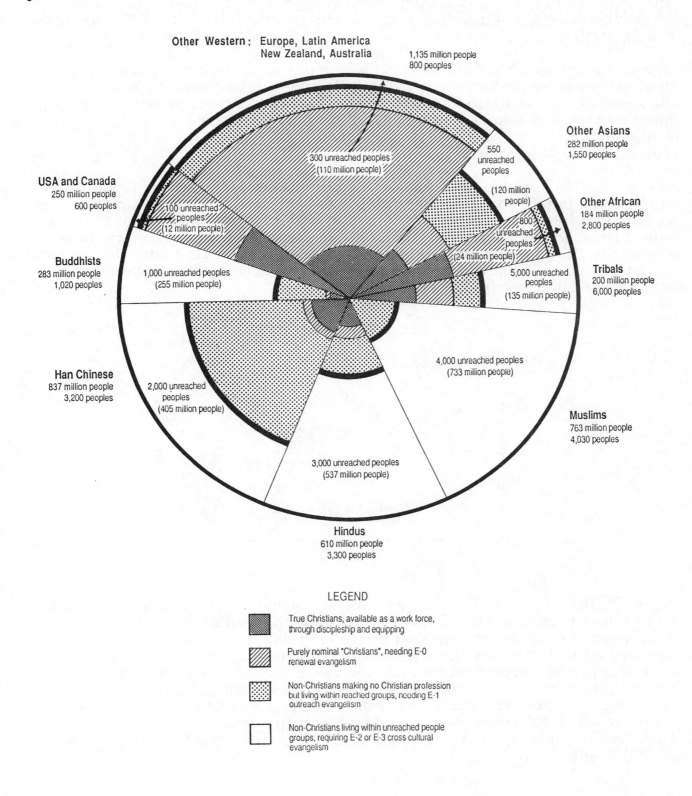

LEGEND

True Christians, available as a work force, through discipleship and equipping

Purely nominal "Christians", needing E-0 renewal evangelism

Non-Christians making no Christian profession but living within reached groups, needing E-1 outreach evangelism

Non-Christians living within unreached people groups, requiring E-2 or E-3 cross cultural evangelism

Each section of the globe represents a cultural megasphere, a people who have one major distinctive which allows them to be grouped together for our purposes. You will notice on the chart that the greatest proportion of unreached belong to the Buddhist, Han Chinese, Hindu, Muslim, and tribal megaspheres. Within these five megaspheres, we can count 15,000 unreached people groups.

Unless we live in a part of the world where one of these megaspheres predominates, we probably know very little about these peoples. What are they like, and what will it take to reach them? To begin answering some of these questions, we will take a look at each of these megaspheres.

The Buddhist Megasphere

The world's 235 million Buddhists are found primarily in the Far East. This religion was founded by Buddha in the sixth century B.C. Buddhism originated in Northern India and eventually spread in several forms throughout India and into Burma, Sri Lanka, China, Japan, Korea, Nepal, Thailand, Vietnam, Laos, Cambodia, Tibet, and Mongolia. There are relatively few Buddhists left in India today, but the religion has taken strong root in the countries where it was spread by Buddhist missionaries.

Figure 7.6

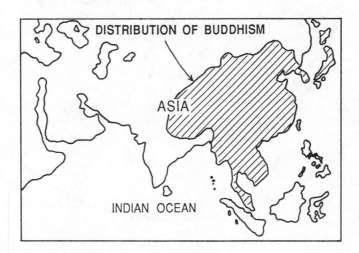

Although Buddhism is classified as a world religion in its own right, its origins lie in ancient forms of Hinduism. Presumably, the Buddha founded his religion in response to his observation that man's lot in life was to suffer. He was dissatisfied with the way the religion of his homeland dealt with this problem and thus began searching for an answer. He came to the conclusion that suffering was caused by selfish desire and that in order to be released from suffering, one must renounce that desire. He established an austere "Eightfold Path" by which followers could be saved. To help stay on the path, many of the Buddha's disciples gathered into monasteries, thereby greatly aiding the spread of Buddhism.

For the Buddhist, salvation consists of escaping from the "Great Sea of Birth, Death and Sorrow." This concept is founded on the philosophy of "reincarnation," the endless cycle of birth and rebirth in which the soul passes from life to death to life again, constantly working out the consequences of its past lives. To become free of this endless "Wheel of Becoming" is the object of Buddhism, and this is accomplished by attaining "Nirvana," a state of enlightenment.

It is generally true that where Buddhism has prevailed, Christianity has languished. Although Roman Catholic missions had some success in French Indochina, as a whole, traditional Buddhist populations have shown resistance to the gospel. Only where Buddhist influence has been weak, such as among the Koreans and animistic tribal groups, has Christianity made significant inroads. However, in recent times, the catastrophic wars which have engulfed the countries of Indochina have shaken Buddhists out of their religious self-complacency. An effectual door for the gospel has been opened, particularly through ministries to the thousands of refugees fleeing their war-torn homelands.

The Chinese Megasphere

The majority of the nearly one billion Chinese still live in the country of China, although more than 40 million others are scattered around the globe. During its 5,000-year history China has known tremendous upheavals, the most recent of which was the Communist takeover in 1949. Nearly 10,000 Christian missionaries were at work in China prior to that takeover, and about five million Chinese were protestants or Roman Catholics.

Figure 7.7

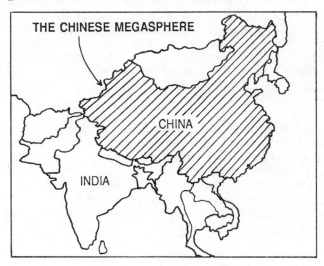

The expulsion of the missionaries by the Communists was followed by 30 years of intense persecution and silence from the church. In 1979, that silence was broken, and to the astonishment of many, the Chinese Church had not only survived but had grown substantially under the persecution! The following overview of Chinese evangelization is excerpted from a report emerging from the Consultation on World Evangelization (COWE) held at Pattaya, Thailand in 1980.[4]

Christian Witness to the Chinese People

Lausanne Committee for World Evangelization[5]

INTRODUCTION

The Chinese constitute the largest single segment of the human race. Their unbroken history of more than 5,000 years marks a culture that is durable and resilient. They have survived the ravages of countless internal struggles and foreign invasions and remain today a distinct people.

And yet, throughout their long history, the God and Father of our Lord and Saviour Jesus Christ has been almost a total stranger to them. True, there have been periods in which those who knew the true and living God dwelled in their midst, but for a variety of tragic reasons, the great majority of Chinese learned little of Christ's name and salvation. Jewish synagogues and Nestorian merchant communities were scattered throughout China during the Tang dynasty (seventh to ninth centuries) when Chinese civilization was more advanced than anything Europe had to offer. Franciscan missionaries struggled to survive on the fringes of that empire during the years of Mongol dominance (13th century), while creative Jesuits followed in the 16th and 17th centuries. Nevertheless, these relatively brief periods of Roman Catholic missionary presence produced little lasting spiritual benefit for the common people.

It was only when Protestant and renewed Catholic missions came to China in force in the 19th and 20th centuries that it could be said that the Christian church had at long last been planted among China's millions. Even then, this church was more identified with Western cultural influence than with any spontaneous acceptance by the Chinese themselves. It was during those decades prior to the Japanese invasion of Northeast China in 1937 that the church began to loosen its Western moorings. This was largely due to the emergence of an able and vigorous Chinese leadership that began to take over responsibilities of the formerly mission-oriented churches, as well as to produce a variety of independent Christian movements. Through their widespread influence, they prepared the whole church to meet the forthcoming anguish which occurred after 1949.

Since then, during the past three decades, the people of mainland China have experienced a series of painful convulsions under revolutionary fervor. In the anguish of life under these protracted and trying circumstances, Chinese people have at long last become deeply disenchanted with revolutionary rhetoric and social manipulation, and the euphoria originally generated by the Maoist triumph has evaporated. Today, the official line has been reduced to "Four Modernizations"; the call to make economic growth and military security virtually the sole objectives of all collective activity.

---

[4]Lausanne Committee for World Evangelization, "Christian Witness to the Chinese People," *Lausanne Occasional Papers, No. 6* (Wheaton, IL: Lausanne Committee for World Evangelization, 1980). Used by permission.

[5]This report is one of the series of Lausanne Occasional Papers emerging from the Consultation on World Evangelization (COWE) held at Pattaya, Thailand, in June 1980. The report was drafted by members of the "Mini-Consultation on Reaching Chinese" under the chairmanship of Thomas Wang. The excerpts included here focus on ethnic Chinese in the People's Republic of China.

Touching the church in China, we must be particularly sensitive to the implications of God's evident control of recent history. It was in His providence that all Western missionaries were removed from China (largely completed by 1951). He allowed the church there to be severely tested by man ever since the authorities determined to break its ties with the West and make it subservient to the state. Many suffered for their faith and some died in prison. During the period of the Cultural Revolution, some theologians overlooked the wide scale oppression and tended to identify the emergence of a new political order with the coming of the kingdom of God. Others, however, rejected it in its totality as incompatible with Christian faith.

As the years passed, Christians on the outside lost contact with the actual situation in China. Most could only pray and wait. Many asked whether all those years of sacrificial labor on the part of thousands of foreign missionaries and Chinese workers had been in vain. They waited over 30 years for an answer.

Today at this Pattaya Consultation, we rejoice that the silence has been broken. Government strictures against public worship have to some extent been relaxed. We now find nothing less than a living, growing church, with thousands upon thousands of Christians courageously confessing that Jesus Christ alone is Lord!

Among the more than 40 million Chinese outside of the mainland, God has seen fit to work in different patterns. Over the years, He has pursued those Chinese in such ways that many feel they are being prepared for a significant role in His kingdom in the days ahead. He has placed them in positions of leadership in various fields. Moreover, He has made them receptive to the Christian message, and churches made up of these people now exist in more than 80 countries of the world. Indeed we cannot but believe that what God has been doing in recent years in China to glorify His name through a suffering church and among other ethnic Chinese to bring about a growing church will be seen to be intimately interrelated in the days ahead.

Having said this, we at the same time must not ignore the fact that the Chinese churches (both in the mainland and outside) are still occupied with issues and problems which must be objectively analyzed and studied. They must humbly seek the Lord's guidance into viable strategies and work very hard for their ultimate realization, with cooperation from churches of the West and the Third World.

Our primary concern is with the evangelization of the Chinese people, both in the mainland and throughout the world. In our judgment, we believe we stand today on the threshold of the greatest ingathering into Christ of the Chinese people this world has ever known. But more, our larger concern is that in these last days, God will transform the Chinese church into a missionary vehicle through which the Christian gospel will be brought to the forgotten and hidden peoples of this generation.

1. What does this introduction suggest regarding evangelization of the Chinese people in the near future?

_____

_____

REACHING THE CHINESE ON THE MAINLAND

Reaching the Chinese people on the mainland of China is, perhaps, one of the most difficult and challenging tasks in world evangelization. It is difficult because the one billion people in China live under a socialist system; and it is challenging because of the changing situation that is developing in China. In thinking and planning for the evangelization of China, we must, therefore, do so with these two realities held in proper tension.

In addition, it is absolutely mandatory that we do not think of the evangelization of China as something to be done primarily from the outside. We must keep in mind that these Christians in China, who have remained faithful to the Lord despite many trials of faith and much suffering, are already busily engaged in this task. Hence, the central challenge for Christians outside China is to learn how to work with them.

In seeking to find answers to this central question, we at COWE have reviewed Chinese attitudes toward religion, Chinese receptivity to the gospel, and the current state of the church. We have sought to identify the issues involved in the evangelistic task and also to work out realistic goals and strategies for its accomplishment.

CURRENT OFFICIAL ATTITUDE TOWARD RELIGION

Recent official publications indicate that the Chinese Communists have not abandoned their Marxist interpretation of religion. In fact, they have recently related their traditional position: religion is an erroneous worldview held by people not yet liberated by science and culture. They concede a distinction, however, between world religions such as Christianity, Buddhism, and Islam, and traditional Chinese superstitions such as geomancy, fortune telling, etc. The former are accorded legal status while the latter are to be suppressed by science and education.

This current policy of toleration toward the world religions is being implemented as part of the Party's revived "united front" policy, in a reversal from that of the 1971-1976 days. This return to the pre-1966 religious policy is also a natural consequence of China's adoption of the "Four Modernizations" program.

The influence of the Marxist interpretation of religion, particularly of Christianity, nevertheless still is strong among the Chinese people. This is inevitable, following three decades of Marxist indoctrination. Today, instruction in atheism is being stepped up. Government religious officials continue to link the missionary movement in China with Western imperialism.

To be realistic about the future evangelistic task in China, therefore, we must understand the implications of this official attitude toward religion in general and toward Christianity in particular. We should expect the government to set limits upon Christian activities in China and upon evangelistic efforts from outside China.

2. What two major factors must be considered in the evangelization of mainland China, and how do these affect foreign missions to China?

_____

_____

The report on Chinese evangelization goes on to describe the receptivity of different sections of Chinese society and the current condition of the church and evangelization. Although the report estimates that there are four to six million Chinese Christians on the mainland, later investigations have shown that there may be as many as 50 million Chinese Christians today!

The report also mentions four avenues by which Christians outside China are encouraging the ongoing evangelization of China:

Radio--Since the Communist takeover, The Far East Broadcasting Corporation has directed Christian radio broadcasts toward the Chinese mainland. These broadcasts have been an effective tool for evangelization as well as for encouraging believers. This ongoing ministry is of vital importance.

Prayer--Prayer for China has been offered widely by churches throughout the world. China's national transformation, as well as the church, have become the focus of prayer in recent years. This ministry is not only a tremendous encouragement to believers on the mainland, but is also deemed essential to China's evangelization.

Bible Distribution--Most Bibles and Christian literature in China were destroyed during the "Cultural Revolution." When China began opening its doors to travel in 1977, Christians started taking Bibles into the country. Today, visitors continue to carry in Bibles as well as send them to friends and relatives.

Visits--China has opened its doors wide to tourism. Christians are taking advantage of this opportunity to visit Chinese Christians. Through these contacts, the Chinese church's sense of isolation is being broken, and the visitors themselves are often greatly encouraged by the testimony of Chinese believers.

With a vital, growing church in China and an ongoing negative stance by the Communist government towards foreign influences, the wisest course of action at this time appears to be to continue focusing on ministries of encouragement to the church rather than attempting overt evangelistic efforts from the outside.

III. HINDU, MUSLIM, AND TRIBAL MEGASPHERES

The Hindu Megasphere

Hinduism, the ancient religion of India, traces its origins back 4,000 years. It entered India during the third century B.C. and presently claims the vast majority of that country's 600 million inhabitants. The complex Hindu caste system is the backbone of Indian social organization. This rigid system divides its adherents into an estimated 3,000 distinct people groups.

Figure 7.8

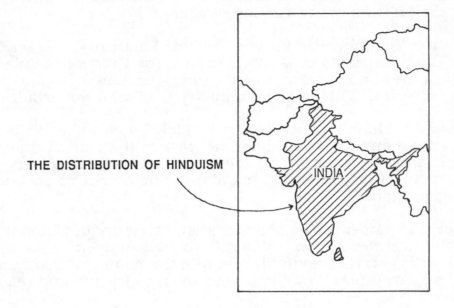

THE DISTRIBUTION OF HINDUISM

INDIA

Because Hindus comprise a significant percentage of the unreached peoples, a special report entitled "Christian Witness to Hindus" (1980) was produced by the Lausanne Committee for World Evangelization. Much of the following information is condensed from that report.[6]

Generally speaking, the growth of Hinduism has been biological. In the past, this pattern of expansion had a tendency to confine the religion to the borders of India. But large exportation and migration of Indians during this century have produced pockets of Hindus all over the world. As a rule, these Hindu minorities seldom draw converts from other religions. However, in recent times, the popularity of Eastern thought and religion in the West has produced conversions to certain Hindu sects. These sects are led by "gurus," Hindu mystics who claim supernatural powers.

It is impossible to define Hinduism in concise terms because the religion is a conglomeration of ideas, beliefs, convictions, and practices. Its many forms fall into six general classifications:

Philosophic Hinduism--This form of Hinduism is dominated by ancient "Vedas" and "Upanishads" (scriptures). These writings teach that there is a spark of divinity in each man. To call a man a sinner is therefore blasphemous. Since man cannot be considered a sinner, this branch of Hinduism thus finds no use for a savior.

---

[6]Lausanne Committee for World Evangelization, "Christian Witness to Hindus," *Lausanne Occasional Papers, No. 14* (Wheaton, IL: Lausanne Committee for World Evangelization, 1980).

Religious Hinduism--This branch of Hinduism adheres to "Puranas," or epics which they claim are revelations from God. They have a strong belief in "avatars," incarnations of gods. They hold to a pantheon of 330 million gods, of which man is free to worship any. Salvation is gained through three paths: the way of knowledge, the way of devotion, and the way of good deeds.

Popular Hinduism--This form of Hinduism is adhered to by the majority of Hindus. Followers are influenced by ancestral traditions, animal worship, temple cults, magic, exorcism, etc. Their concern is primarily with the gods who protect them, bless them, and make them prosperous.

Mystic Hinduism--Hindu mystics, known as "gurus," draw many followers. They often claim that they are incarnations of gods and that they possess supernatural abilities to heal, perform miracles, read the inner thoughts of men, and prophesy the future.

Tribal Hinduism--This type of Hinduism is greatly influenced by animism, spiritism, the occult, necromancy, and animal worship. The dread of the unknown pervades the minds of the adherents of tribal Hinduism.

Secular Hinduism--Adherents to this form of Hinduism are only nominal Hindus and are indifferent to religious practices. The few religious practices they perform are materialistically motivated.

Several forces affecting the evangelization of Hindus are at work. Hinduism easily absorbs philosophies and trends and has therefore been influenced by the different movements in parts of India in recent decades. The India of today can be described as a secular democracy with agnostic leadership. Urban populations are quickly becoming nominal Hindus, open to new influences. Rural populations, oppressed by poverty and corruption, seek a liberating gospel. Unrest and political instability are softening the Hindus to the gospel.

1. Social unrest, wars, famines, and other catastrophes often provide an open door for the gospel. On the other hand, advanced education, stability, and material prosperity frequently have the reverse effect. How do you explain this phenomenon?

   _____

   _____

   _____

The following excerpt[7] outlines 10 proposals for Hindu evangelization.

TEN PROPOSALS

These 10 proposals might become the tools to disciple the responsive populations of India.

Let the Church in India Be a "Waiting" Church

By that I mean let the Indian church be a church that is waiting on God for an outpouring of the Holy Spirit. A great spiritual awakening among the Christians can result in passion for souls and sacrifices for the cause of evangelism in India.

Go, Preach, Disciple, Teach

With this fourfold ideal strategy, we not only go to the people and preach to them, but when they put their trust in Christ we disciple them by baptizing them in the name of the Father, the Son, and the Holy Spirit. Then we continue to teach them to grow into perfection. Discipling and teaching should not be confused with each other. Teaching is a follow-up of discipling.

Focus on the Common People, Even the Depressed Classes

Much of the energies of the evangelizing agencies are dissipated by not focusing on the responsive. "Win the winnable while they are winnable," says Dr. McGavran. The Harijans and the other depressed castes of India, by the most sober estimate, are the responsive communities in India. No time must be lost in multiplying churches among these people.

Make Conversions Within the Social Structure

People need not be asked to change their social customs and other traditional behaviors. To become a Christian does not mean to wear pants and coats. Men and women may be asked to follow Christ still being proud of their culture or caste to which they belong. So let us strive to make conversions with minimum social dislocation.

Christ Must Increase, Christianity Must Decrease

I am not saying that Christianity must be done away with. I am only saying that a Christianity which is closely identified with the West must be eventually shipped back to where it came from. When Christ is "lifted up" as the liberator of India, as already He has been, He is going to attract millions of people to Himself. This I can give in writing in my own blood. Christ must be proclaimed as the God of our salvation and as liberator from social, political, and economic depression. Cells of Christians must be formed. The Indian church must be formed in its own biblical molds.

Plant Churches That Plant Churches

A church is not an end in itself; it is only a means to an end. The church is a missionary community. Wherever this principle has been applied, the newly organized churches produced daughter churches rapidly. Our ultimate aim must be to plant churches which in turn would plant churches and on and on without end.

---

[7]Ezra Sargunam, "Strategy for India," *Multiplying Modern Churches in India* (Publisher unknown, 1974). Used by permission.

This could be brought about only through a lay movement. Therefore, it is imperative to keep hammering along at the priesthood of all believers.

Strategize People Movements

People in India are not just individuals. There is the extended family and the clan and the caste. The street corner preachings and bazaar preachings and the handing out of tracts to the passersby may bring in a few stray individuals to the Christian fold. But the most effective and successful way to evangelize is through the families and caste groups who are responsive to the gospel. Mobilize the Christians to bring their relatives to Christ. Our slogan must be "Families for Christ" and "Relatives for Christ."

Minimize "Service Missions"

We are not saying that the social gospel must be completely done away with. We only say let these things be done in proportion. Let not priority be given to "service mission."

Restructure Seminaries

Seminaries should not be centers of academic pursuit, but idea factories which produce men of action with missionary zeal and vision. If a student has not gained practical knowledge in discipling non-Christians and striven to become an active church planter while in the seminary, he is not going to learn it out in the field. To our knowledge, church planting ministry has been carried out by two of the seminaries in Latin America.[8]

Seminaries in India also should open out-stations to carry out theological education by extension programs.

Indigeneity in Theology, Worship, and Mission

Much has been said about the need of indigenous theology and worship these days, but no one seems to be concerned for an indigenous mission. This is very important in these days when national feelings are so high. We must constantly expose ourselves to new national methods to reach the nationals.

The one I think would be effective along this line is a *Padayatra* (foot pilgrimage), which I myself feel burdened to carry out in a few years when the situation ripens. I may begin from Cape Comerin and walk five or 10 miles a day, visiting village after village, proclaiming the "good news" and establishing churches on the way, finally reaching Madras.

I am sure there must be still better Indian methods through which the people of India may be discipled. We have to constantly keep ourselves open to the leading of the Holy Spirit to show us new strategies by which an effective church planting ministry may be set in motion. The future of mission in India depends upon our ability to use indigenous methods to disciple the population of our beloved land.

---

[8]Roger S. Greenway, *An Urban Strategy for Latin America* (Grand Rapids: Baker Book House, 1973), p. 152.

2. In his "Ten Proposals," what message does the author communicate to traditional foreign missions?

_____

_____

3. What is his message to the Indian church?

_____

_____

The Muslim Megasphere

Most of Islam's 700 million adherents are spread from North Africa to the Far East islands of Indonesia. Mohammed, a seventh century Arab, founded this religion after claiming to have received direct revelation from God through the Archangel Gabriel. Through military means, Mohammed and his successors united the factious, polytheistic Arab tribes, converting them in the process to the new monotheistic religion. Islam's "jihad" or "Holy War" did not stop in the Arabian Peninsula. Fired by a fanatical new religious zeal, the Arabs boiled out of their homeland and, within a hundred years, had conquered the entire Eastern Mediterranean region, India, parts of China, all of North Africa, and Spain. They were finally stopped at the gates of France.

Figure 7.9

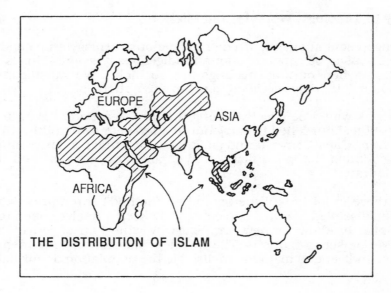

THE DISTRIBUTION OF ISLAM

The conquered people were given a choice of converting to Islam or retaining their own religion. If they retained their religion, special taxes were levied against them, including a heavy tax imposed on each family member. Under this kind of economic pressure, most conquered peoples converted to Islam.

Where the Muslim conquerors met with Christian populations, only those who were firmly rooted or who had the means to escape the economic pressure of the initial onslaught survived the centuries of Muslim dominance. The best example is the Egyptian Coptic Church which, largely due to its monastic structures, was able to survive and today is a growing body, embracing hundreds of newly converted Muslims. As a whole, however, where the Arabs conquered, Christianity was extinguished or faded into a small, ingrown minority.

At the end of the 11th century, Christianized Europe began sending its armies to the Middle East in an attempt to regain control of some of the conquered lands. The special objective of the "Holy Wars" was Jerusalem and the "Holy Lands." Although these crusaders succeeded in reclaiming their objective for a time, they were expelled in the 13th century. They left behind a bitter Muslim resentment toward Christians, which has continued to be a major stumbling block in successful Muslim evangelization. This antipathy, combined with the fact that most Arab countries came under European domination during the colonial era, has decreased the success of current Western missions. Only recently have real breakthroughs in Muslim evangelization been noted.

Islam has its roots in Judaism and Christianity. Its chief doctrine is, "There is no God but Allah (Arabic for God), and Mohammed is His prophet." Muslims are monotheistic and believe in the absolute sovereignty of God. The faithful are those who submit themselves totally to God's will. All others are infidels.

The sermons and sayings of Mohammed are collected in Islam's sacred book, the Koran. The Muslims also believe in the Bible and the prophets, of whom they consider Jesus one of the greatest, but Mohammed is the last and therefore the most authoritative. Although there is much agreement between the Koran and the Bible, there are also significant contradictions. Perhaps the greatest is the Koran's denial of Christ's crucifixion. Muslims believe that, although the Bible was inspired originally, Christians and Jews have corrupted it to serve their own purposes. In spite of these differences, most missiologists believe that the Koran can be used successfully to bridge the gap in the Muslim's understanding of the person and work of Christ.

In the following article,[9] Michael Youssef[10] describes the opportunities for Muslim evangelism today.

Muslim Evangelism

Michael Youssef

In any attempt to evangelize Muslims today, we can hardly afford the mistakes of the past. One of our greatest mistakes has been that of not sufficiently taking into

---

[9]Michael Youssef, "Muslim Evangelism in the 1980's," in *Unreached Peoples '80*, ed. C. Peter Wagner and Edward R. Dayton (Elgin, IL: David C. Cook Publishing Co., 1980), pp. 38-48. Used by permission.

[10]Born in Egypt and ordained to the Anglican ministry in Australia, Michael Youssef has been special assistant to the President of the Haggai Institute for Advanced Leadership Training in Atlanta, Georgia. He is a researcher and lecturer on Muslim evangelism.

account cultural, linguistic, ethnic, and sociological factors in the background of the people. Nor can we afford the luxury of ancient but erroneous prejudices against the Muslim world.

Perhaps the most damaging mistake of all has been our neglect of Muslims. Hiding behind excuses such as "monolithic Islam," and "Muslims are resistant to the gospel," we have invested less than two percent of North American Protestant missionaries in reaching Muslims. There has been little sowing; there has been little reaping.

The Muslim world, however, has been subjected to the secularizing influences of the West. Past Western domination of present-day independent Muslim nations has not helped the Christian mission, but it did transmit Western ideas and values to a whole generation of Muslim elite.

Some observers felt that these secularizing influences, which have eroded the faith of many in the West in Christ, might well erode Islamic beliefs too. Little did they suspect the opposite reaction, a revival within Islam in reaction to the secularizing influence of the West.

And yet, in the midst of our miscalculations, prejudices, and neglect, I believe God has made this the hour for Muslim evangelism. Surprising stories from Muslim countries tell us of unprecedented events in the evangelization of Muslims. They reveal that the Muslim world is not everywhere resistant. They give hope to the church to redeem her neglect, to erase her prejudices, and to turn back from former mistakes.

THE IDEOLOGICAL STRUGGLE IN THE MUSLIM WORLD--GOD'S OPPORTUNITY

We have observed an increase in Islamic militancy in the past 10 years. In Pakistan, Iran, Iraq, Egypt, Libya, and Indonesia, militant movements are spreading, some more extensively than others. Ironically, even though most Muslim nations are the signatories of the U.N.'s Declaration on Human Rights, they interpret that declaration in a distinctive way. They reason that, since Islam is a total way of life, the people of a given nation are free under Islam, and since God's law is above human laws and declarations, whatever Islam says is right.

I believe the problem is complicated by more than Islamic militancy. In many cases, Muslim countries that are suspicious of Western influence and Western missions are also susceptible to association with the Russian communist regime. This is illustrated by countries such as Libya, Afghanistan, Algeria, Syria, and Iraq. And although some other countries, such as Indonesia, Egypt, Sudan, and the United Arab Emirates, have not yet opened their doors to missionaries, they are at least allowing them in.

Secularization, both capitalistic and communistic, contributes to the ideological struggle going on in some Muslim countries. The current situation in Iran is a good illustration of this struggle.

In the midst of this kind of struggle and anxiety, the Christian gospel can be very attractive. We should be watching for stress points in the ideological struggles of the Muslim world. Rather than pulling our people out of such situations, we need to persevere as witnesses. In Iran, for example, a young believer recently led 20 people to Christ in a period of six months! In America, where many Iranians have been stranded by the present government, there are Iranian converts to Christ in almost every major city. Stress produces openness. Restless hearts in search of meaning and peace are finding their rest in Christ.

Another place to watch in the coming days is Afghanistan. Conservative Muslim tribals are up in arms against the Marxist-oriented government of Taraki. After the uprising in Heerat, Russian planes strafed the city for two days, leaving a thousand dead. The general populace, terribly offended by both their own Muslim leaders and their allies, the Russians, have recently shown an uncommon friendliness to Christians passing through the area. There is some sense in which such tragedies can become God's opportunities.

4. What does the author suggest is bringing some openness to the gospel among Muslims, and how can we take advantage of this situation?

_____

_____

_____

THE ISLAMIC MONOLITH: FACT OR FANCY?

Underlying our concern for culturally sensitive models is the awareness of the rich diversity within Islam. Muslims are divided into hundreds of "homogeneous units" that differ from each other geographically, ethnically, ideologically, culturally, and often theologically. Iran, for example, cannot be called a monolithic society. Ethnic Persians make up only 48 percent of the population. Eight percent of Iran's population is Kurdish, 19 percent Turkish-speaking, 18 percent tribal Gulani, Baluchi, and Luri, and the remaining are divided among many smaller groups. Religiously, Iran's Muslims are divided into Shias, Sunnis, Bahais, Ismailis, Ahl-i-Haqq, Yezidis, communists, secularists, and both progressive and conservative Muslims. This kind of diversity can be observed in dozens of Muslim countries.

Other examples of surprising diversity are the 20,000 Chinese Muslims who have migrated and presently live in Saudi Arabia, 145,000 Kurds living in Kuwait, and 20,000 Circassian Muslims living in Jordan. The 720 million Muslims of the world speak at least 500 different languages and are subdivided into probably 3,500 different homogeneous units.

DIFFERING KINDS OF SOILS – A CLUE

Just as there were different kinds of soil in Jesus' parable, so we are likely to find many different kinds of Muslim peoples. Unfortunately, some people treat the whole Muslim world as if it were a single type of soil and erroneously attempt to use only one method on it. It is not, as many who are currently involved in a ministry to Muslims can testify.

Indonesia, for example, is the largest Muslim country in the world, with 121 million Muslims, over 87 percent of the population. Yet Indonesia is not an Islamic state. The number of responsive Muslims to the Christian faith in Indonesia is quite astounding. The Sundanese of Java, for example, long considered resistant to the gospel, are of varying levels in their commitment to Islam. Some areas are highly orthodox and resistant to Christianity. Others are far less Islamicized. House churches have been successfully planted in nonresistant areas.

The point is that we can find responsive people (good soil) even in the world's most populous Muslim nation. This does not mean we should neglect the unresponsive segment of the population. But it does mean that we should invest our greatest efforts on the fruitful ground and encourage our converts, who appreciate the reasons for resistance to the gospel, to evangelize the less responsive areas. And we must simultaneously experiment with new strategies.

5. What does the great diversity among Muslims suggest about the kind of strategies we need to plan in reaching them?

_____

_____

OPPORTUNITIES FOR CROSS-CULTURAL WORKERS OF ALL NATIONALITIES

Sometimes we can learn from our Muslim friends. For example, there is a growing effort by Saudi Arabia and other Mideastern countries to strengthen the growth of orthodox Islam within Indonesia. Most of the missionaries in that movement are Cairo-trained Arabs sent to Indonesia to teach the Arabic language and Islamic theology.

A suggested strategy, in this case, would be to send Arab Christians as missionaries to these heavily populated Muslim islands of Indonesia. They, too, can teach Arabic, and preach the gospel. They will be very acceptable because it is prestigious to be an Arabic-speaking person.

Korean Christians are making a far greater impact upon the Muslims in Saudi Arabia than any other group. Saudis expect the adherents of the Greek, Coptic, and Syrian orthodox churches along with the Armenians to be Christians. They expect the Americans, Germans, and British to be at least nominally Christians. But what is baffling to them is how the Koreans, having no Christian background or history, can be dedicated believers in Christ. What could be more significant than a Korean mission in Saudi Arabia, in the form of technical advisors, laborers, doctors, engineers, etc.?

An article by Norman Horner gives some excellent statistical information concerning the Arabian Gulf states. His conviction is that, while these are "arid and sparsely populated regions where the economic and cultural character has undergone more rapid and far-reaching change in the last 10 years than has happened almost anywhere else on earth, yet they look to be the promised land for so many foreigners." Of course, the reason for this is obviously the production of oil and all the economic prosperity that accompanies that product. Cultural, economic, and sociological change should be viewed very seriously by missionary-minded people. I believe that cultural distortion and disorientation often provide fertile ground for the Christian advocate of a culturally relevant evangelism.

However, this is not the only good news about prospects of evangelism in the Gulf area. Horner explains that a large influx of foreigners, primarily from India, Pakistan, Iran, Egypt, Lebanon, Europe, and America, now vastly exceeds the population of the natives. Among these people are a sizable number of Christians. In Kuwait, for example, it is estimated that five percent of the population is Christian. In Bahrein, about two percent of the population are Christians; in Qatar, over two percent; in Abu Dhabi, about four percent; in Dubai, a little over three percent. Mind you, the vast majority of these Christians are foreigners. There are very few native Christians, if any. The largest Christian community by far in the Arabian Gulf area is the Indian Christian community. It is estimated that over 30 percent of all Indians living in the Arabian Gulf are Christians.

This is, in my judgment, one of the greatest opportunities for Indian missionaries. That is, Indian missionaries, preferably converts from Islam themselves, should be prepared to work in this area of the world where relative freedom is enjoyed, and there witness for Christ and build His church.

6. What strategies for evangelism are suggested by the phenomenon of the oil-rich Arab states hiring thousands of foreign workers as technicians and laborers?

_____

_____

The Tribal Megasphere

The word "tribe" in its popular sense is a designation for a primitive, isolated, and superstitious people who are generally organized under a chief or headman. This popular designation is not strictly accurate since tribes and clans in many countries transcend social levels, are found in the major cities, and often adhere to one of the world's leading religions such as Islam, Hinduism, or Christianity.

For our purposes, we will narrow the definition to those groups of people who have not yet demonstrated adherence to one of the world's leading religions, but worship spirits which they believe have direct influence on their lives. Because tribal peoples often attribute life or "spirit" to inanimate objects, their religion is generally classified as "animism." They are frequently found in isolated places such as tropical jungles, barren deserts, and rugged mountains.

Although we are excluding tribes that adhere to one of the world's major religions, it is important to note that this adherence is often a thin veneer covering traditional animistic practices. It is estimated that 70 percent of the Islamicized peoples fall into this category. The same can be said for the majority of Latin American Indian societies "Catholicized" at the time of the Spanish conquest. Popular Hinduism and ancestor worship are also closely related to animism. When developing strategy for evangelizing any of these groups, it is imperative that the animist view of the world be considered.

There are some 6,000 tribal groups scattered throughout the globe. They range in size from several million down to a mere handful of people. With the relentless advance of "civilization" and "commerce" into every corner of the globe, hundreds of tribes have disappeared. The introduction of diseases against which they had no resistance, deliberate genocide by majority populations pushing into their territories, and the introduction of corrupting influences from the outside have taken their toll of millions of tribal people. This process continues, and time is running out for many of the approximately 5,000 tribes which still remain to be evangelized.

There is no doubt that tribal peoples are some of the most responsive to the gospel. In many cases, they have developed such strong Christian convictions that they have become cross-cultural missionaries and have successfully evangelized other tribes.

Dr. Alan Tippett spent over 20 years as a missionary on the Fiji Islands and is recognized as a leading authority on animism. In an article entitled "The Evangelization of Animists,"[11] he outlines six essential concepts to keep in mind in evangelizing animists. The following list is a brief summary of these concepts.

The Problem of Encounter--Animists cannot drift into Christian faith. Conversion must be demonstrated through a clear-cut separation from the past. Since animists are subject to the influence of many gods or spirits, upon conversion they must demonstrate that the old ways no longer have power over them and that they are now God's people.

This biblically supported concept (Jos. 24:14-27; Acts 19:18-19; Eph. 4:22-24) is demonstrated by a "rite of separation," which is usually marked by some dramatic encounter such as fetish-burning, burial of ancestral skulls, casting sacred paraphernalia into the sea or river, or eating the forbidden totem fish or animal. This symbolic rejection of the old ways serves as a continual reminder that Christ is not just added to their pantheon of gods; He stands alone as their Lord and Savior. Only through this kind of spiritual encounter can syncretism (the mixing of two religions) be avoided.

The Problem of Motivation--Not all converts from animism have the right motivation in becoming Christians. Some convert for materialistic reasons. Others come to Christ out of a misunderstanding of Christianity, a misunderstanding of salvation, or even a misperception of their own need. They may want to receive medical help or have a trade store set up in their village. They may perceive the Christian God as superior in warfare and therefore one to be cultivated. They may simply seek to advance in status or wealth or to have a better job, and they may see Christianity as a means to that end. Still others, observing the vast wealth (in their estimation) the missionaries possess and mystified by the technologies they bring with them, become Christians in hopes of learning some of the missionary's magical secrets.

This is not to say that all animists convert out of wrong motivation. There are thousands of warm-hearted Christians who really know Jesus as Lord. But the problem of motivation does exist and needs to be addressed when animists first indicate a desire to become Christians.

The Problem of Meaning--Whenever the Christian message is proclaimed in a new language, it runs the risk of misinterpretation. The person communicating the message must necessarily use words from the totally secular vocabulary of his audience. The words for God, spirit, sin, love, prayer, forgiveness, etc. must be provided from a vocabulary which expresses a non-biblical world view. The problem is further complicated by the audience's perception of the messenger and by what they think he might represent.

---

[11] Alan R. Tippett, "The Evangelization of Animists," in *Let the Earth Hear His Voice*, ed. J. D. Douglas (Minneapolis: World Wide Publications, 1975), pp. 844-857.

The evangelist himself may present the gospel in a manner totally incompatible with the way animists view the world. It is generally true that because animists believe spiritual beings demonstrate their power through observable acts, they expect the spirit which the missionary advocates to do likewise. It is unlikely that they will be convinced through mere rhetoric. The message must be communicated in such a way that it fits in with the hearers' world view. In order to do this, the missionary must understand his audience thoroughly.

The Problem of Social Structure--The people the evangelist goes to probably organize their lives quite differently from the way the evangelist himself does. The missionary's individualistic outlook may contrast sharply with the group mentality typical of the animist. Instead of cultivating a group decision by consensus, which is normal in that culture, the evangelist may try to get individuals to make decisions. If he is successful in challenging the social structure and a church is formed, he may seek the bright young men to lead the new church, rather than respecting the tribal practice of elder rule. In such a process, the culture and the church suffer painful conflict.

An effective church planter will avoid these problems if he pays close attention to social structures and allows the church to take on indigenous cultural forms from the beginning.

The Problem of Incorporation--The task of evangelism is not complete until converts are incorporated into a body of fellowshiping believers. This "church" must meet the converts' need for a sense of belonging and must lead them into participation, worship, witness, and service in ways that are consistent with their kind of world. Lack of sensitivity to the challenge of incorporation will lead to a sterile church with a legalistic adherence to form.

The Problem of Cultural Void--In their zeal for a pure church, missionaries have often prohibited the incorporation of cultural values and the use of cultural art forms in the church because of past association with pagan practices. When the church is thus stripped of tribal skills and cultural heritage, there is little left to express the worshiper's Christian faith. The consequence is a church dependent on foreign forms and funds for its perpetuation.

Preservation of traditional techniques and values in a situation of changing cultures is necessary if the church is to be dynamic and self-sustaining. The missionary must make value judgments based on the question of whether retention of a particular practice or form will lead to syncretism, or whether the practice can be adapted to Christian expression. A balance must be maintained which eliminates those things not compatible with biblical faith, yet allows those practices which are not expressly forbidden by Scripture.

Much of what Tippett has to say is not limited to the evangelization of animists. His principles are missiologically sound and are applicable to many new mission situations as well as to older churches. Indeed, it might be worthwhile for older, established churches to subject themselves to the scrutiny of these six principles. Such churches may become ingrown, rigid, and inflexible and may begin to lose their young people, who are changing with the times and feel that the church is no longer relevant to their needs.

7. Think through the preceding six principles carefully. Then write a description of what kind of church you think should be established in your own "pagan" society to minister effectively to your culture.

_____

_____

_____

_____

_____

_____

_____

_____

The Great Imbalance

Why have we focused on the five megaspheres having the smallest Christian populations? Don't the descriptions prove that these people are hard, resistant populations, nearly impossible to reach? This may be our initial response, but a further look at statistics will show that pathetically little has been done to reach any of these people. Take a look at the following graph

Figure 7.10

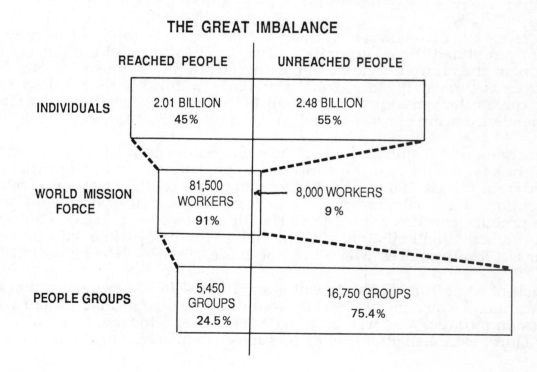

THE GREAT IMBALANCE

	REACHED PEOPLE	UNREACHED PEOPLE
INDIVIDUALS	2.01 BILLION 45%	2.48 BILLION 55%
WORLD MISSION FORCE	81,500 WORKERS 91%	8,000 WORKERS 9%
PEOPLE GROUPS	5,450 GROUPS 24.5%	16,750 GROUPS 75.4%

These figures are a reflection of what Western missions have been doing for the last few decades. The statistics speak loudly for themselves. Only one missionary has been sent to work with unreached peoples for every seven who have been sent to work among peoples with an established church. When we consider that a large proportion of missionaries working with unreached peoples have been sent to work with tribal groups, the ratio of missionaries to the unreached among Buddhists, Muslims, and Hindus climbs to one worker for hundreds of thousands!

In light of these facts, we cannot lightly dismiss these people as unresponsive. They may not be easy to reach, but until the church makes a concerted effort proportionate to the vast need, she stands convicted of negligence in communicating the gospel to those who have never heard the saving name of Jesus Christ.

SUMMARY

A biblical understanding of the word "nation" will dispel the naive notion that, because the church is established in most of the countries of the world, the Great Commission has been completed. There are still thousands of biblically defined nations, or "people groups," which lie outside the witness of the established church. They will not be reached unless the church is willing to extend her witness beyond her own cultural frontiers through E-2 and E-3 evangelism.

Hundreds of these unreached peoples can be found surrounded by Christian populations. They are "hidden peoples" which the church has not been able or perhaps willing to see. It will take more than an "open door policy" to draw these people into the kingdom. Beyond these hidden peoples are huge megaspheres of unreached peoples where there are so few Christians that it will take a massive new thrust of E-2 and E-3 evangelism to reach them. The Buddhist, Chinese, Hindu, Muslim, and tribal megaspheres deserve the church's urgent and immediate attention. The church cannot continue to neglect this great responsibility.

INTEGRATIVE ASSIGNMENT

1. To what people group do you belong? What are some of the ethnic and cultural distinctives of this group? Using this information as a point of reference, identify and briefly describe another people group with whom you would have to engage in E-2 evangelism. Do the same for a people who would require you to engage in E-3 evangelism.

2. List each of the five megaspheres studied in this chapter. Then beside each one, list the important factors mentioned that should be considered in planning a strategy for that megasphere.

3. Make an outline for a brief talk entitled, "The Importance of Cross-Cultural Evangelism to the Completion of the Great Commission." Use biblical as well as statistical evidence to support each point.

QUESTIONS FOR REFLECTION

The introduction of terminology such as "hidden" or "unreached" people can dim the fact that the Bible calls these people "damned." Thousands of souls pass each day into a Christless eternity, never having had the opportunity to know their Savior. The horrible specter of masses of humanity passing into eternal punishment is something from which we all recoil. This grim reality should drive us to desperate efforts on their behalf. Unfortunately, the church's response is often tokenism or callous indifference. Does the plight of the lost make any difference to you? Meditate on John 3:16-18, 35-36. Record your thoughts in your journal.

CHAPTER 8

TO REACH THE UNREACHED

INTRODUCTION

In the last chapter we looked at the mission task remaining. We saw that an accurate picture of what remains to be done can only be achieved by considering the world in light of the biblical definition of nations. Such a view shows us a world with thousands of culturally defined nations which have not yet been discipled. It also shows us the priority of cross-cultural mission in fulfilling the Great Commission.

In this chapter we will seek to understand how best to plan a strategy to reach the unreached. Our previous study has given us a general idea of how to approach the Buddhist, Chinese, Hindu, Muslim, and tribal megaspheres. Now we will begin to focus on the specifics of strategy. To do this, we will consider what factors must be evaluated in targeting a people to be reached, how to define our objectives, and how to determine what methods we should use to reach those objectives.

In the first part of this chapter, Peter Wagner outlines four mission strategies. In the second part, Dr. Donald McGavran shares insights on mission goals and objectives which should greatly influence our choice of methods. Lastly, Edward Dayton presents five questions which form the basis of a worksheet you may be using in selecting a people group and planning a strategy for evangelization.

I. THE FOUR STRATEGIES OF MISSIONS

In the following excerpt,[1] Peter Wagner shows us four areas of strategy to consider in accomplishing the mission task effectively and efficiently.

THE FOUR STRATEGIES OF MISSIONS

Modern missionary strategy is not simplistic. As a matter of fact, it is helpful to look, not at one strategy only, but at four strategies. I will list them here for convenience, then explain each one in detail:

Strategy I: The Right Goals

Strategy II: The Right Place at the Right Time

Strategy III: The Right Methods

Strategy IV: The Right People

STRATEGY I: THE RIGHT GOALS

Every one of Jesus' commands to His people contains a goal of some kind. There are hundreds of them in the New Testament, and faithful servants will want to obey them all in every way possible. But one command above all others contains the goal for missions, and against that goal we must evaluate all missionary strategy. This commandment is known as the "Great Commission," and it is found in Matthew, Mark, Luke, John, and Acts.

A proper understanding of the Great Commission will give us a clear picture of what God's goals for missions are. It goes without saying that God's goals are the *right goals.*

The place to start is Matthew 28:19-20, the most detailed and complete summary of the Great Commission. A proper interpretation of these verses will provide us with the key needed to understand the others in context. Here is what the text says: "Go therefore and make disciples of all nations, baptizing them in the name of the Father and of the Son and of the Holy Spirit, teaching them to observe all that I have commanded you. . . ."

Notice that the passage contains four action verbs: *go, make disciples, baptize,* and *teach.* In the original Greek only one of them is imperative, and three are participles. The imperative, *make disciples,* is at the heart of the command. The participles, *going, baptizing,* and *teaching,* are helping verbs.

Making disciples, then, is the end. It is the *right goal* of mission strategy. Going, baptizing, and teaching are means to be used toward accomplishing the end. They are also necessary components of missionary strategy, but they are not ends in themselves.

The other four appearances of the Great Commission do not expand on the right goal. They do add to the list of the means available to reach it. Mark 16:15, 16

---

[1]C. Peter Wagner, *Stop the World, I Want to Get On* (Glendale, CA: Regal Books, 1974), pp. 77-87. Used by permission.

repeats baptizing, but adds preaching. Luke 24:47, 48 repeats preaching, but adds witnessing. John 20:21 mentions sending. Acts 1:8, also written by Luke, repeats witnessing and adds the geographical aspect of Jerusalem, Judea, Samaria, and the uttermost part of the earth.

Now I will make a rather bold statement. *In my judgment, the greatest error in contemporary missionary strategy is the confusion of means and end in the understanding of the Great Commission.*

In other words, some missions and missionaries have set up their programs as though some of the means were ends in themselves. They have not adequately articulated what they are doing in terms of making disciples. Some, for example, have contented themselves with preaching the gospel whether or not their preaching makes disciples. Some have very meticulously counted "decisions," but they make no corresponding effort to count and report *disciples*. This is why some evangelistic reporting seems inflated. Just to know how many attended an evangelistic crusade or how many signed decision cards is helpful but inadequate. The Lord of the Great Commission, in the final analysis, is interested in *disciples*, not simply *decisions*.

Don't forget, when we talk about right goals, we are talking about goals for the whole body, not just for individuals. The doctrine of spiritual gifts teaches us that we all make different contributions. But as all members of the body work together, the final result should be new disciples. Success or failure must be measured ultimately in those terms. One entire mission might concentrate on translating the Bible, for example. Bible translation is an essential function of the body, for without the Word of God in the language of each people, they will not be able to hear the message of salvation. But proper strategy will coordinate this work with that of other members of the body so that translated Bibles become, not just some more exotic contributions to the literature of mankind, but effective instruments for making disciples.

At this point be careful of the definition of *disciple*. If the right goal of missionary strategy is to make *disciples*, you absolutely have to know what Jesus was talking about if you plan to obey Him. You have to know how you can tell when you have made one. Nebulous ideas of what disciples are only serve to blur good strategy.

A person is not a disciple just because he has been born in a Christian country or, in many cases, even if he is a church member. We have already mentioned that decisions in themselves do not necessarily lead to disciples. Not everyone who prays to receive Jesus ends up a disciple. The basic meaning of disciples in the New Testament is equivalent to a true, born-again Christian. Everyone whose name is written in the *Lamb's Book of Life* is a disciple. Those who are not are not disciples in the Great Commission sense of the word.

In order to make a disciple, you need to go to the people not yet true Christians. Unsaved people are the raw material, so to speak, for fulfilling the Great Commission. The instant one becomes a "new creature in Christ" (II Cor. 5:17), you have made a disciple.

Some have confused "making disciples" with "discipleship." *Making disciples* is the right goal of evangelism and missions according to the Great Commission. Once disciples are made, they then begin the lifetime road of *discipleship*. Helping people along the road is another important Christian ministry, an essential function of the body, but one step past the goal of the Great Commission. Even the participle "teaching" in the Great Commission itself does not refer to the details of the road of discipleship, as some might think. The thing taught in that verse is "to observe," not "all things I have commanded you." Part of becoming a disciple is to be disposed to obey Jesus. The details come later as the new disciple travels down the road of discipleship.

What does a disciple look like? How can you tell one when you see him? Acts 2 gives us a helpful indication. On the Day of Pentecost 3,000 disciples were made. The reason we know they were disciples and not just people who made "decisions" is that when Luke looked back in preparation for writing the book of Acts, they were "continuing steadfastly in the apostles' doctrine and fellowship and breaking of bread and prayers" (Acts 2:42). Outsiders can recognize disciples because "they have love one for another" (John 13:35).

If a mission society moves into a pagan village one year and moves out three years later leaving a group of 250 people who declare that Christ is their Lord, who meet together regularly for worship, who read the Bible and pray--they have made 250 disciples and to that degree have fulfilled the Great Commission. These disciples might lack a great deal of polish. They might not act like Wheaton, Illinois Christians. They might have a long way to go down the road of Christian discipleship, but nevertheless they are disciples. If the mission in question reports its results in such terms, it has properly understood Strategy I. It is aiming for the *right goals*.

1. What is the "right goal" of the missionary task, and how will we know when we have reached it?

_____

_____

STRATEGY II: THE RIGHT PLACE AT THE RIGHT TIME

Strategy II is best understood in agricultural terms. It comes out most clearly in some of Jesus' rural-oriented parables. As a farmer myself (my college degree is in dairy production!), I often jestingly suggest that being a farmer is more helpful in interpreting the parables than knowing Greek! The helpful aspect is that every farmer, by nature, has what I call *the vision of the fruit*.

No farmer works his field for the fun of it--he works for the payoff, which is the fruit. A man buys a farm with the anticipation that it will produce fruit. He may enjoy mechanics, but he works on his machinery only because it will help him get the fruit. He sows his seed and cultivates his crops, not because he thinks it's fun to ride tractors, but because if he doesn't there will be no fruit. "He that soweth and he that reapeth rejoice together" (John 4:36). Why? Because they gather fruit together.

Sound missionary strategy never loses the vision of the fruit. Strategy I teaches us that in missionary work this fruit is *disciples*. Keep this vision foremost in sowing, pruning, and reaping.

The Vision in Sowing

The Parable of the Sower appears in Matthew, Mark, and Luke. The briefest summary is in Luke 8:4-15. It tells of a farmer who sowed seeds on four different parts of his farm, but got fruit on only one. Anyone with the vision of the fruit will instantly ask, "Why?" Jesus' disciples undoubtedly asked the same thing when they first heard it.

According to Jesus' interpretation, the variable factor was not the sower, nor was it the seed (which is described as the "word of God"), nor was it the method. It was the soil. No matter how good the seed is, any farmer knows it will not bear fruit on roadways, on rocky soil, or among thorns. In order to produce fruit, good seed must be sown in fertile soil.

The obvious lesson for missionary strategy is that the seed of the Word must be concentrated on fertile soil if fruit is to be expected. Some peoples of the world are receptive to the gospel while others are resistant. The world's soils must be tested. Concentrating, come what may, on rocky soil, whether or not any disciples are made, is foolish strategy. Farmers who have the vision of the fruit do not make that mistake too often, but some missiologists unfortunately do. This is the "right place" aspect of Strategy II.

The Vision in Pruning

The Parable of the Fig Tree in Luke 13:6-9 is seen as a threat by some missionaries. If they are guided by the vision of the fruit, however, it should not be.

The farmer who came along and saw a beautiful fig tree was forced to look a little deeper. The problem there was comparable to many mission fields. The fig tree had grown well, but there were no figs! Much missionary "work" has likewise developed to a high degree, but there is no fruit--there are no disciples. The farmer in the parable is a good strategist. When there is no fruit after much work and a prudent time lapse, he says cut it down--change your program. He operates on the basis of the vision of the fruit. His hired man does not share the vision because his income depends not so much on harvest as on a salary. His strategy is to continue the work as long as he can. He, like many missionaries, is program-centered, not goal-centered.

Missionaries who are comfortably settled into a certain "program" or "missionary work" would do well to examine what they are doing in terms of the vision of the fruit. It is not easy to change a program, especially when you have been hoping against hope that in a year or so it will begin bearing fruit. But too often these years have stretched out into lifetimes. Missionaries who could have spent 10 years making disciples spend the same 10 years simply doing "mission work" because they lack the courage to cut the barren fig tree down and change their program.

The Vision in Reaping

When Jesus talks to His disciples about reaping, for the first time He mentions the need for praying that the Lord of the harvest will "send forth laborers into His harvest" (Matt. 9:37-38). When the "laborers are few," the farmer runs the risk of losing some of the harvest. The Strategy II aspect in this case is the "right time." Laborers are not needed when the harvest is still green, nor are they needed when the harvest has passed. Timing is of utmost importance in any harvest.

Suppose, for example, that you owned an apple orchard. In Field A, a worker could harvest five bushels in an hour. In Field B, it would take him five hours to harvest just one bushel. In Field C, he couldn't harvest anything because the apples are all still green. If you had 30 workers today, where would you send them? I think I would send 29 of them to Field A so as not to lose the fruit there. I would send the other one to do what he could in Field B and also to keep his eye on Field C. His job would be to let me know when those fields were ripe so I could redeploy the personnel.

Parallel situations arise time after time in missionary work. Some peoples are ready to be harvested today, some are not yet ready. These "unresponsive peoples" should not be neglected--someone should be there who is expert enough to tell when they are becoming ripe for the gospel. In one sense you need the very finest workers in the unresponsive fields. But no one who takes strategy seriously would advocate a massive labor force in green fields. Jesus wouldn't. He does not tell us to pray for more laborers to go to green fields or to fallow fields. The laborers are needed for the *ripe* harvest fields.

Right after Jesus says that in Matthew 9, He sends His own harvesters out in Matthew 10. There were three fields in those days: Jews, Gentiles, and Samaritans. Only the Jews were ripe at the time. Jesus specifically tells His disciples not to go to the Gentiles and Samaritans (Matt. 10:5, the green fields), but to go to the Jews (Matt. 10:6). Later on both the Gentiles and the Samaritans ripened and bore much fruit, but not at that time.

Granted, it is not always the easiest thing to tell which soil is most fertile or just when a particular harvest is going to ripen in missionary work. Agricultural testing methods are much more advanced today than missiological testing methods. But missiologists are improving their methods all the time and making encouraging advances. A good deal is now known about testing peoples as to their degree of resistance or receptivity to the gospel. Up-to-date missions will take full advantage of such expertise, thus applying Strategy II--the right place at the right time.

THE VISION IN REAPING

2. Why is the "vision of the fruit" so important in considering where we will place our mission effort?

_____

_____

3. How do the "vision in pruning" and the "vision in reaping" affect our ongoing efforts?

_____

_____

STRATEGY III: THE RIGHT METHODS

When there is much work and little or no fruit, something is wrong. Careful analysis will usually pinpoint the trouble as either working in unripe fields or working in ripe fields but using wrong methods. You can go into a perfectly ripe field of wheat and work your head off, but if you are using a cornpicker, you will get nothing. Potato diggers are useless in apple orchards.

Around the world there are peoples who would gladly receive the gospel and become Jesus' disciples, but missionaries among these people are not making disciples because they are using inappropriate methods.

The wrong language is one of the common methodological mistakes. In many cases on record the missionary thought that preaching in the trade language would be adequate for making disciples. Only when he switched to the local dialect, the language of the heart, however, did the fruit begin to come. If he had refused to change his methods, no amount of hard work would have done the job.

Mixing peoples has often proved to be another wrong method. For many years, for example, the Oregon Friends were reaping a great harvest among the Aymaras of Bolivia, while others working equally as hard were not. It was then discovered that the Friends insisted on keeping their churches purely Aymara, while others thought it well to mix mestizo believers with Aymaras. Missiologists call this *the principle of homogeneous unit churches*. Churches of one kind of people only are more effective in winning others of the same people. In Bolivia the method made the difference.

The list could be multiplied, but let's take a case closer to home. In 1959, D. James Kennedy was called to pastor the Coral Ridge Presbyterian Church in Florida. He began with a congregation of 45, but within a year it had dwindled to 17. He was so discouraged he considered leaving the ministry. A harvest field? Kennedy might well have concluded there was none at all.

But he changed his method. For one thing, he realized that if there was a harvest out there, it wouldn't come walking to him. He had to go out into the field and reap it. For another, he realized that the pastor can't do it all, and if effective evangelism is going to be done, the church has to begin functioning as a body. He then began a systematic program of house evangelism and trained a core of church members to help him. Strategy III worked. The harvest began to come in, and in 10 years the church had grown from 17 to 2,500!

Kennedy found a method that worked in his place at that particular time. Some fellow ministers have tried it with similar success, but others have tried it and have had scant results. Whenever a method is successful, the temptation arises to think it will work anywhere at any time. Strategy III is more complex than that, however. Every new situation requires a new evaluation and often new, tailor-made methods.

Methods must be selected on largely pragmatic factors, since the Bible does not pretend to give 20th century instruction. Therefore, it is good strategy not only to set measurable goals, but also to build in from the start of the effort instruments for measuring its success or failure. Only by doing this will it be possible to look back and know which methods God has blessed and which methods He has not blessed. One of the most curious facts in modern missions is that this simple procedure is so seldom carried out.

4. What two reasons does Wagner give to explain why a field may be unfruitful?

   _____

   _____

5. There is a natural tendency to blame lack of results in mission work on the hardness of the people rather than honestly evaluate our methods. What does Wagner suggest that missions do in order to overcome the lack of objectivity in evaluating mission efforts?

   _____

   _____

STRATEGY IV: THE RIGHT PEOPLE

Some things God does by Himself; some things He does by using human beings.

It seems, for example, that the difference between fertile and barren soil is basically a matter of divine providence. The ripening of certain harvest fields at certain times can be attributed only to the sovereignty of God. "I have planted, Apollos watered," writes Paul, "but *God gave the increase*" (I Cor. 3:6).

God brings the harvest to ripeness, but He does not harvest it. He uses Christian people to accomplish that task, and He is glorified when His people "bear much fruit" (John 15:8). He is particularly interested in "fruit that remains" (John 15:16). But how does this fruit come? The servant of God can only bear fruit if the branch abides in the vine. Jesus is the vine, and Christian people are the branches.

Strategy IV, then, stresses the right people. The right person is the person entirely filled with the Holy Spirit. He abides in Jesus. He is fully committed. He takes up his cross daily and follows his Master. Without Strategy IV, the first three strategies are dead letters. That is why Jesus insisted that His disciples not begin their missionary work until they were "endued with power from on high" (Luke 24:49).

6. Why does the success of the first three strategies hinge on the fourth strategic consideration?

   _____

   _____

It is apparent that to carry out God's mission successfully, we must be clearly aware of what the objective is, where and when an effort should be made, what tools are most appropriate for the task, and what qualifications are required of the laborers. If we ignore any of these strategy areas, the entire mission effort may be doomed to ineffectiveness and failure from the start.

Unreached Does Not Mean Unreachable

Because some megaspheres of unreached peoples have developed a reputation for being resistant, it is easy to conclude that these peoples represent "unripe" fields, and therefore should be bypassed for riper fields. The assumption is that the right strategies have been deployed in attempting to reach such people. Well documented cases have shown, however, that failure to reap a harvest has often had more to do with wrong goals, methods, or personnel than with lack of a receptive target group. Frequently a conscious effort to deploy right strategy among people believed to be "unreceptive" has resulted in a fruitful harvest.

The following case study describes a mission launched toward a people who had developed a reputation as "unreceptive." The mission, known as the "Tonga Team," gives rightful credit to the Lord for having prepared this people to receive the gospel message. But it took the right strategy to reap the harvest others had not been able to gather.

The Tonga Team was formed in 1967, when Phil and Norma Elkins joined two singles and two other couples to target and plan to reach an unreached people group. This initial banding together was followed by three years of study and preparation. In 1970 the team members were sent out by their "Antioch," a church in San Fernando, California. The following describes the results of their efforts.[2]

EARLY DECISIONS AND CONVICTIONS

As the team searched for an unreached people (two years), they concluded the Holy Spirit was leading them to a segment of the Tonga tribe (one of the largest in Zambia, numbering over 300,000) called the Toka-Leya. Ninety-five percent of these people were adherents of an ethnic, or localized, folk-religion (some would use the term *animistic*). Within a 12-mile radius of where the team settled (the primary target area) were 100 villages with four small congregations that had not grown for several years (a total of 75 Christians).

The team spent most of the first two years (1970-71) learning the language and culture, without engaging in overt evangelistic activities. By the end of 1973 there were four times as many churches (16) and six times the membership (450). Beyond this immediate 12-mile area, completely new movements were started. For example, in the Moomba chieftaincy, 70 miles to the north, newly trained national Christians planted six churches with 240 members within a few months. This was done in 1973 and involved winning the chief, a third of all the village headmen, and both court judges.

I mention this early rapid response to show that we were indeed led to a "ripe pocket" in God's mosaic of peoples. We knew that the national church, motivated and trained, had to be the vehicle to gather the harvest. By 1974 we felt most of the American team could pull out. By 1979, the last two "foreign" families felt they

[2]Phillip Elkins, "A Pioneer Team in Zambia, Africa," in *Perspectives on the World Christian Movement*, ed. Ralph D. Winter and Steven C. Hawthorne (Pasadena, CA: William Carey Library, 1981), p. 683. Used by permission.

could responsibly move on to another new people to begin the process again. Today a national church continues the process of winning and discipling "to the fringes."

"Methods," "approaches," and "strategy" may be "unspiritual" words in some Christians' vocabulary. I feel in the context of this effort there was validity in the strategy and specific methods followed by the team. In addition to what has been described, I think the first two years in which we were involved as in-depth "learners" of the Tonga world view (language, lifestyle, values, politics, social structure, beliefs, educational systems, and other aspects of culture) were essential to our efforts as church planters. My wife and I lived in a village of 175 people and followed a lifestyle closely identified with that of other Toka-Leya families. We learned to "hurt" where they hurt and "feel" what they felt. We identified, not so much to be "accepted," though that is important, but to understand and appreciate their culture for its finest and best dimensions. We had to know what parts were already functioning positively within the will and purpose of God. We needed to know what had to be confronted and changed to fit the demands of the kingdom of God.

Perhaps most critical was the need to learn where people had "felt needs" through which God's message of redemption could be accepted as good news. The message that had been proclaimed as "gospel" by earlier Christian efforts was in fact perceived as "bad news." The gospel was perceived as God calling men to have one wife and not to drink beer. Though Christians were saying many other things, this was perceived as the "banner" of the message. Because missionaries showed a major interest in setting up schools for children, the adult population found the message all right for children but almost unthinkable for adults.

7. According to the preceding account, where had earlier missions to the Tongas concentrated their efforts, and what was the overall effect?

_____

_____

8. Why was the gospel perceived as "bad news"?

_____

_____

9. How did the Tonga Team differ in their approach?

_____

_____

II. PEOPLE MOVEMENTS

The failure of mission ventures to produce a viable church among a people even after many years of work may betray an ignorance of the right goal. In the following article,[3] Dr. Donald McGavran[4] illustrates how one's understanding of the long-range objective in mission has a significant effect on the overall success of the mission effort.

A Church in Every People: Plain Talk About a Difficult Subject

Donald A. McGavran

In the last 18 years of the 20th century, the goal of Christian mission should be to preach the gospel and by God's grace to plant in every unchurched segment of mankind--what shall we say--"*a church*" or "*a cluster of growing churches* "? By the phrase "segment of mankind" I mean an urbanization, development, caste, tribe, valley, plain, or minority population. I shall explain that the steadily maintained long-range goal should never be the first but should always be the second. The goal is *not* one small sealed-off conglomerate congregation in every people. Rather, the long-range goal (to be held constantly in view in the years or decades when it is not yet achieved) should be "*a cluster of growing congregations in every segment.*"

As we consider the question above, we should remember that it is usually easy to start one single congregation in a new unchurched people group. The missionary arrives. He and his family worship on Sunday. They are the first members of that congregation. He learns the language and preaches the gospel. He lives like a Christian. He tells people about Christ and helps them in their troubles. He sells tracts and Gospels or gives them away. Across the years a few individual converts are won from this group and that. Sometimes they come for very sound and spiritual reasons, sometimes from mixed motives. But here and there a woman, a man, a boy, a girl do decide to follow Jesus. A few employees of the mission become Christian. These may be masons hired to erect the buildings, helpers in the home, rescued persons, or orphans. The history of mission in Africa is replete with churches started by buying slaves, freeing them, and employing such of them as could not return to their kindred. Such as chose to could accept the Lord. A hundred and fifty years ago this was a common way of starting a church. With the outlawing of slavery, of course, it ceased to be used.

One single congregation arising in the way just described is almost always a conglomerate church--made up of members of several different segments of society. Some are old, some young, orphans, rescued persons, helpers, and ardent seekers. All seekers are carefully screened to make sure they really intend to receive Christ. In due time a church building is erected, and lo, "a church in that people." It is a conglomerate church. It is sealed off from all the people groups of that region. No segment of the population says, "That group of worshipers is *us* ." They are quite right. It is not. It is ethnically quite a different social unit.

This very common way of beginning the process of evangelization is a slow way to disciple the peoples of earth--note the plural, "the peoples of earth." Let us observe

---

[3]Donald A. McGavran, "A Church in Every People: Plain Talk About a Difficult Subject," in *Perspectives on the World Christian Movement*, ed. Ralph D. Winter and Steven C. Hawthorne (Pasadena, CA: William Carey Library, 1981), pp. 622-628. Used by permission.

[4]Known worldwide as perhaps today's foremost missiologist, Donald McGavran was born in India of missionary parents and returned there as a third-generation missionary himself in 1923, serving as a director of religious education and translating the Gospels into the Chhattisgarhi dialect of Hindi. He founded the School of World Mission of Fuller Theological Seminary, of which he is now Dean Emeritus. McGavran is the author of several influential books, including *The Bridges of God, How Churches Grow*, and *Understanding Church Growth.*

closely what really happens as this congregation is gathered. Each convert, as he becomes a Christian, is seen by his kin as one who leaves "us" and joins "them." He leaves our gods to worship their gods. Consequently his own relations force him out. Sometimes he is severely ostracized; he is thrown out of house and home; his wife is threatened. Hundreds of converts have been poisoned or killed. Sometimes, the ostracism is mild and consists merely in severe disapproval. His people consider him a traitor. A church which results from this process looks to the peoples of the region like an assemblage of traitors. It is a conglomerate congregation. It is made up of individuals, who one by one have come out of several different societies, castes, or tribes.

Now if anyone, in becoming a Christian, is forced out of or comes out of a tightly structured segment of society, the Christian cause wins the individual but loses the family. The family, his people, his neighbors of that tribe are fiercely angry at him or her. They are the very men and women to whom he cannot talk. You are not of us, they say to him. You have abandoned us, you like them more than you like us. You now worship their gods, not our gods. As a result, conglomerate congregations, made up of converts won in this fashion, *grow very slowly* . Indeed, one might truly affirm that where congregations grow in this fashion, the conversion of the ethnic units (people groups) from which they come is made doubly difficult. "The Christians misled one of our people," the rest of the group will say. "We're going to make quite sure that they do not mislead any more of us."

One-by-one is relatively easy to accomplish. Perhaps 90 out of every 100 missionaries who intend church planting get only conglomerate congregations. Such missionaries preach the gospel, tell of Jesus, sell tracts and Gospels, and evangelize in many other ways. They welcome inquirers, but whom do they get? They get a man here, a woman there, a boy here, a girl there, who for various reasons are willing to become Christians and patiently to endure the mild or severe disapproval of their people.

If we are to understand how churches grow and do not grow on new ground, in untouched and unreached peoples, we must note that the process I have just described seems unreal to most missionaries. "What," they will exclaim, "could be a better way of entry into all the unreached peoples of that region than to win a few individuals from among them? Instead of resulting in the sealed-off church you describe, the process really gives us points of entry into every society from which a convert has come. That seems to us to be the real situation."

Those who reason in this fashion have known church growth in a largely Christian land, where men and women who follow Christ are not ostracized, are not regarded as traitors, but rather as those who have done the right thing. In that kind of a society every convert usually can become a channel through which the Christian faith flows to his relatives and friends. On that point there can be no debate. It was the point I emphasized when I titled my book *The Bridges of God.*

But in tightly structured societies, where Christianity is looked on as an invading religion, and individuals are excluded for serious fault, *there* to win converts from several different segments of society, far from building bridges to each of these, erects barriers difficult to cross.

1. What are the main problems associated with "one by one" conversion in a society where Christianity is viewed as a foreign religion?

_____

_____

_____

Now let us contrast the other way in which God is discipling the peoples of Planet Earth. My account is not theory, but a sober recital of easily observable facts. As you look around the world, you see that while most missionaries succeed in planting only conglomerate churches by the "one-by-one out of the social group" method, here and there clusters of growing churches arise by the people movement method. They arise by tribe-wise or caste-wise movements to Christ. This is in many ways a better system. In order to use it effectively, missionaries should operate on seven principles.

First, they should be clear about the goal. The goal is not one single conglomerate church in a city or a region. They may get only that, *but that must never be their goal.* That must be a cluster of growing, indigenous congregations, every member of which remains in close contact with his kindred. This cluster grows best if it is in one people, one caste, one tribe, one segment of society. For example, if you were evangelizing the taxi drivers of Taipei, then your goal would be to win not some taxi drivers, some university professors, some farmers, and some fishermen, but to establish churches made up largely of taxi drivers, their wives and children, and their assistants and mechanics. As you win converts of that particular community, the congregation has a natural, built-in social cohesion. Everybody feels at home. Yes, the goal must be clear.

2. How does the goal of the "people movement" method differ from the goal of the "one by one" method?

_____

_____

The second principle is that the national leader or the missionary and his helpers should concentrate on one people. If you are going to establish *a cluster of growing congregations* amongst, let us say, the Nair people of Kerala, which is the southwest tip of India, then you would need to place most of your missionaries and their helpers so that they can work among the Nairs. They should proclaim the gospel to Nairs and say quite openly to them, "We are hoping that within your great caste there soon will be thousands of followers of Jesus Christ, who also remain solidly in the Nair community." They will, of course, not worship the old Nair gods; but then plenty of Nairs don't worship their old gods. Plenty of Nairs are Communist and ridicule their old gods.

Nairs whom God calls, who choose to believe in Christ, are going to love their neighbors more than they did before and walk in the light. They will be saved and beautiful people. They will remain Nairs, while at the same time they become Christians. To repeat, concentrate on one people group. If you have three missionaries, don't have one evangelizing this group, another that, and a third 200 miles away evangelizing still another. That is a sure way to guarantee that any churches started will be small, non-growing, one-by-one churches. The social dynamics of those sections of society will work solidly *against* the eruption of any great growing people movement to Christ.

3. How does the second principle of the "people movement" method affect the deployment of personnel?

_____

_____

The third principle is to encourage converts to remain thoroughly one with their own people in most matters. They should continue to eat what their people eat. They should not say, "My people are vegetarians, but now that I have become a Christian I'm going to eat meat." After they become Christians they should be more rigidly vegetarian than they were before. In the matter of clothing, they should continue to look precisely like their kinsfolk. In the matter of marriage, most peoples are endogamous; they insist that "our people marry only our people." They look with very great disfavor on our people marrying other people. And yet when Christians come in one-by-one, they cannot marry their own people. None of them have become Christian. Where only a few of a given people become Christians there, when it comes time for them or their children to marry, they have to take husbands or wives from other segments of the population. So their own kin look at them and say, "Yes, become a Christian and mongrelize your children. You have left us and have joined them."

All converts should be encouraged to bear cheerfully the exclusion, the oppression, and the persecution that they are likely to encounter from their people. When anyone becomes a follower of a new way of life, he is likely to meet some disfavor from his loved ones. Maybe it's mild; maybe it's severe. He should bear such disfavor patiently. He should say on all occasions:

"I am a better son than I was before; I am a better father than I was before; I am a better husband than I was before; and I love you more than I used to do. You can hate me, but I will not hate you. You can exclude me, but I will include you. You can force me out of our ancestral house, but I will live on its veranda. Or I will get a house just across the street. I am still one of you; I am more one of you than I ever was before."

Encourage converts to remain thoroughly one with their people in most matters.

Please note that word "most." They cannot remain one with their people in idolatry or drunkenness or obvious sin. If they belong to a segment of the society that earns its living by stealing, they must "steal no more." But in most matters (how they talk, how they dress, how they eat, where they go, what kind of houses they live in) they can look very much like their people and ought to make every effort to do so.

4. What is the aim of this third principle?

_____

_____

The fourth principle is to try to get group decisions for Christ. If only one person decides to follow Jesus, do not baptize him immediately. Say to him, "You and I will work together to lead another five, or 10, or God willing, 50 of your people to accept Jesus Christ as Savior so that when you are baptized, you will be baptized with them." Ostracism is very effective against one lone person. But ostracism is weak indeed when exercised against a group of a dozen. And when exercised against 200 it has practically no force at all.

5. What is the strength of a "group decision"?

_____

_____

The fifth principle is this: Aim for scores of groups of that people to become Christians in an ever-flowing stream across the years. One of the common mistakes made by missionaries, Eastern as well as Western, all around the world is that when a few become Christians, perhaps 100, 200, or even 1,000, the missionaries spend all their time teaching them. They want to make them good Christians, and they say to themselves, "If these people become good Christians, then the gospel will spread." So for years they concentrate on a few congregations. By the time, 10 to 20 years later, that they begin evangelizing outside that group, the rest of the people no longer want to become Christians. That has happened again and again. This principle requires that from the very beginning the missionary keeps on reaching out to new groups. "But," you say, "is not this a sure way to get poor Christians who don't know the Bible? If we follow that principle we shall soon have a lot of "raw" Christians. Soon we shall have a community of perhaps 5,000 people who are very sketchily Christian."

Yes, that is certainly a danger. At this point, we must lean heavily upon the New Testament, remembering the brief weeks or months of instruction Paul gave to his new churches. We must trust the Holy Spirit and believe that God has called those people out of darkness into His wonderful light. As between two evils, giving them too little Christian teaching vs. allowing them to become a sealed-off community that cannot reach its own people, the latter is much the greater danger. *We must not allow new converts to become sealed off.* We must continue to make sure that a constant stream of new converts comes into the ever-growing cluster of congregations.

6. What great danger does the fifth principle attempt to combat?

_____

_____

Now the sixth point is this: The converts, five or 5,000, ought to say or at least feel: "We Christians are the advance guard of our people, of our segment of society. We are showing our relatives and neighbors a better way of life. The way we are pioneering is good for us who have become Christians and will be very good for you thousands who have yet to believe. Please look on us not as traitors in any sense. We are better sons, brothers, and wives, better tribesmen and caste fellows, better members of our labor union than we ever were before. We are showing ways in which, while remaining thoroughly of our own segment of society, we all can have a better life. Please look on us as the pioneers of our own people entering a wonderful Promised Land."

7. What effect do you think the demonstration of the above attitude would have on the evangelization of a people?

_____

_____

The last principle I stress is this: Constantly *emphasize* brotherhood. In Christ there is no Jew, no Greek, no bond, no free, no Barbarian, no Scythian. We are all one in Christ Jesus. But at the same time let us remember that Paul did not attack all imperfect social institutions. For example, he did not do away with slavery. Paul said to the slave, be a better slave. He said to the slave owner, be a kindlier master.

Paul also said in that famous passage emphasizing unity, "There is no male or female." Nevertheless Christians in their boarding schools and orphanages continue to sleep boys and girls in separate dormitories!! In Christ, there is no sex distinction. Boys and girls are equally precious in God's sight. Men from this tribe and men from that are equally precious in God's sight. We are all equally sinners equally saved by grace. These things are true; but at the same time there are certain social niceties which Christians at this time may observe.

As we continue to stress brotherhood, let us be sure that the most effective way to achieve brotherhood is to lead ever-increasing numbers of men and women from every *ethnos*, every tribe, every segment of society into an obedient relationship to Christ. As we multiply Christians in every segment of society, the possibility of genuine brotherhood, justice, goodness, and righteousness will be enormously increased. Indeed, the best way to get justice, possibly the only way to get justice, is to have very large numbers in every segment of society become committed Christians.

8. Why are we more likely to achieve brotherhood through Christian witness than through attacking unjust social institutions?

_____

_____

As we work for Christward movements in every people, let us not make the mistake of believing that "one-by-one out of the society into the church" is a bad way. One precious soul willing to endure severe ostracism in order to become a follower of Jesus, one precious soul coming all by himself is a way that God has blessed and is blessing to the salvation of mankind. But it is a slow way. And it is a way which frequently seals off the converts' own people from any further hearing of the gospel.

Sometimes one-by-one is the only possible method. When it is, let us praise God for it and live with its limitations. Let us urge all those wonderful Christians who come bearing persecution and oppression to pray for their own dear ones and to work constantly that more of their own people may believe and be saved.

One-by-one is one way that God is blessing to the increase of His church. The people movement is another way. The great advances of the church on new ground out of non-Christian religions have *always* come by people movements, never one-by-one. It is equally true that one-by-one-out-of-the-people is a very common beginning way. In the book, *Bridges of God*, which God used to launch the Church Growth Movement, I have used a simile. I say there that missions start out proclaiming Christ on a desert-like plain. There life is hard; the number of Christians remains small. A large missionary presence is required. But, here and there, the missionaries or the converts find ways to break out of that arid plain and proceed up into the verdant mountains. There large numbers of people live; there great churches can be founded; there the church grows strong; that is people movement land.

I commend that simile to you. Let us accept what God gives. If it is one-by-one, let us accept that and lead those who believe in Jesus to trust in Him completely. But let us always pray that, after that beginning, we may proceed to higher ground, to more verdant pasture, to more fertile lands where great groups of men and women, *all of the same segment of society*, become Christians and thus open the way for Christward movements in each people on earth. Our goal should be Christward movements within each segment. There the dynamics of social cohesion will advance the gospel and lead multitudes out of darkness into His wonderful life. We are calling people after people from death to life. Let us make sure that we do it by the most effective methods.

9. Most missionaries would be delighted if a "people movement" for Christ occurred among those with whom they are working. Assuming they are in a

situation which deploys a "one by one" methodology, what changes should be made in a conscious effort to pursue the goal of a people movement?

_____

_____

_____

_____

Planning for People Movements

Historically, most observable people movements seem to have happened almost by accident. Sometimes a missionary "accidentally" stumbles on a key cultural concept whose long-awaited fulfillment is embodied by his own coming and presenting the gospel. This happened to Albert Brant, sent to the Dorsa tribe in Ethiopia. Upon arrival, he decided to camp under a certain sycamore tree. Little did he know that Dorsa tradition stated that someday God the Creator would send a messenger who would camp under that very tree, a fact which established immediate credibility for Brant's gospel message. Within a few years, hundreds of churches were established among the Dorsas.

Other people movements have been started by a convert who is won through the "one by one" approach. Then, quite apart from the missionaries' efforts, the convert returns to his own people with a message presented in a manner uniquely suited to the people's needs. The story of pioneer missionary Adoniram Judson is a perfect example of this. While Judson struggled to win the Burmese, his houseboy, who was a member of a tribal group, was converted and quietly began to lead his tribe's people to a knowledge of Christ. Within a few decades, the vast majority of his tribe had become Christians.

God desires that the *nations* be discipled. People movements reflect the fulfillment of that desire. In recent years, missionaries have begun to pray, plan, and work purposefully towards starting people movements among specific peoples. The results have been rewarding. Without minimizing the patient work of evangelism which has already been accomplished through a "one by one" approach, let us trust God for people movements among those peoples who have yet to be reached.

III. THE UNIQUE SOLUTION STRATEGY

Our mission objective has a profound effect on the methods we deploy for evangelization. If our objective is to see a people movement for Christ, we cannot simply assume that "standard" approaches to evangelization will automatically produce the desired effect. In fact, many of the methods Western missionaries have traditionally used may prove quite ineffective in bringing about people movements for Christ. To reach unreached peoples, we must understand that each group is unique and will therefore require a unique strategy of approach.

In the following excerpt[5] Edward Dayton explains how to formulate unique strategies for specific peoples.

HOW DO WE REACH THEM?

The world we are concerned with is the world of unreached people. Some of these groups are large. Some are small. The point is that we need to *discover God's strategies*, His best way for reaching these people. Certainly if the God of the universe is capable of being concerned with each individual in the world, He is just as concerned for the peoples of the world.

How do we reach them? Through their need.

By trying to know them as God knows them.

By attempting to meet their need as they see it.

By communicating the saving power of Jesus Christ in their language and in their cultural understanding and in terms of where they are.

Too often some forms of evangelism have been carried out by people who had a solution and were looking for a problem. In other words, they assumed that there was one particular evangelistic method that would be appropriate in every setting. Evidently, God has not ordained it so. God's great love for humanity is expressed by His willingness to accept people wherever He finds them.

In order to communicate to people we have to begin where *they* perceive their need. We have to reach them *through* their need. We need to *know them* as *God knows them* and to begin by *attempting to meet their need as they see it*. When we have done this, we will have the potential for communicating the saving power of Jesus in their language, and their cultural understanding, and in terms of where they find themselves. Understanding a people through their need is basic to the strategy that we are presenting here, a strategy that is useful anywhere in the world.

How do we discover their needs? What do we need to know about them?

Where they are

Why they should be considered a people group

Where they are in their movement toward Christ

Their potential receptivity to the gospel

Their perceived spiritual needs

---

[5]Edward R. Dayton, "To Reach the Unreached," in *Unreached Peoples '79*, ed. C. Peter Wagner and Edward R. Dayton (Elgin, IL: David C. Cook Publishing Co., 1978), pp. 25-31. Used by permission.

Where they are geographically is, of course, of first importance. But we need to go further and understand *why they should be considered a people group.* We need to put some boundaries around them.

A group of people is not static. Even in so-called traditional societies there is always movement. So we need to understand where this people is in terms of *their movement toward Christ.* Are they on the brink of receiving Him, or are they completely unaware of His existence? The situations within which people find themselves will have a great deal to do with their receptivity to new things and thus their receptivity to the gospel. We need to make some statements about that.

Finally, we need to understand their *perceived spiritual needs.* Jesus Christ is the answer to everyone's needs. But people have different needs at different times, and we must begin where they presently are.

1. Why are the needs of a people the key to developing a strategy for reaching them?

    _____

    _____

    _____

The Engel Scale

In recent years some new tools have been developed to help us to better describe and thus better understand a people. One of these tools helps us to understand where people are in their movement toward Christ.

Notice that this scale shows a progression from no awareness of Christianity to being an active propagator. The scale is not special or peculiar to religion or Christianity. All of us, in making major decisions, go through some steps like this. And if we think back on our own conversion experience, we will discover that there were different people, different situations that moved us toward Christ.

Figure 8.1

WHERE IS THIS PEOPLE IN THEIR MOVEMENT TOWARD CHRIST?

The Engle Scale*

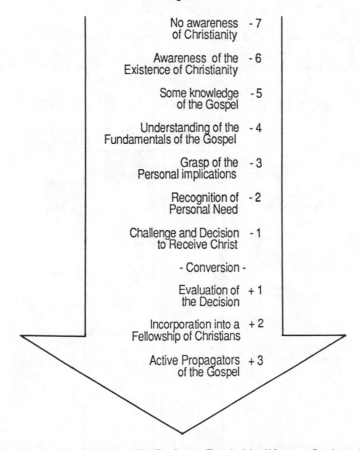

No awareness of Christianity	- 7
Awareness of the Existence of Christianity	- 6
Some knowledge of the Gospel	- 5
Understanding of the Fundamentals of the Gospel	- 4
Grasp of the Personal implications	- 3
Recognition of Personal Need	- 2
Challenge and Decision to Receive Christ	- 1
- Conversion -	
Evaluation of the Decision	+ 1
Incorporation into a Fellowship of Christians	+ 2
Active Propagators of the Gospel	+ 3

*This scale was originally proposed by Dr. James Engel of the Wheaton Graduate School.

There was a day when, either because of ignorance or because of our extreme youth, we had absolutely *no awareness of Christianity* (-7 on this scale).

Most Westerners are aware or have some *awareness of Christianity* (-6 on our scale), and most Americans have *some knowledge of the gospel* (-5). The day came when some of us had an understanding of the *fundamentals of the gospel* (-4). What happened next and in what sequence is very difficult to tell. It varies tremendously from individual to individual. But in addition to an intellectual understanding, each of us had to understand that this gospel was meant for us; we had to *grasp the personal implications* (-3). But even that is not enough. We must also have a *recognition of personal need* (-2) that we think the gospel can meet. Only then are we ready to have a *challenge and decision to receive Christ* (-1).

What takes place next is, in purely religious terms, called "conversion." In more biblical terms we would call it regeneration, a new birth.

93

But as is the case in most major decisions, there is almost always an *evaluation of the decision* (+1). Research has shown that this is the key time in the life of a new Christian. How we minister to people as they go through this evaluation will have a major impact on their future.

Once this decision is past, people move on to being *incorporated into a fellowship of Christians* (+2) and then *become active propagators* (+3).

We have described this decision-making process in terms of individuals. Actually, groups of people go through this same type of *group process*, and so this scale becomes even more useful to us. Let's look at some examples, using the following illustration.

Figure 8.2

EXAMPLE OF THE USE OF THE ENGEL SCALE

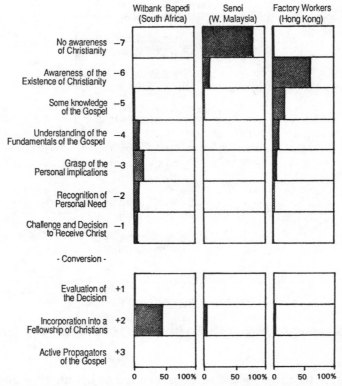

Here are three different groups of people: Witbank BaPedi in South Africa, the Senoi in West Malaysia, and factory workers in Hong Kong.

The people in the first group are almost all Christians. Only a small percentage are still back in that category of having not moved beyond some knowledge of the gospel (-5). Approximately 45 percent of them have been incorporated into a fellowship of Christians (+2). This is a *reached people.*

The Senoi are at the other extreme. At best we can tell, about 80 percent of them are absolutely unaware of any existence of Christianity. True, there is a very small church (+2), but there is very little movement towards Christ.

The factory workers of Hong Kong, on the other hand, are surrounded by Christian symbols. Large numbers of them have an awareness of Christianity (-6). But the church is very small, although it appears that there are numbers of people who are moving towards Christ.

Now the advantage of these descriptions of people is that it helps us to *tailor our message.* We are much like the manufacturer of a product or a provider of a service. They have to know where the people are in order to do a good job of marketing. In the best sense of the word, we want to be outstanding marketers of the gospel! But still another factor must be considered. What is the *potential receptivity of a people to the gospel?*

2. Why is the Engel scale useful in planning strategy?

_____

_____

_____

The Resistance/Receptivity Scale

Missionary research all over the world has shown us that there are many indications of a people's potential receptivity or resistance to the gospel. For example, we know that people who are undergoing a great deal of economic stress or upheavals in their way of life are more open to a new understanding of the world.

The *resistance/receptivity* scale helps us know how much research we are going to have to do in order to reach a particular people. Although it is a generalization, we can say that people who are highly receptive will probably respond to almost any evangelistic method, while people who are highly resistant are going to need a great deal of special care.

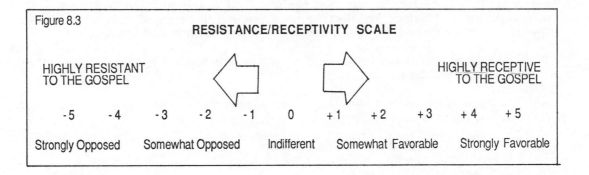

Underneath the scale, we have listed peoples in these various categories. There are tremendous opportunities for the gospel around the world! Here are a few:

Figure 8.4   PEOPLE KNOWN TO BE OPEN TO THE GOSPEL

COUNTRY	GROUP	POPULATION	PERCENT CHRISTIAN
China (Taiwan)	Hakka	1,750,000	(1%)
India	Kond	900,000	(3%)
Philippines	Cotaboto Manobo	10,000	(1%)
Thailand	Lepers of Northeast	390,000	(.5%)
Indonesia	Sundanese	25,000,000	(1%)
Benin	Boko	20,000	(2%)
Ethiopia	Shankilla	500,000	(1%)
Kenya	Fishing Turkana	20,000	(4%)
Germany	Koreans	10,000	(8%)
U.S.A.	Racetrack Residents	50,000	(10%)
Mexico	Azteca	250,000	(2%)
Belize	Black Caribs	10,000	(1%)
Colombia	Coreguaje	500	(1%)
Guatemala	Quiche	500,000	(7%)

3. How will the resistance or receptivity of a people to the gospel affect our strategy?

_____

_____

DESIGNING KEYS AND UNLOCKING DOORS

There are peoples all over the world who are "locked out" from the gospel; they are hidden people, because no one has really found a key to open the door of their understanding to Christ's love for them. They will be reached only when they are approached as unique people groups with their own culture and sense of unity.

With God's help you can design keys which will unlock the door for a particular people to whom God has called you.

There are some obvious questions that can be asked that will enable the Holy Spirit to give us the mind of Christ:

1. What people does God want us to reach?
2. What is this people like?
3. Who should reach them?
4. How should we reach them?
5. What will be the result of reaching them?

These five steps can be thought of as a planning process. The emphasis is placed on asking the right questions, for as each people is unique before God, so will be the answers to the questions.

The five steps we have just listed are all intertwined: what people we want to reach, what the people are like, the means and methods we would use to reach them, and who should reach them are not questions that can be asked one at a time. That is just not the way we think. Obviously, our ability to reach a people will have something to do with which people we try to reach. If we cannot discover God's way of reaching them, then we will have to search for a different people.

A much better way to think of these questions would be to see them arranged in a circle. Each question leads to the next, with the last leading back to the first. It is a *process* that needs to be repeated over and over.

So although the questions are presented in a sequence, you will discover that you will often be asking many different questions at the same time. Don't let the sequence of the questions keep you from allowing the Holy Spirit to lead your mind and heart.

Figure 8.5

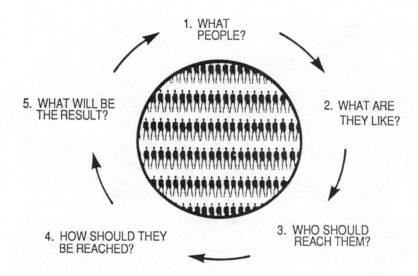

1. WHAT PEOPLE?

2. WHAT ARE THEY LIKE?

3. WHO SHOULD REACH THEM?

4. HOW SHOULD THEY BE REACHED?

5. WHAT WILL BE THE RESULT?

4. Why are the five questions in this section better placed in a continuous circle than in a list?

_____

_____

THE MYSTERY OF EVANGELIZATION

Planning strategies for evangelization is no substitute for the powerful presence and action of the Holy Spirit! If anything, the more carefully and prayerfully we try to think through the evangelization of a specific group, the more keenly we feel our dependence upon God.

There is a *mystery* to evangelization. The Spirit moves as He sees fit (John 3:8). It is God who is at work to do His perfect will. In ways that we cannot understand, He uses imperfect, sinful men and women to communicate His love and the good news of salvation through His beloved Son to all who will receive Him.

There is a mystery to what happens as the Holy Spirit transforms lives of individuals and nations. We can many times see only the *results* of the Spirit's work. The finger of God writes across the pages of history, and we can see what He has done. But so often we are unable to understand fully what has happened.

But there is *mystery* too in the fact that God has charged His church to go into all the world to preach and make disciples, trusting Him for results and yet at the same time praying, dreaming, anticipating, longing into the future. And as we respond to the command of God's Word and the prompting of His Spirit within us, we are expected to bring our *total being* to bear on the task before us, to think, to pray, and to plan. Jesus spoke to this when He said that a man should not start to build a tower or engage an enemy without first considering the possible outcomes (Luke 14:28). It was said of the early church that they outlived, outdied, and outthought the Roman Empire.

There is a *mystery* about God's action in society through the society itself. Many times God uses changes in the society to prepare people to receive His Word.

Finally, there is *mystery* about the person of the evangelist. The Word of God has as much to say about what we are to *be* as what we are to *do*. The gospel is proclaimed through the spoken word. People cannot come to a knowledge of the Savior unless they hear (or read) that He is. But they are often attracted to Him by the love they find among His disciples.

Remember, each disciple is called upon to see himself or herself as part of a larger body (I Cor. 12:12). Within that body each has a special place, and in the process of evangelization different persons play their special role at different times. "I sowed, Apollos watered, but God gave the increase" (I Cor. 3:6, RSV).

Let us then use *all* the gifts that God has given us, both individually and corporately. Let us try to think God's thoughts after Him. Let us attempt to uncover God's strategy--to think about the people to whom we may be called, to earnestly consider their needs, to take into account all that God might do to reach them. Let us make certain that we are clean vessels, fit for His use. And then let us go forward believing that God will be faithful, and GIVE HIM THE GLORY.

5. How should the "mystery of evangelization" affect our attitude towards planning strategy?

_____

_____

The Tonga Team in Zambia used an approach similar to the one Edward Dayton suggests to determine the best way to present the gospel to the Tongas. They spent two years learning the language and culture in an effort to understand the people and their view of the world. During this time they discovered that Tonga culture is permeated by fear of evil spirits. The Tongas feared the *isaku* in particular, evil spirits commanded by humans who had won their allegiance through a gruesome ritual involving, among other things, the head of a human corpse.

In the following excerpt[6] Phil Elkins describes how presentation of the gospel from an understanding of the people's needs produced the desired result.

RESPONDING TO FELT NEEDS

From all of the above insights a picture of *felt needs* emerged to which God could speak meaningfully. The first *Good News* from God for the Tonga was that He had given to us a *Holy Spirit*. The Tongas knew nothing of a good spirit, much less a *Holy Spirit* from God Himself as a gift. We shared that we were not afraid, as they were, of *isaku* spirits because we had residing in us continually a *Spirit* that would not tolerate other spirits. The Spirit in us was more powerful than any other spirit. This explained the lack of fear they had seen in our lives, the joy, the confidence, and hope.

The second part of our *Good News* was that the God, which they already knew by name, had *not abandoned them*. The Tonga had left God, but He was willing to live among them again. He had already proved His willingness by sending a Son who lived as a human and showed humans how to really live. We explained that one can now talk directly to God about their needs and that this *Son* also serves as a person's special advocate before God. We further explained that God's Son was so concerned to remove the sin and guilt for all of the offensive ways that we live that He Himself accepted the punishment on our behalf.

The Tongas began to realize the verification and proof of what we said was the *Holy Spirit* which lived in us. Lest I be misunderstood by a reader of this, I am not talking about a special gift of speaking in tongues. I am speaking of that which every Christian receives at his *new birth.*

We also spoke of the verification that would come from knowing the Bible. This had little immediate impact, as most of the people could not read. However, the Word is not confined to the printed page. The Word was communicated daily by a God who was willing to reveal Himself in their lives. He revealed Himself one day as we went to a village where we were stopped by a drunken woman who forbade us to come into her village. She said they followed Satan and not God. That night she died and the next day hundreds of people came wanting to know more of God's will for their lives.

The major political leader of our area had been leading the people to the graves of their ancestors annually to solicit rain. When he accepted the *Good News*, he demonstrated his faith by leading his people in a new way. When the first drought occurred he called the people together to spend a day calling to God to give them rain. This was a bold move which exceeded the faith of some of the missionaries. But God honored the boldness, and before the sun set the earth was drenched in rain.

In the village where we made our home, almost half of the adult population accepted baptism. At their initiative we all spent a night in prayer before going out as a group to share our faith with another village.

As our team of American missionaries saw more and more churches planted, we began to modify our role as leaders in evangelism and church planting. I believe it was a good strategy for us to identify with the Tongas physically and to provide a physical and spiritual model for evangelism. I know this is a concept that is considered "past" in many circles, but I feel it should still be an emphasis in pioneer mission efforts.

---

[6]Elkins, pp. 686-687.

To train an indigenous leadership we set up 16 extension centers for training every Christian in the basics of the Christian faith and instituted a special course for those who emerged as church leaders. This was done with the new Christians bearing the cost of the courses. We followed the practice of not subsidizing the construction of buildings or providing funding for those who entered the preaching ministry.

6. In the preceding account, why was understanding the people's felt needs essential to effective communication of the gospel?

_____

_____

SUMMARY

How do we go about reaching an unreached people group? There are several factors which affect the development of our strategy. First, we must fully understand the goal. Secondly, we must keep clear the vision of the harvest, pruning, and reaping. Thirdly, we must develop the right methods to reach the people. Last but not least, we must make sure we understand the qualifications required of those who are sent to perform the task.

Although we may have in mind the immediate goal of making disciples, consideration of the long-term goal of evangelization will greatly affect the methods we use. "One by one" methodology is sometimes appropriate where the church is an accepted part of the culture, but where the church is still considered a foreign entity, a "people movement" approach is most desirable. Such an approach will require that new strategies be developed for each people, because many traditionally applied methods will not be effective.

We must evaluate each people on the basis of their needs in order to discover how to evangelize them. This approach will lead us to an in-depth understanding of the people and their culture. The use of newly developed tools such as the Engel scale and the resistance/receptivity scale can also help us assess a people's spiritual condition and determine how the gospel should be presented in order to meet felt needs. By asking basic questions such as what people God wants us to reach, what these people are like, who should reach them, how we should reach them, and what the results of reaching them will be, we can fine tune the process of targeting an unreached people with the gospel. However, this planning must be balanced with the recognition that the Lord often works in mysterious ways to bring about His purposes. We must remain flexible in our planning and must give God the freedom to work as He sees fit in each situation.

INTEGRATIVE ASSIGNMENT

The following assignment will require a great deal of initiative on your part. In essence, we are asking you to target a people and develop a strategy for reaching them appropriate to their culture and situation. In this exercise you will apply to a practical situation many principles you have been learning.

We recognize that there are severe limitations in this kind of exercise. To develop an actual strategy, you would need to spend a good deal of time among the people you are targeting. This will not be possible for most of you. However, if you *have* spent extended periods of time among the people you choose, or if you are a member of the unreached people group itself, then this exercise should challenge you to a greater depth of understanding and a perceptive strategy for the evangelization of that people group.

Most of you will need to undertake this assignment through the avenue of research. You will discover what the people is like by interviewing either members of the group or those who are intimately acquainted with them. If you have access to a university or good public library, you may be able to select a people from recorded ethnographic studies. If you are taking this course in a formal setting, your instructor may want to assign a people group to you and personally direct your research. In some cases, it may be desirable to have students work together as teams in their research and planning.

Some of you may already be burdened for a specific people group. For you, this exercise may be a small step in fulfilling the desire which God has placed in you to reach this group. For others, this will be primarily an intellectual exercise. We trust, however, that it will stimulate all of you to become interested in other people groups and, through prayer and planning, to become advocates for their redemption.

This assignment is based on the five questions Edward Dayton asks:

1. What people?

2. What are they like?

3. Who should reach them?

4. How should they be reached?

5. What will be the result?

The assignment will be spread over the next two chapters. As you finish this workbook on strategy, you will be asked to turn in a report entitled:

"TO REACH THE _____" (name of the people group).

The report will have five sections:

I. Targeting a People Group

II. People Group Description

III. The Force for Evangelization

IV. Approach and Methods to Evangelization

V. Timetable and Timeline

For each section of your report, a worksheet is provided to help you organize your research and thoughts. Since the research for this assignment is to be spread out over chapters 8 and 9, for the present you will only be doing worksheets covering the first two sections. You will finish researching the last three sections in chapter 9 and will complete your written report by the time you finish chapter 10.

Purpose of the Project

The object of this exercise is to anticipate how God might work in a given situation if a sound strategy for evangelization were developed and applied. The worksheets are based in part on a questionnaire designed for actual use in the identification and targeting of unreached peoples. When this tool is used as the basis of an actual mission effort, it is crucial that the questions be answered as accurately as possible. In this exercise, however, the accuracy of the information is not critical. Some answers, in fact, will not be available without research well beyond the limits of this course. In such cases, supply information which seems realistic. We are more interested in the *process of selecting a group and planning strategy* than we are with detailed accuracy of information.

Given the above limitations, we urge you to make a reasonable effort to become knowledgeable about your people group. The approach and methods you choose will be based on the information you gather and on what you are learning in this study regarding successful approaches. The projected results and timetable for evangelization will, of course, be entirely conjecture on your part. However, you should attempt to be realistic in your expectations.

WORKSHEET #1: TARGETING A PEOPLE GROUP

The first question you must seek to answer is, **"What people?"** If you agree that the priority today should be the "hidden" or "unreached" peoples, then your selection should be made from the thousands of groups in this category. But how do you narrow the field to just one group? Since your opportunities for research are limited, availability of information is a major consideration. Another limitation may be a people's receptivity. Attempt to select a group which you believe is already receptive or is becoming receptive to the gospel. Another consideration is the strategic importance of the people to the spread of the gospel. Reaching a specific group or stratum of a society may offer a key for the spread of the gospel throughout that society.

As you begin considering a specific people group, answer the following questions. Remember, if you don't have enough information for some answers, just make a calculated guess.

A. Reachedness

1. Is anyone currently attempting to reach this people group? If so, who? Are they being successful, or is a new effort desirable?

2. Is there a "viable" church among this people, one which can adequately carry on evangelization?

3. Based on the Engel scale, where are the majority of these people in their movement toward Christ?

4. In your estimation, is this a reached or unreached group? Explain your answer.

B. Receptivity

1. Is this people open to religious change of any kind?

2. What is the current attitude of this people towards Christianity? (Use the resistance/receptivity scale.)

3. Do you believe this people is or can become receptive to the gospel? Explain your reasoning.

C. Strategic Considerations

1. Are there other strategic considerations, related to the spread of the gospel in this area of the world, that should be taken into account in targeting this people?

103

2. Are these other strategic considerations significant enough to override other factors such as apparent low receptivity?

WORKSHEET #2: PEOPLE GROUP DESCRIPTION

Once you have determined what people you are targeting, you will want to answer the question, **"What are the people like?"**

A. General Physical Description

1. What is the name or descriptive title of this people group?

2. What is the approximate size of this people group?

3. Of what race, class, caste, nationality, etc. are they members?

4. What is their first language? What other languages do they speak?

5. Where do these people live? What is their environment like?

6. What is the economic situation of this people group? Is there a specific profession which characterizes them?

7. What other physical distinctives are part of these people's cultural boundaries?

B. Religious Background

1. Describe the religion or religions to which these people adhere.

2. What percentage adhere to each religion? How many people are nominal in their faith, and how many are sincere practitioners of their religion?

3. Do the people seem satisfied with their religion and its practices? How does their religion cope with issues of illness and death?

C. Cultural Practices Influencing Conversion

1. What cultural values, beliefs, structures, or practices might provide a bridge for the gospel?

2. What cultural values, structures, or practices are the greatest hindrances to the gospel? Are some of the practices in direct contradiction to Scripture?

3. Are there cultural practices or structures which could be reinterpreted and incorporated into Christian lifestyle or worship?

4. What is the most appropriate language to use for evangelization of these people? Why?

D. External Influences on Evangelization

1. Are there government-imposed restrictions on evangelizing these people? If so, what are they?

2. Are there sociological or economic factors inhibiting the evangelization of these people?

3. Are there sociological, economic, or political factors that can be used to advantage in the evangelization of these people?

4. Are there translated portions of Scripture, medical work, schools, or other aids to evangelism that are present due to other Christian influences?

Your answers to the previous questions should give you enough information to write the introductory part of your report. Start with the rationale you have for targeting this particular people group, followed by a general description of the people, where and how they live, their religion, etc. Conclude this section by evaluating cultural factors influencing conversion as well as internal and external influences on the evangelization of the people. You should now be ready to describe a strategy for reaching these people with the gospel.

QUESTIONS FOR REFLECTION

Turn to I Timothy 2:1-4. Paul firmly urges Timothy to pray for all men everywhere so that we may lead a quiet and tranquil life. Prayer for all men is good and acceptable to God, "who desires all men to be saved and come to a knowledge of the truth" (I Tim. 2:4). As you begin researching a people group, commit yourself to pray for them. Think of specific ways you desire God to work among them. Then record your prayer for this people group in your journal.

CHAPTER 9

EVANGELISM, DEVELOPMENT, AND CHURCH PLANTING

INTRODUCTION

Thus far in our study we have learned basic principles which form the backbone of our approach to the remaining task of mission. We have attempted to look at the world as God sees it, nation by nation. We know that there are at least 16,750 unreached people groups and that these groups can be classified into five major megaspheres. We have examined aspects of strategy vital to reaching those still unreached with the gospel. Finally, a method has been suggested for targeting a specific people and for beginning to plan for their evangelization.

Beyond targeting a people and finding out as much as possible about them, we must face the question of how to go about evangelization. It's important to bear in mind that our goal is not single converts, or even a single church, but a cluster of culturally relevant churches. We want to aim for a "people movement," but between the identification of a people and the accomplishment of this goal will lie years of dedicated effort. Not only must we plan a general strategy to implement and support a mission to a people; we must also decide on the specific tactics we intend to employ. These are what will occupy our time from day to day and week to week.

The most significant factor in the development of tactics is our understanding of the people we hope to reach. What are they like? What are their needs? How is their society structured? What emphasis will be necessary so that the gospel will penetrate and then permeate the group? What would the church look like among these people? These questions can only be answered by living with the people, learning their language, adopting their lifestyle, gaining their confidence, and seeking to know them better than they know themselves. Each people is unique, and the tactics we employ for each group will also be unique.

The whole subject of knowing a people and identifying intimately with them is so important that the last five chapters of this course will be devoted to it. If God Himself deemed it necessary to become a man in order to know our frailties and bring salvation to us, then we can place no lesser emphasis on the necessity of knowing and identifying intimately with a targeted people group in order to reach them.

In this chapter, then, we will discuss tactics of evangelization in a general sense. We will not suggest the specific means of implementation, for that cannot be done until time is actually spent with a people. We will, however, outline principles which will help you know what to consider as you plan tactics and methodology. First, a comparison will be made of two methods used for evangelization in Northwest China. Then we will look more closely at how meeting basic human needs figures into the task of evangelization. In the final section, we will consider principles of church planting that have led to the spontaneous multiplication of churches in Honduras. You will also be completing the remaining worksheets for your report on reaching an unreached people group.

I. EVANGELISM

The Great Commission of Mark 16 says, "Go ye into all the world and *preach* the gospel . . ." (Mark 16:15). A simple interpretation of this passage and others such as Romans 10:13-15 might lead to the conclusion that all a missionary has to do is set up shop and start preaching to whomever will listen. But the way one goes about proclaiming the gospel has a significant effect on the response to the message. For example, the gospel can be interpreted as "bad news" if the bearer of the message proclaims it inappropriately. What the messenger does is often more important than what he says. The following article[1] demonstrates the importance of using methods of evangelism which truly present the gospel as "good news."

Evangelization of Whole Families

Chua Wee Hian[2]

Year: 1930

Locality: Northwest China

Case Studies:

1. The approach and strategy of two single European lady missionaries.

2. The approach and strategy of the Little Flock Assembly of Chefoo, Shantung.

Objectives: Identical--to plant local churches and to engage in extensive village evangelism.

---

[1]Chua Wee Hian, "Evangelization of Whole Families," in *Let the Earth Hear His Voice*, ed. J. D. Douglas (Minneapolis: World Wide Publications, 1975), pp. 968-971. Used by permission.

[2]Chua Wee Hian is General Secretary of the International Fellowship of Evangelical Students (IFES). An Asian from Singapore, he has served as an associate secretary for IFES in East Asia and as editor of *The Way*, a quarterly magazine for Asian students.

Case Study 1

Two gifted and dedicated lady missionaries were sent by their missionary society to Northwest China. Their mandate was to evangelize and plant congregations in a cluster of villages. They spoke fluent Chinese; they labored faithfully and fervently. After a decade, a small congregation emerged. However, most of its members were women. Their children attended the Sunday School regularly. The visitor to this small congregation would easily detect the absence of men.

In their reports and newsletters, both missionaries referred to the "hardness of hearts" that was prevalent among the men. References were made also to promising teenagers who were opposed by their parents when they sought permission for baptism.

1. From this brief description, why do you think that some Chinese parents might perceive the gospel to be "bad news"?

_____

_____

Case Study 2

In 1930 a spiritual awakening swept through the Little Flock Assembly in Shantung. Many members sold their entire possessions in order to send 70 *families* to the Northwest as "instant congregations." Another 30 *families* migrated to the Northeast. By 1944, 40 new assemblies had been established, and all these were vitally involved in evangelism.

Now, in terms of dedication and doctrinal orthodoxy, both the Europeans and the Little Flock Assembly shared the same commitment and faith. But why the striking contrasts in results and in their strategies of church-planting?

Consider the case of the two single lady missionaries. Day by day, the Chinese villagers saw them establishing contacts and building the bridges of friendships with women, usually when their husbands or fathers were out working in the fields or trading in nearby towns. Their foreignness (dubbed "red hair devils") was enough to incite cultural and racial prejudices in the minds of the villagers. But their single status was something that was socially questionable. It was a well-known fact in all Chinese society that the families constitute basic social units. These units insure security. In Confucian teaching, three of the five basic relationships have to do with family ties--father and son, older brother and younger brothers, husband and wife. The fact that these ladies were making contacts with individual women and not having dialogues with the elders would make them appear to be foreign agents seeking to destroy the fabric of the village community. A question that would constantly crop up in the gossip and discussion of the villagers would be the fact of the missionaries' single state. Why aren't they married? Why aren't they visibly related to their parents, brothers and sisters, uncles and aunts, and other relatives? So when they persuaded the women or the youth to leave the religion of their forefathers, they were regarded as "family-breakers."

By contrast, the Little Flock Assembly in sending out Chinese Christian families sent out agents that were recognizable socio-cultural entities. Thus the 70 families became an effective missionary task force. It is not difficult to imagine the heads of these families sharing their faith with the elders of the villagers. The grandmothers could informally transmit the joy of following Christ and of their deliverance from demonic powers to the older women in pagan villages. The housewives in the markets could invite their counterparts to attend the services that were held each Sunday by the "instant congregations." No wonder 40 new assemblies were established as a result of this approach to church-planting and evangelism.

2. Why were the two women missionaries perceived as a threat to Chinese social structure?

_____

_____

3. What built-in success factors did the missionaries from the Little Flock Assembly have?

_____

_____

EVANGELIZING FAMILIES IN OTHER CULTURES

The strategy of evangelizing whole families is applicable not only in Chinese communities. It is also effective in other Asian communities, African villages and tribes, Latin American *barrio* and societies. Writing on the rapid spread of the Christian faith in Korea, Roy Shearer observed: "One most important factor governing how the church grew is the structure of Korean society. In Korea, we are dealing with a society based on the family, not the tribe. The family is strong even today. The soundest way for a man to come to Christ is in the setting of his own family."[3]

He went on to relate repeated situations when heads of families returned to their clan villages and were successful in persuading their relatives and kinsmen to "turn from idols to serve the living God." He concluded: "The gospel flowed along the web of family relationships. This web is the transmission line for the current of the Holy Spirit that brought men and women into the church."[4]

In her book *New Patterns for Discipling Hindus*, Miss B. V. Subbamma categorically asserted that the Hindu family might be the only social institution through which the gospel could be transmitted and received. Not all would agree with this assertion, because there are evidences of university students who have professed faith in Christ in the great university centers of India. Some could take this step of faith because they were free from parental pressures. However, as a general rule, Miss Subbamma's observation and deduction are correct.

Evangelizing whole families is the pattern of current missionary outreach in parts of Latin America. There in the Roman Catholic culture of web-relationships, family structures are strong. Exploiting this social pattern, the Chilean Pentecostals, like the Little Flock Assembly in Shantung 40 years ago, dispatch *families* from among their faithful to be agents and ambassadors of church

---

[3]Roy E. Shearer, *Wildfire: Church Growth in Korea* (Grand Rapids: Wm. B. Eerdmans Publishing Co., 1966), p. 146.
[4]Shearer, p. 150.

expansion. Through these evangelizing families, many assemblies and congregations have been planted in different parts of that continent. The phenomenal growth of the Pentecostal movement in Latin America reflects the effectiveness of using families to evangelize families.

At times it is difficult for individualistic Westerners to realize that in many "face to face" societies religious decisions are made corporately. The individual in that particular type of society would be branded as a "traitor" and treated as an outcast if he were to embrace a new religious belief. After the Renaissance, in most Western countries, identity is expressed by the Cartesian dictum *Cogito ergo sum:* I know, therefore I am. Man as a rational individual could think out religious options for himself and is free to choose the faith that he would like to follow. This dictum does not apply in many African tribal communities. For the Africans (and for many others) the unchanging dictum is, *I participate, therefore I am.* Conformity to and participation in traditional religious rites and customs give such people their identity. So if there is to be a radical change in religious allegiance, there must be a corporate or multi-individual decision.

This is particularly true of Muslim families and communities. The one-by-one method of individual evangelism will not work in such a society. A lecturer friend of mine who teaches in the multi-racial university of Singapore once made this significant remark, "I've discovered that for most Malay students (who are nearly all Muslims) Islam consists not of belief in Allah the supreme God--it is *community*." Ambassadors for Christ in Islamic lands should cope not only with theological arguments concerning the unity and nature of God; they should consider the social and cultural associations of Muslims. Where sizable groups of Muslims had been converted, their decisions were multi-individual. An excellent illustration would be that of Indonesia. During the past 15 years, wise missionaries and national pastors had been engaging in dialogues and discussions with the elders and leaders of local Muslim communities. When these decision-makers were convinced that Christ is the only way to God and that He alone is the Savior of the world, they returned to their villages and towns and urged all members to turn to Christ. So it was not surprising to witness whole communities being catechized and baptized together.

Such movements are termed as "people movements," and many years before the Indonesian happening, Ko Tha Byu, a remarkable Burmese evangelist, was instrumental in discipling whole Karen communities and villages to Jesus Christ. Today the Karen church is one of the strongest Christian communities in Southeast Asia.

4. What is the basic difference between Eastern and Western perceptions of the relationship between an individual and the group?

_____

_____

_____

5. What strategy for evangelism is needed to penetrate cultures which highly value "family" and "community"?

_____

_____

THE BIBLICAL DATA

When we turn to the biblical records, we shall discover that families feature prominently both as the recipients as well as the agents of salvation blessing.

To begin with, the family is regarded as divinely instituted by God (Eph. 3:15). In fact, all families owe their descent and composition to their Creator. By redemption, the church--God's own people--is described as "the household of God" (Eph. 2:19) and the "household of faith" (Gal. 6:10).

In the Pentateuch, great stress is laid on the sanctity of marriage, the relation between children and parents, masters and slaves. This emphasis is underscored in the New Testament (see Col. 3:18-4:1; Eph. 5:22-6:9; I Pet. 2:18-3:7).

It is the family or the household that pledges its allegiance to Yahweh. Joshua as head of his own household could declare, "As for me and my house, we will serve the Lord" (Jos. 24:15). Through Joshua's predecessor Moses, Yahweh had taught His people to celebrate His mighty acts by sacred meals and festivals. It is interesting to observe that the Feast of the Passover (Ex. 12:3-4) was a family meal. The head of the family was to recite and reenact the great drama of Israel's deliverance at this family gathering. Through Israel's history, even until New Testament days, family feasts, prayer, and worship were regularly held. Thus the Jewish family became both the object of God's grace and the visual agent of His redemptive actions. Their monotheistic faith expressed in terms of their family solidarity and religion must have created a tremendous impression on the Gentile communities. One of the results was that large numbers of Gentiles became proselytes, "associate members" of the Jewish synagogues. Jewish families made a sizable contribution to the "missionary" outreach.

The apostolic pattern for teaching was in and through family units (Acts 20:20). The first accession of a Gentile grouping to the Christian church was the family of the Roman centurion Cornelius in Caesarea (Acts 10:7, 24). At Philippi, Paul led the families of Lydia and the jailer to faith in Christ and incorporation into His church (Acts 16:15, 31-34). The "first fruits" of the great missionary apostle in Achaia were the families of Stephanas (I Cor. 16:15), Crispus, and Gaius (Acts 18:8; I Cor. 1:16; Rom. 16:23). So it was clear that the early church discipled both Jewish and Gentile communities in families.

It was equally clear that households were used as outposts of evangelism. Aquila and Priscilla used their home in Ephesus and Rome as a center for the proclamation of the gospel (I Cor. 16:19; Rom. 16:5). Congregations met in the homes of Onesiphorus (II Tim. 1:16; 4:19) and Nymphas (Col. 4:15).

As the above article demonstrates, the Bible strongly supports the concept of family. Where family and community are highly valued, the gospel does not need to be perceived as a threat to the social structure. In fact, it can actually be presented in such a way that it strengthens this structure. Due respect for the head of the household or the elders of the community should be shown by communicating and discussing the gospel first with them. If a household accepts the gospel, then worship and religious ceremony should incorporate the family unit.

6. What tactical changes might the two women missionaries discussed in the preceding article have made, had they understood the importance of family to the Chinese?

_____

_____

_____

The above case studies could lead one to the conclusion that unmarried women should not have been sent into the situation described. The only practical tactical change might seem to be for the women to have gotten married or to have returned to their homeland. But it is often not possible, practical, or desirable for Western women to initiate a change of their singleness. It is also inconsistent with Scripture to deny them missionary service because of their singleness, since Scripture commends the single state for service to God (I Cor. 7:32-35).

The dilemma of the missionaries' "inexplicable" singleness might have been solved had these women realized the problem it caused in the minds of the Chinese. It is probable, however, that their Western orientation prevented them from recognizing the problem, since being single in the West is acceptable, particularly for those devoted to religious work. Perhaps the first failure of the women, then, was not understanding that they, as messengers, would be perceived in such a way that their message would be discredited. Later, when young people became Christians and were baptized against their parents' wishes, the missionaries changed from being a cultural enigma and became an absolute threat.

Understanding this problem would perhaps have led the women to seek a creative solution. One such solution would have been "adoption" into a Chinese family. When confronted with similar situations, other single missionaries have occasionally placed themselves under the authority and protection of the head of a family. By doing this, they have eliminated some of the mystery surrounding their presence, and an acceptable niche has been found for them within the existing society. Still other missionary women have faced the problem by seeking respectable roles such as teacher or tutor. By providing a needed service, they have done much to gain acceptance into the life of the society.

The main point is that whatever social structure is present, it is of utmost importance that the gospel be presented in such a way that it is not perceived unnecessarily as a threat to that society. When the messenger cannot be understood, it is likely that the message will not be understood either.

A comprehensive mission strategy should consider who is best able to reach a given people group. If the national church in that country, at E-1 or E-2 distance, is able to reach them, then every effort should be made to encourage them to do so before an E-3 effort is initiated from the outside. Unfortunately, missions are often launched without a real attempt to understand who is in the best position to reach a particular people. The national church may be considered too weak or unmotivated to do mission work, so the foreign mission society takes it upon itself to enter the new field. Unfortunately, through this process the national church may come to believe that it is incapable of doing mission work, thus reinforcing the whole problem.

A neglect of mission work by the national church may not be due to lack of vision, lack of confidence, or past failures. Rather, incomplete understanding of mission methods may have led to the use of wrong tactics. Inexperience may have caused the personnel to become discouraged. Lack of resources may not have allowed a sustained effort. Tragically as well, older missions often have stood by with little or no interest in the struggles of fledgling agencies except perhaps to criticize their failures.

Some missions are finally awakening to such problems and neglect and are starting to support the development of mission agencies among young churches. Expatriate mission personnel are being loaned to the young agencies in support roles. Training programs, sponsored by older missions, are being offered to national believers who are seeking to enter cross-cultural mission work. If we are to take the remaining task of world evangelization seriously, it is imperative that we see much more of this international and inter-agency cooperation.

7. In the above case studies, who was in the best position to reach the Chinese of the Northwest, and in what ways could the two missions possibly have combined efforts?

    _____

    _____

    _____

The following case study[5] further illustrates some principles we have been discussing. In this particular case, God placed a vision for an unreached people in the heart of a young Indian, Prem Sagar. The way Prem undertook this mission was somewhat unorthodox, but this was certainly not the first time God led an individual believer to circumvent "bureaucracy" in order to do what God had asked him to do. Let us pray for the sensitivity to encourage such men from the outset to pursue their mission vision.

A Flaming Fire in the Maredumilli Jungles

Ezra Sargunam

Prem Sagar, a young man of 22, was called of God for full-time ministry. He came from the West Godavari District of Andhrapradesh to the city of Madras to undergo ministerial training at one of the Bible schools. During his summer vacation in 1979, he traveled about 100 miles to spend the holiday at the home of one of his relatives in the East Godavari District. This uncle of Prem Sagar was a forest officer with the government and was living with the family in a forest area called Maredumilli Samithi.

A FLAMING FIRE

During the time he stayed with his uncle and family, Prem Sagar came to know about the tribal people living in the jungles of Maredumilli Samithi. He met some of these groups, and the Lord placed a special burden in his heart to return to work among these tribal people after his seminary training. While he was at the Bible school, Prem Sagar kept talking to me and my colleagues about these hidden people of Maredumilli. However, after seminary training he was appointed to serve as a member of one of the gospel teams in the city of Madras. Since our committee wasn't too happy to send Prem Sagar to serve in the midst of tribal people all by himself and because no one else came forward to go with him for pioneer ministry in this region, he was stuck with the team in Madras.

Prem Sagar kept praying for these tribal people. As the burden in his heart grew for these unreached and as he began to find out that it might take years before the "bureaucrats" would approve the project of reaching the Maredumilli tribals, Prem Sagar determined before God to do it on his own.

Initially Brother Prem wanted to move to Maredumilli, live with his uncle, and so begin the ministry. It was a real test for him when he came to discover that his uncle had transferred to another area. Nevertheless, the "fire" for ministry among the Maredumilli tribals that was burning in his heart could not be put out. Prem Sagar finally wrote a prayer letter to all of his friends and Christian relatives about his decision, resigned from his services with the gospel team, and went entirely on his own in a step of faith to work among the Maredumilli.

[5]Ezra Sargunam, "A Flaming Fire in the Maredumilli Jungles," in *Perspectives on the World Christian Movement*, ed. Ralph D. Winter and Steven C. Hawthorne (Pasadena, CA: William Carey Library, 1981), pp. 697-701. Used by permission.

It needs more than vision and courage for one to be called to serve among the hidden peoples. One needs to become a "flaming fire." The history of the church has proved that the Lord "maketh His ministers a flaming fire" (Ps. 104:4).

Before I elaborate on how this came to be true in the life and ministry of Brother Prem Sagar, let me state briefly here certain characteristics of the people to which he intended to go.

CUSTOMS AND CULTURES OF THE MAREDUMILLI TRIBAL PEOPLE

Maredumilli area covers about 590 square miles and lies on the northeast side of Andhrapradesh and southwest of Orissa. The entire area is covered by hills and dense forest at an altitude of 1,500-4,000 feet above sea level. According to India's 1971 census, within these jungles are about 30,000 tribal people in 5,800 families living in approximately 330 villages. There are at least two or three legends told about the antiquity of the people. One of the traditions states that these people are descendants of groups who once lived in the plains. They moved with their families into the jungles several hundred years ago when the Muslims carried out a mass killing of people who did not embrace Islam. Once they got settled in these jungles, the tradition said, they never again returned to the plains.

Though the caste system is not commonly found among the tribal people of India, the Maredumilli appear to practice caste to some degree. This is one of the strong arguments in favor of the theory that they once came from the plains. The highest of the caste groups among them are the *Konda Reddies*, and the lowest are *Valmikis*.

Since the response to the gospel has been mostly among the *Koyas* and the *Valmikis*, we shall consider briefly the cultural features of these people. They live in huts and lead simple lives. The huts are scattered over hills without regard to caste distinctions. Their clothes are never removed until they are torn or worn to threads. Women wear earrings, nose rings, and bracelets made of various metals. The people go hunting for wild pigs, deer, and birds in bands and share the prey among themselves. Both men and women consume "toddy" (an alcoholic beverage made from the *Zeelugu* palm tree). The Koyas and Valmikis do feast on both marriage and funeral occasions. Though they do not have periodic or annual festivals, they observe the harvest of every crop as a time for "merry-making." The crop will not be eaten before the sacrifice of a cock has been made and the blood is sprinkled over the crop, after which they will eat, drink, and dance together. They put on tiger and cheetah skins, wear bison horns and peacock feathers, and dance in groups.

Marital relations are strictly endogamous. During festivals an unmarried young man (*govu*) can take away the hand of any unmarried maid (*gubbatty*) and take her as his wife irrespective of the will and pleasure of the maid and her family. He can also send her away if he is not pleased with her.

The language they speak is a mixture of Telugu and Oriya and has no script. From the Konda Reddies to Valmikis, they do not have any religion in the strict sense of the term, but they fear the supernatural element. Sacrifices are made to the supernatural powers like lightning, thunder, and rain. Until 1970 these tribes also offered human sacrifices. Though they do not have a clear monotheistic understanding of God, they seem to fear a particular deity by the name of Khonda Raju, who is plural. Interestingly enough, they never worship idols, though certain sacred trees are selected under which the sacrifices are made.

They do not follow modern trade systems, since they are scattered in remote areas where there is no proper communication system. They bring such produce as oranges, poultry, and herb medicines, and what they have hunted, on *shanti* days (market days) and barter their goods with the people from the plains for salt, kerosene, and clothes.

THE VISION BECAME A REALITY

Prem Sagar left Madras and came to Maredumilli. Living in a small hut under the most trying conditions, Prem began his ministry among the Maredumilli tribes. A few of the Christian relatives and friends back in his home town got behind him by sending him a little money and food. One of his more practical approaches was to meet these tribals on *shanti* days when they would come walking more than 30 miles to barter their goods with the people of the plains.

Since most of the people could neither read nor write, the only method of communication that was open to him was to preach to them at the market on Saturdays. So Prem would stand every Saturday night in one of the entrances to the market and would sing along with the help of a tambourine which produced more noise than his singing did. Most of the tribals, on their return journey back into the jungles, would lay down their headloads and listen attentively to the gospel stories. Brother Prem preached to them in the Telugu language which was understood by both the people from the plains as well as the tribals. He followed this with prayers for the sick. Well! Wouldn't anyone like to find healing for their bodies without bothering to give away their wealth to the witch doctor? Many knelt down in prayer for healing, for protection, and for good crops. Several found their prayers answered. The news about the new "Christian Witch Doctor" spread like wildfire throughout the jungles.

Meanwhile, Prem Sagar came across two or three tribals who had apparently attended Christian schools and who had lived and were raised in Christian hostels in Rajamundry, which was about 150 miles away from Maredumilli. These few precious people who were exposed to the message of the gospel still remembered some of the Christian songs. Though they had not become Christians, one of them hung a picture of Christ on the mud walls of his hut. Prem Sagar got all the more excited by the fact that God had already begun His work in the Maredumilli area. This particular individual, who also happened to be a tribal leader, had a teen-age daughter who had bad dreams in the night and was filled by the evil spirit. Brother Prem Sagar fasted and prayed for the deliverance of this dear little girl from the demon possession, and she was completely delivered. This tribal leader and his family put their trust in Jesus Christ. More and more began to happen.

During these months, Prem Sagar never failed to be in touch with us back in Madras. He had written to us a number of times, challenging us to pray for him. We were left without any option but to get behind this "rebel" who left us before formally informing us of his departure and who had only sent his letter of resignation a month after he had begun his ministry in the Maredumilli area.

Early in the 1980's, I did make an effort to survey Maredumilli area with some of my colleagues. After we had seen and were convinced of God's mighty works, we were definitely prompted by the Holy Spirit to get behind Brother Prem's ministry. Meanwhile, the chief of one of the tribes, who had accepted Christ along with his family, came forward and donated a piece of land, where a semi-permanent church building has since been built. The first converts, 17 members of five families, were baptized in the summer of 1980. Subsequently 40 other adults have been baptized. Three churches have been planted. Prem Sagar is now married to a very gifted lady, who, though a university graduate, has graciously accepted the call of God to serve with her husband to serve the Lord in the jungles. Three other full-time national missionaries have been appointed by the Indian Missionary Movement, an indigenous mission agency and the missionary arm of the Evangelical Church of India.

The World Evangelical Outreach, who are doing a tremendous ministry among certain hidden peoples around the world, have now taken up the challenge to work alongside the Evangelical Church of India in discipling 30,000 tribals of Maredumilli. The dream of one man, Prem Sagar, is now becoming a reality.

IN CONCLUSION

The strategies employed and the missiological factors behind the Maredumilli movement are obvious.

1. It takes more than a call, vision, courage, conviction, personnel, and finances to disciple a hidden people. It takes ministers with a flaming fire. Those whom the Lord makes a flaming fire become so obsessed with the call and purpose in their life that nothing can stop them until they fulfill that assignment. This was very true in the case of Prem Sagar.

2. The powers of darkness in animistic cultures have to be counteracted with power-encounter ministry. Many sick people whom Prem Sagar prayed over were miraculously healed. Demons were cast out also, as in the case of a tribal chief's daughter. Another person was bitten by a poisonous cobra, and his life was spared because of prayer.

3. The Maredumilli tribals have some kind of monotheistic belief, which was some preparation for them to accept the Christian faith. According to missiological principles, such animistic groups who are remote and do not identify themselves with the mainstream of any one of the major religions, like Hinduism, Buddhism, or Islam, are most responsive to the message of the gospel. This has been very well proven with the Maredumilli tribals.

4. Though the Lord has used Prem Sagar in initiating the movement, he was wise in linking his efforts with a much larger indigenous church planting group, namely, the Evangelical Church of India. He was not fighting the battle on his own. There were others who stood with him in the cause of discipling these precious Maredumilli tribal people.

The Evangelical Church of India, with OMS International at the world level and the Indian Missionary Movement at the national level, are marching towards the goal of 1,000 churches by the turn of the century. Two hundred of these churches have already been planted. More hidden peoples continue to be identified, and disciples for Christ and multiplied churches are appearing among them. May the Lord of the harvest continue to make His ministers a flaming fire who win the winnable while they are winnable.

8. Describe Prem Sagar's strategy for evangelism. Why did it succeed?

_____

_____

_____

9. How was the mission venture strengthened and expanded through inter-
    agency cooperation?

_____

_____

The initial strategy for evangelism needs to incorporate more than just
"preaching." It also requires sensitivity to the target culture and an
understanding of the best way to communicate the gospel within the cultural
context, since the way the messenger is perceived determines to a large extent
the effectiveness of the gospel penetration. A comprehensive strategy will also
consider who is best suited to minister the gospel to a particular people. It will
evaluate how the Spirit of God is leading individuals to commit themselves to
the evangelization of a people, and it will reinforce that vision and leading.

II. DEVELOPMENT

Ministering to the physical needs of people is undeniably part of the missionary
task. There was a time when evangelical missions in the West argued over
whether evangelism or "social action" best defined the mission of the church.
Conservative evangelicals argued against a "social gospel" which merely aimed
at improving the temporal conditions of societies with little concern for their
eternal well-being. More liberal evangelicals argued against a spiritual message
which had no concern for a man's physical well-being.

As in most such arguments, neither extreme can be adequately defended. Just
as Christ balanced His ministry on earth by meeting both spiritual and physical
needs, so must the mission of the church include both aspects of outreach. As
we consider the subject of meeting human need through mission, we will see
that this focus on need can play a significant role in our strategy.

Many areas of the world are in desperate need of personnel with the skills to
meet basic human needs at the community level. Often such areas are closed to
conventional missionaries, particularly missionaries from North America.
Frequently, however, the governments will permit foreign workers to enter on
the basis of a needed skill. Thus, social action can become the "means" to a
church planting "end."

In the following article[6] the authors define the term "development" and show which kind of development is most likely to complement evangelization.

Helping Others Help Themselves:
Christian Community Development

Robert C. Pickett and Steven C. Hawthorne[7]

Evangelical Christians are recognizing that social action and evangelism are not opposite poles. They are complementary partners in the task of the church. The task of the church cannot be split into the "social" and "spiritual" dimensions. We are to be the preserving "salt of the earth" as much as we are to be the evangelizing "light of the world." In many cases, costly service must accompany the gospel proclamation. In almost all cases, tremendous benefit to the well-being of society can and should result from making obedient disciples.

But just what is meant by "social action"? Mentioning the term brings to mind tired warnings against diluting the truth with the "social gospel." Social action is best associated with constructive social change, but the term is used to mean anything from working for women's rights to delivering baskets of food to poor families at Christmas. The term is sufficiently vague to be nearly useless.

Another term is headed to the oblivion of multiple meaning: Development. We hear of International Development and Christian Development. We read of Developed Countries and Less Developed Countries and even Least Developed Countries.

WHAT IS DEVELOPMENT?

There are basically four strategies of alleviating the suffering of a needy world. Each of them has been called "development." These can be considered on a matrix setting two basic methods against two basic foci of action. Our tactics can bring aid from outside the country, or we can seek changes in the structures and life patterns of the people, helping them to effect the changes that they desire. We can either focus on socio-political structures or on meeting basic needs.

The matrix only attempts to begin to distinguish the four approaches. A complete definition of each is beyond the scope of this article.

Each of the approaches has a certain validity. They are, to a great extent, interdependent and complementary. A look at the potential of each approach can help the Christian worker meet basic needs.

[6]Robert C. Pickett and Steven C. Hawthorne, "Helping Others Help Themselves: Christian Community Development," in *Perspectives on the World Christian Movement*, ed. Ralph D. Winter and Steven C. Hawthorne (Pasadena, CA: William Carey Library, 1981), pp. 747-753. Used by permission.

[7]Robert C. Pickett was a professor of agronomy at Purdue University for 22 years. He has worked as a consultant for crop improvement and community development projects in over 100 countries. Steven C. Hawthorne is pursuing a degree in cross-cultural studies in the School of World Mission at Fuller Theological Seminary. He co-edited *Perspectives on the World Christian Movement*, a well known reader on missions.

Figure 9.1   FOUR STRATEGIES OF DEVELOPMENT

	METHOD:	
	HELP FROM WITHOUT	CHANGE FROM WITHIN
STRUCTURES	**STRATEGY I** ECONOMIC GROWTH	**STRATEGY II** POLITICAL LIBERATION
NEEDS	**STRATEGY III** RELIEF	**STRATEGY IV** COMMUNITY DEVELOPMENT

FOCUS: (STRUCTURES / NEEDS)

STRATEGY I: ECONOMIC GROWTH

"Economic growth" often is reflected by improvements in the macro-statistics of a country such as higher per capita income level or an improvement in the balance of trade.

The concern for economic growth in the sense of Christian Community Development is for "micro-economic" factors such as adequate food, fuel, and health for each family provided locally on a sustainable basis. Any economy must reach decisions about what goods are to be produced, in what quantities and by what methods, and how much of these goods will go to each person or family.

In the Third World or developing countries an accurate assessment must be made of both human and natural resources, along with present problems or limiting factors. The people must be motivated toward development and involved in planning for economic development or growth. Finally, the people must then be adequately trained in the best systems of efficient and sustainable use of the natural resources about them.

One basic problem often overlooked is the effect of grossly inadequate production of many if not most basic items in developing countries. This makes the choice among alternative uses of scarce resources much more difficult. The distribution in most Third World countries becomes inadequate, with many (poor) people being left out and confusion setting in.

The 1960's "Decade of Development" was a period of massive injections of wealth into the economics of the less developed countries. It was thought that benefits derived from booming industry and trade would "trickle down" to the poor. The effort largely failed to bring substantial improvement to the quality of life for the suffering masses. The blessings rarely trickled down to where they were most needed. But economic growth is indeed a viable course of action, when accompanied by careful attention to development on the community level.

STRATEGY II: POLITICAL LIBERATION

Strategy I aims to bolster the national economy and government. Strategy II tends to see the basic problem to be this very system of national government and commerce. The call is for liberation from oppressive regimes and international trade agreements which intensify the gap between the "haves" and the "have nots." So many have so little. And the gap is widening. The "haves" continue to accumulate. The "have nots" get poorer. But Strategy II is overwhelmingly complex. It includes a wide spectrum of activity from violent revolution to quiet lobbying for human rights.

Christian missions have been a powerful force in matters as varied as land reform, refugees' rights, and the abolition of slavery. Christian missions should continue to be this kind of force. But they must help cultural "insiders" take the leading role in such change; otherwise, such force is a reverse imperialism that still imposes the will of outsiders on the people. Today's missionary force is wise to avoid such interference. Yet, in still another sense, few oppressive political structures stand apart from certain multi-national corporations and international trade agreements. Christians can and should seek to end the injustices in international trade and commerce.

Strategy II is indeed complex, but one thing is clear. It holds little promise of lasting hope without Strategy IV. Time after time, one regime is replaced by one even more oppressive. The Liberation all men seek can only be known in the perfect rule of the Messiah Himself at the end of the Age. We are justified in working toward justice and peace; we know that we work with God in doing so. But our efforts will never usher in the Kingdom. Even redeemed humanity cannot govern with the righteousness we ultimately long for.

The converse is also true in many places. (Strategy IV is in some ways contingent on the success of Strategy II.) Development efforts can often come to naught without some attention to the system that may prevent people from partaking of the fruits of community development. It is one thing to give a man rice (Strategy III), it is another thing to help him grow more rice (Strategy IV), and then it is quite another thing to ensure that he may partake of the harvest of rice (Strategy II).

Both Strategies I and II are concerned primarily with structures. A direct focus on either strengthening or overturning structures can often backfire, even with an intention to see needs met. Injustices can be reinforced on the one hand or repeated on the other. Unless people are *enabled* to help each other live better lives, changes in the system will make little real difference.

1. How workable for an average church or mission society are Strategies I and II? Why?

   _____

   _____

   _____

2. What dangers does a foreign or cross-cultural mission risk in basing tactics on Strategy II?

   _____

   _____

STRATEGY III: RELIEF

Strategy III aims at survival for victims of war, disaster, and prolonged injustice. Massive relief efforts have been launched by Christian organizations, but they have been called nothing more than a "band-aid" on the desperate wound of humanity. Many such efforts treat the symptoms rather than the disease. Some even feel that relief, if continued, is detrimental in the long run because it takes away the incentive for local production and development. Some say doomed communities should be allowed to pass away to insure the survival of others. However, this "lifeboat" mentality has no place in Christian strategy. It amounts to genocide at worst and the "euthanasia" of an entire community at best. Some have justly criticized relief efforts coupled with evangelism for producing "rice Christians." A "rice Christian" has become a Christian to assure himself and his family of getting a daily dole of food. This is obviously not the best sort of evangelism. At worst it is rank manipulation. If done in this way, evangelism aggravates the situation.

But relief is necessary to break the vicious cycle of survival. An infusion of aid is needed to help people stop "eating their seed-corn;" otherwise there is no hope for long-term growth and life. But it is this long-range hope that moves Christians to search for answers to deep-seated problems.

STRATEGY IV: COMMUNITY DEVELOPMENT

Many factors point to the need for "Community Development." In the Third World the poorest and those unreached by development are mostly (80 percent plus or minus) in remote rural areas which suffer from lack of transportation and communication. There is little hope for them to enter into the international trade and buy their basic needs--they must be shown how to produce and meet their own needs themselves in the context of Christian sharing. Development seldom continues well or far if the spiritual needs are not simultaneously being met.

Many people in developing countries become defeatist or fatalistic and think of themselves as poor and incapable. They think their country or area is also poor and lacking in resources. The challenge for the Christian (who ideally is also a developer) is to help the local people see hope--for the abundant life here on earth as well as for the life eternal. After hope comes the need for the local people to become motivated to contribute to their own development. Then comes the adequate assessment of their own personal talents, abilities, and resources as well as the natural resources about them. This can bring release from the syndrome of "we're a poor people in a poor country and cannot improve."

Another factor hindering development is the tendency of many people to look at factors limiting food production, for example, and then blame the lack of adequate programs or performance on the "flood, drought, pests, diseases, etc." The challenge is to adequately assess these problems, make plans to overcome them, and begin adequate production on a renewable basis. The tendency to "find a scape-goat" must be overcome if adequate development is to take place.

There is a place for Christian involvement in all four strategies. But Strategy IV, i.e., Christian Community Development, is the key. Evangelism, in turn, is the key to Strategy IV, when people are freed from their fears or indifference--or even hate-- to truly help one another. Community development begins when and where there are hearts of love and hope in a community.

3. What is the inherent danger of evangelization based on Strategy III?

_____

_____

4. Why do the authors believe that Strategy IV best harmonizes the goals of evangelization and development?

_____

_____

PHYSICAL DEVELOPMENT FACTORS

Christian Community Development efforts must address themselves to the whole need complex of a community. Care must be taken to work with the cultural "givens" of the community. Changes must be proven to be desirable. The survival patterns of many communities are so fragile that unforeseen side effects of improvements can prove disastrous. The risk of doing things differently often appears too great to those at or under a subsistence level of living. Any tools, foods, and new technology must be carefully studied to insure that they are appropriate culturally and are renewable and sustainable physically. But most community development is a simple matter of a partnership of strengths and common sense of different cultures. Several basic development factors should be coordinated for holistic development:

1. **Water**

Pure drinking water is a daily necessity, and water for at least garden irrigation is desirable. Nonpotable water is perhaps the greatest purveyor of human physical misery. Diseases and parasites from the water lead to lethargy. Pure water can often be provided by constructing protected wells. Communities can be instructed on how to boil, filter, or chemically treat their water.

2. Sanitation

The prevention of contamination of water and food by diseases and parasites is largely a matter of education. Simple instruction in proper washing of hands and food and the proper disposal and isolation of human and animal wastes can make a great difference.

3. Food

Both the amount of food, i.e., total calories, and the nutritional balance are important. Many people do not have enough to eat, but many more suffer from nutritional deficiencies of protein, vitamins, and minerals not present in the usual basic diet of cereals, or in roots and tubers which are high in carbohydrates and starch but deficient in the other necessities. Thus, improvements must be made both in amount of food and in a proper balance of protein, vitamins, and minerals. These nutrients can be provided by such foods as grain legumes (beans, peas, etc.), green leafy vegetables, and other fruits and vegetables that can be grown in intensive home gardens if not generally available. Simple plans for crop rotation and storage can alleviate the "feast or famine" syndrome.

4. Fuel

Wood is by far the number one cooking fuel in the world, particularly in the "hungry half." Native forests are rapidly being cut down in many developing areas and are long gone in more ancient areas of civilization. The hope for *renewable* firewood production lies in several promising species of fast growing tropical trees including Eucalyptus, Leucaena, Melina, and Pinus species. Several of these are already widely used and are being replanted on hundreds of thousands of acres each year.

5. Health

Westerners are conditioned to think of health as a gift. Health care then is focused on curing diseases with expensive hospital and clinic complexes. In community development efforts, the stress should be in *preventive* medicine. Important components are teaching sanitation and public health, inoculations, parasite and disease control, and nutrition training. These should be added to whatever curative medicine is present.

6. Shelter and Clothing

These should be designed and provided by making maximum use of local crops, e.g., cotton for cloth and bamboo for buildings. Many other plant materials can be used in addition to rock, clay bricks, etc., where available for buildings.

7. Income Production

Cash crops are the primary exports and cash earners for most developing countries (except oil-exporting countries). Typical cash crops include coffee, cocoa, sugar cane, rubber, tea, and palm oil, as well as some of the very food crops developing countries need most, such as beans. "Cottage" industries and village cooperatives can be encouraged. Using local labor and materials, these arrangements hold great promise with good marketing technique.

8. Education

In many needy countries there is insufficient education, and literacy rates are very low. Thus literacy often gets first attention in education improvement. Next comes the choice between so-called classical education toward skills useful only at government desks (the biggest employer in many countries) or education toward meeting the needs of the people. The latter desperately needs expansion.

9. Communication and Transportation

These two interacting factors are almost unbelievable in their negative effects on the welfare of the people in remote areas. The majority of the people in developing countries live in these areas. Regional or national programs are often necessary to make improvements, but the possibilities for local action should be thoroughly studied.

A TEAM STRATEGY

There are three kinds of gifts that are needed in Christian Community Development. One is the gift of bringing others to Christ and planting churches. Another is a gift in a needed technical area like food production, health care, literacy, or vocational training. The third is a gift of administration in order to design, implement, and evaluate programs to help the people.

A key strategy is to organize teams that have people with special gifts in these three areas of church planting, needed technical expertise, and management. While all these gifts may be found in one person, it would be more advisable to have these tasks assigned to specific members of a team.

Each committed Christian should strive to spread the gospel of Jesus Christ as his first priority. Each member of a team is best trained first as a "generalist" in addition to being trained as a specialist in a specific task. General training can be given to teach basic and practical skills and information that can be shared with the people. This can be on witnessing for Christ, small-scale family food production, health promotion, disease prevention, first aid, and simple treatment. Each member can also be trained to be more effective in planning and organizing his or her own work, in leadership, and in controlling (or getting the desired

THE HUNGRY HALF AND THE HIDDEN PEOPLE

Thus, while all four strategies for development are necessary, and while all four have weaknesses, community development holds the most promise for the Christian worker desirous of promoting fundamental change in human societies. Community development is consistent with the posture of humility and involvement that Jesus modeled for His disciples. Community development revolves around vigorous yet sensitive evangelism. And the "hungry half" that are most in need of community development are more often than not the "hidden peoples" that are justly receiving increased attention by the church of Jesus Christ today.

5. The article lists nine areas of community development. For each of these areas, list at least one technical skill or professional role which could be deployed in meeting needs in these areas. For example:

   1. _Water--well driller, water purification technician_

   _____

   _____

   _____

   _____

   _____

   _____

   _____

   _____

6. Why do the authors suggest a "team strategy" in pursuit of Christian community development objectives?

   _____

   _____

The Bible strongly supports the concept of expressing Christian love through meeting basic human needs. Matthew 25:31-40 hardly allows us to treat this practice as "optional." The fact that meeting human need through Christian community development can also open the doors to unreached people should stimulate the church to pursue this channel for evangelization actively. It is not unreasonable to expect every missionary to develop a profession or skill of direct use in community development in addition to obtaining the usual Bible and church related training.

III. CHURCH PLANTING

Let us now project ourselves beyond the initial stages of evangelization. Let us assume that we have worked hard at understanding the people. We have learned their language and culture, gained their acceptance, understood their felt needs, applied our skills to communicate Christian love, and seen families come to Christ and organize into a church. How do we go about seeing these initial results multiplied throughout the people group?

In the following article[8] veteran church planter George Patterson[9] outlines the principles behind the spontaneous multiplication of churches.

The Spontaneous Multiplication of Churches

George Patterson

Christ commands us: "Lift up your eyes, and look on the fields" (John 4:35). A brief glance at the "fields" of over two and a half billion unreached people is awesome. Just the mathematics involved forces us to the conclusion that it is not enough simply to *go* to a mission field or to *send* someone else. It is not even enough to go to a mission field and start a few churches. Obedience to the Great Commission will mean that we either send and train, or go as, the type of missionary that can start churches that will grow and reproduce normally (as churches will) and start daughter churches and granddaughter churches and great-granddaughter churches and on and on and on until you have reached enormous population areas. There is no other way that we can obey Christ.

I have been working in Honduras directing a Bible institute which is our tool for church planting. Our field is not highly responsive. Ordinary traditional missionary methods get very little results. Our people are very poor, semi-literate, subsistence-level farmers. Even though most of our churches are small, in small villages, we have developed a strategy to enable the churches to multiply. We start an average of one new church every three or four months. We have been doing this now for over 10 years.

Fifteen years ago, we ran a traditional Bible institute which was similar to seminaries and Bible institutes in the United States. It was a residence program where students would come in, live and study, and so forth. We saw very negative results. The students that graduated simply did not go out and start churches, nor could the majority of them pastor churches. The same thing had been happening throughout Latin America. And so we changed to a TEE program, that is, Theological Education by Extension. We took the studies to the people who lived in the villages and in the mountains and in the cities. We went primarily to older family men instead of the single young men who had been coming to our Bible

---

[8]George Patterson, "The Spontaneous Multiplication of Churches," in *Perspectives on the World Christian Movement*, ed. Ralph D. Winter and Steven C. Hawthorne (Pasadena, CA: William Carey Library, 1981), pp. 601-616. Used by permission.

[9]Since 1965 George Patterson has worked in northern Honduras under the Conservative Baptist Home Mission Society. He has developed a special kind of theological education by extension program, "Obedience-Oriented Education," that trains Honduran student workers in evangelism and church planting. This program has produced 80 new churches in northern Honduras in the last 15 years.

institute. We focused on men with roots in their village, who could begin pastoring with the respect of the people much more easily than a single young fellow could.

I would like to share some biblical extension principles which have given the best results in Honduras for using TEE to plant churches. The specific methods and forms may not be compatible with your field, but these biblical principles, applied with methods that are compatible with the culture, should foster the spontaneous multiplication of churches in any mission field. Remember, God does not bless methods; He blesses obedience. We have simply taken TEE and combined it with a strong discipling program focused on obedience, and, with hard work, churches have resulted. These principles are not only for those of you going to the field. They are just as important to those continuing at home, either in multiplying disciples in your area or in molding your church to train and send missionaries capable of planting self-multiplying churches. There are four basic principles to follow: look on the fields, edify the body, aim at obedience, and organize for spontaneous multiplication.

1. Why can't the mission objective stop at the planting of a church or even the planting of several churches?

_____

_____

LOOK ON THE FIELDS

Christ commands a careful scrutiny of the fields (John 4:35). Paul knew his own "sphere" of ministry quite well (II Cor. 10:12-16). He knew what kind of church he wanted to plant and where he wanted to plant them. He had a clear idea of his own ministry.

Define Your Own Area of Responsibility

Every one of us needs to ask the question: "For whom am I responsible?" Many missionaries never learn to define their responsibility. The geographic and ethnic aspects of their ministry are never clear. Some are opportunists, like gold panners running around mining gold, always looking for a richer vein over the next mountain range. I asked one missionary in Honduras, "What is your area of responsibility?" "Oh," he said, "I am going to win Honduras for Christ." And he is going around "winning Honduras for Christ," but he has never started a church and probably never will. He goes to this city, then that city. He hands out tracts in prisons and army camps. But he has never defined his area of responsibility. You must learn to define your area in precise, concrete terms. My area of responsibility, for example, is "the Spanish speaking people of rural north central Honduras." This includes about 400 villages and a few towns and cities. Defining your area will take much study and prayer. Use a map. Confer with mission leaders, colleagues, and national workers. Investigate several areas to find where the population lies, where other missionaries are not working, and where people are responding to the gospel. Be exact. You cannot make practical plans until you know exactly where you are going to work.

Define the Kind of Church You Must Plant

What kind of churches must you plant so that they will multiply themselves spontaneously throughout your area of responsibility? Describe the church in terms of what it is able to do and what it does do, rather than in terms of structure and organization. Please distinguish very clearly between preaching points and genuine New Testament churches. Now, what is a preaching point? A preaching point is a designated place where a missionary or national worker goes weekly to the people who will gather to listen to him preach. They may sing and play the guitar and pray. Local leadership is neither trained nor established. Rarely are new converts baptized. The Lord's Supper is seldom served. And often there is little discernible difference between the Christians and non-Christians. Perhaps as many as 90 percent of church planting missionaries start preaching points with the hope that they will somehow evolve into a church. It does not happen except by the grace of God, if He's merciful. Preaching points tend to perpetuate themselves.

It is imperative to know precisely what you are aiming at so you are not stumbling around with the idea, "I'm gonna go and preach and I hope someone comes." Be careful not to start places where people come to listen to you preach. You really don't need your preaching at all to get a church started. There are many ways of communicating the gospel besides public preaching from a pulpit.

A church is a congregation of disciples who obey the commands of the Lord Jesus Christ. These are repentant, baptized believers who celebrate the Lord's Supper, love one another, show compassion to their neighbors, pray, give, and evangelize. In Honduras we simply define a church as "a group of believers committed to obey Christ." You will want to use your own biblical definition, but make sure that it is concise and precise, so that you will know exactly what you are aiming for on the field.

Define the Shortest Route to Plant a Church

Let's set the stage: you've got a good education behind you; you are on the field; you know some of the language; you have unpacked your suitcases; you walk out of the door and find five million people at your doorstep. What are you going to do? What is the shortest possible route to plant a church that will spark a spontaneous movement to Christ? The steps will vary in every situation. Avoid sidetracking in unnecessary intermediate stages in the evolution of a church. Sometimes some cultural factor absolutely demands an indirect route. Keep the steps short and simple. If you add unnecessary steps, you will fall into the error of starting unnecessary institutions like radio stations or schools or working through medical teams and other indirect means. And when they do start what they think is a church, it is not a church at all. It is a preaching point again, dominated by the missionary, not a real church, growing and reproducing spontaneously as a living body. If there is a need for auxiliary institutions, you can help the national church raise them up later.

In Honduras we multiply churches most rapidly following these five steps:

1. Witness first to male heads of households; go with them to win their friends and relatives. Have no public services until the local men are trained to lead them.

2. Baptize all repentant believers without delay.

3. Organize a provisional board of elders right away (Acts 14:23). Explain that they must win their own people and learn to pastor them themselves. Authorize them to serve the Lord's Supper and to lead their flock in doing the other things Christ commanded. They do not "preach" yet.

4. Enroll these elders in extension training classes. Meet with them every two or three weeks or as often as possible until they are mobilized.

5. Provide a checklist of the congregation activities ordered by Christ and His apostles for His churches. Use this list as a guide to teach and mobilize one of the elders who teaches and mobilizes the rest.

Define Your Ministry

What are you doing? My own ministry is: "To help the Honduran churches train their own workers." I can say it in one sentence. Yours will probably be a bit different. You may work for a time before you discover what you can do. Be flexible. You may be on the field a year or two before you can pin it down, but keep working at it until you can pin it down. Be concise. If you cannot be brief and precise, you have probably taken on too much. Trim your task down to where you can't help but do a good job; then let God open doors to wider fields.

Of course, consider what gifts the Holy Spirit has given you; but remember that we are to seek gifts, not to call attention to ourselves, but only to minister in love to one another in the most practical, edifying way. Make sure your ministry gives first priority to the greatest command: to love (John 17:26).

2. According to Patterson, what steps must be taken in defining church planting tactics?

_____

_____

_____

_____

EDIFY THE BODY

The second principle is to build up the church as a living body. Paul teaches us in Ephesians 4:11-12 that whatever pastors and teachers and missionaries do, they are to train the members of the church for the edifying of the body of Christ.

Build Loving and Serving Relationships Among Church Members

What kind of church organization provides the minimum guidance and coordination necessary to enable the members of an infant congregation to minister in love to one another and to the lost? The key to building edifying relationships among the church members is the pastor. Keep in mind the biblical model for church leadership (Tit. 1:5; Eph. 4:11-16; II Tim. 2:2; Acts 20:17-38). A weak pastor dominates his congregation. A strong pastor promotes ties between all members.

Figure 9.2   **A PASSIVE, PASTOR-CENTERED CHURCH:**

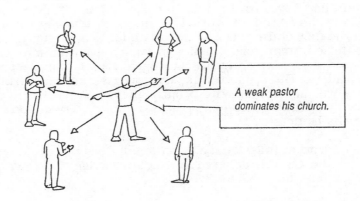

Teach your converts from the beginning to edify one another in love. Building a network of strong relationships provides for the large number of ministries required in the local church in order for it to grow and reproduce daughter churches.

INTERACTION IN A DYNAMIC CHURCH

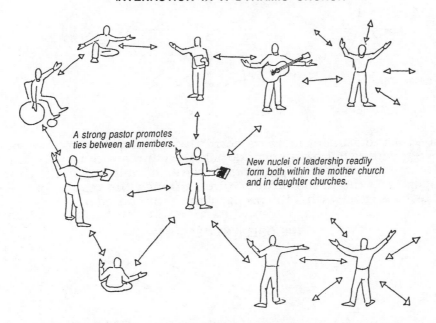

Build a Teaching/Reteaching Relationship With Lay Church Leaders

How can you lead them into those personal, loving relationships through which they can readily serve, teach, and counsel one another? Paul left Timothy behind to work with the elders in several newly planted churches. He charged him: "The things you have heard from me . . . these entrust to faithful men who will be able to teach others also" (II Tim. 2:2). Develop a loving, confidential relationship between teacher and student, a "Paul-Timothy" relationship. This is the "master-apprentice" teaching relationship. Teach the way Christ did. Teach the way the apostles did. Train your men on the job.

In Honduras I have only three students, whom I teach one at a time. They "reteach" the same things in several churches, to men who "reteach" in other churches. We have over 100 active student workers. Whenever we start a new church, a provisional board of elders is organized right away. As soon as possible, the outside worker enrolls the natural leader (most respected and loved by the people) as his own Timothy and student worker. This man teaches the rest of the provisional elders in the new church. Do not worry about "leadership training" as such. Simply organize those human relationships in such a way that many can teach or serve one another and daughter churches are born. Such a project will automatically call forth its leaders. But if you reverse the process, manufacturing the "leaders" first, in hope they will accomplish the project afterwards--you will end up getting things done only by spending enormous sums of money. Trust God's Spirit to raise up and motivate His leaders!

The outside worker (missionary or national) does not decide who these new leaders will be; let the church observe and acknowledge those who best conform to the biblical idea for elders (I Tim. 3:1-7).

Beware of traditional education objectives which focus on educating a *man*. Biblical education objectives seek to edify the *church*. The traditional teacher sees only his student.

Figure 9.3   **THE TRADITIONAL TEACHER**

TEACHER   PASSIVE STUDENT

He is satisfied if the student answers correctly and preaches good sermons. He neither sees nor cares what his student does in the church with what he learns. The obedient teacher sees beyond his student, observing his ministry in the church. The teacher responds to the needs of the church through the reports of the student worker and teaches exactly what the people of the church need.

Figure 9.4   **THE OBEDIENT TEACHER**

TEACHER   CHURCH

STUDENT-WORKER

134

Build Inter-Church Relationships

To establish daughter churches we must build loving, edifying relationships between the mother and daughter churches. We must aim at mutual edification within the body of Christ on the inter-church level.

There are several biblical examples of good inter-church relationships: Acts 11:19-26; 11:29-30; 14:26-27; and 15:1-2, 28-31. There are many ways to give and receive between churches. We do it several ways in Honduras. The simplest way is for an extension worker from the mother church to hold extension classes in the daughter churches every two weeks.

Figure 9.5

MOTHER CHURCH   *Extension worker from mother church holds classes in the daughter church.*

Another way, in case there is no one who can travel freely, is to get the main worker from the daughter church to go every two weeks or so to the mother church.

Figure 9.6

MOTHER CHURCH   *Extension student worker from the daughter church studies in the mother church.*

Of course, these two ways can be combined, especially if churches are a great distance apart (we have several cases of a two days' walk separating churches). One month someone goes from the mother church; the next month someone goes from the daughter church.

These kinds of inter-church relationships are essential to the spontaneous multiplication of churches. You will find that these mother-daughter relationships can rapidly multiply in a spontaneous way. In fact the inter-church relationships are the best way to reach a large field. Beware of the bad strategy of the mother church sending workers to several daughter churches.

Figure 9.7 AN INEFFECTIVE STRATEGY

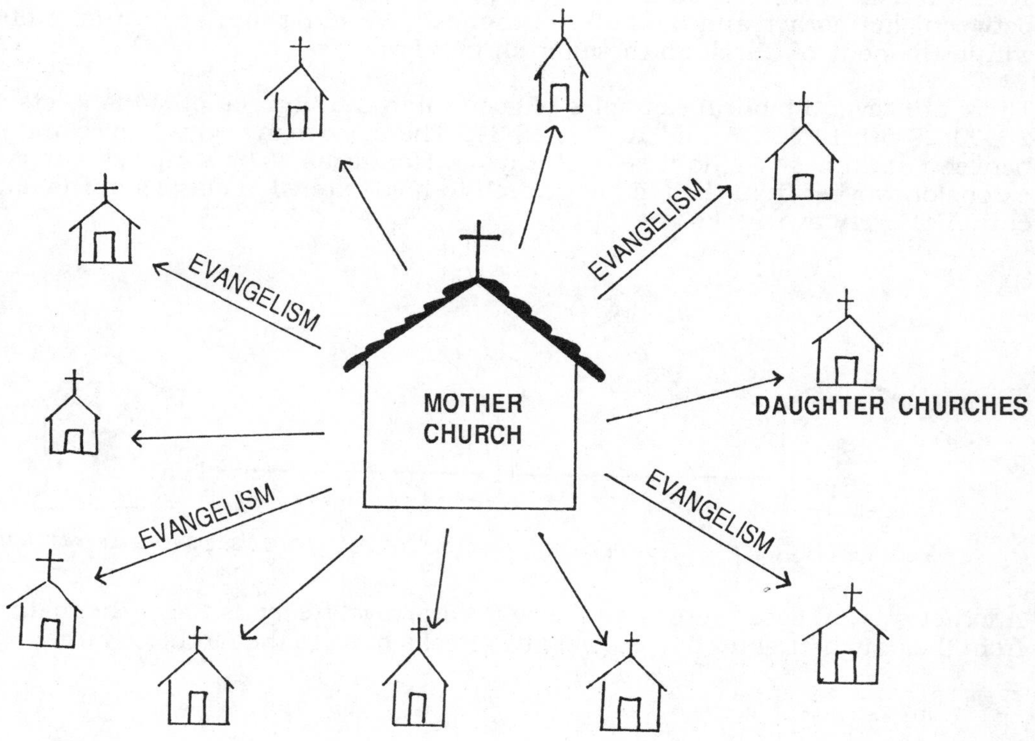

You will wear the workers out and discourage the mother church. It won't work. God's strategy enables a mother church to raise up one or two daughter churches and then make sure these daughter churches repeat the same steps. This will reach granddaughter churches and so on. This does work.

The links in this chain of churches are maintained by volunteer extension teachers from the mother church. We must activate these ties between churches. Help men to know, love, and train each other.

Edify the body of Christ. Let the natural, chosen leaders train the elders. Let mother churches train daughter churches. Allow strong leadership to develop. Don't commit the missionary's greatest sin--controlling the national churches. Keep out of the way. Let them work and grow. That's when you see the "spontaneous" dynamic. By "spontaneous" we mean that the impulse comes from the body itself, indwelt by the Holy Spirit. The controlling impulse does not come from the missionary. You can share your vision and start the ball rolling, and then you've got to step back and let the Holy Spirit work.

One of the several extension chains we have in Honduras has reproduced over five generations and 20 churches.

Figure 9.8   A GOOD STRATEGY

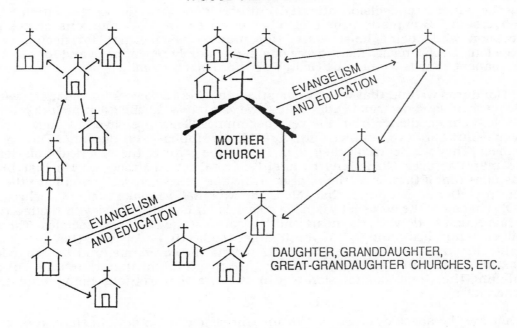

3. What kind of relationship does the author suggest for training workers, and how does this approach contrast with a traditional educational approach found even in Bible schools?

    _____

    _____

    _____

4. Why is the development of church-to-church relationships and the continuous development of leadership essential to sustaining an ongoing church planting movement? How does the missionary's "greatest sin" keep these things from happening?

    _____

    _____

    _____

    _____

AIM AT OBEDIENCE

Jesus sent the apostles to make disciples who would obey all that He commanded (Matt. 28:20). Many missionaries simply preach for "decisions" instead of aiming at making obedient disciples.

Define Evangelism Objectives in Terms of Obedience

In the American decision-oriented culture, decisions for Christ often lead to conversion. But many people of other cultures are not conscious of making a decision while being born again. Repentance is something far deeper than a decision. Decisions are made every day, but you only repent once and for all. It is a permanent change wrought by God. We're born all over again.

In Honduras we find that when we baptize repentant believers immediately, without giving them long doctrinal courses first, we can follow up the great majority, and we teach them obedience from the very beginning. They are saved to obey the Lord Jesus Christ in love, and we don't put a large emphasis on doctrine. The doctrine comes! They will learn all their life. This is the error of the American missionary. He manufactures Christians through an intellectual process. He just blindly assumes that if they learn the right doctrine and believe correctly and have the right interpretation of Scripture, that this is the way that we make them into Christians. NO! That's not the way that we make disciples. It has little to do with the brain, but it has much to do with the heart and the soul. Make obedient disciples. Then you will see churches multiply. If you just get intellectual decisions, they may believe right, they may know all the dispensations and the covenants, and they may know this and that, but what do you have? Are they multiplying churches? Are they fulfilling the Great Commission of Christ? Are they actually doing what Christ ordered?

What are the specific things that Jesus Christ told us to do? In Honduras we ask each new church to memorize the following list of Christ's main commands:

1. REPENT AND BELIEVE: Mark 1:15

2. BE BAPTIZED: Acts 2:38

3. LOVE: John 13:34

4. CELEBRATE THE LORD'S SUPPER: Luke 22:17-20

5. PRAY: John 16:24

6. GIVE: Matthew 6:19-21

7. WITNESS: Matthew 28:18-20

Teach each new believer from the very beginning to obey all these commands. Don't wait for anything. The first few weeks and months of one's spiritual life are the most impressionable; they will greatly determine his future Christian character.

In Honduras we start each new church right away celebrating the Lord's Supper. Most of them serve it every week, by choice. Don't put off training the new elders to serve the Lord's Supper; don't wait to start obeying Christ!

Define Theological Education Objectives in Terms of Obedience

How can you best help your student to train his congregation to *do* those things which Christ orders them to do?

Our Lord's Great Commission in Matthew 28:19-20 requires this orientation. *Education* and *evangelism* married to each other in one extension ministry become an effective church planting tool: combined, one reinforces the other. To teach *biblically*, our primary educational objective must not be to "educate" a student but to edify his church. All basic educational objectives and field plans must be based on the commands of Christ.

Memorize the "commands" of the Lord Jesus Christ for His churches. They are the ABC's of church planting. Only Christ has the authority to ordain what His churches must do.

We must learn to discern three levels of authority:

1. *His Commands*--which carry all the authority of heaven (Matt. 28:18-20): repent and believe, baptize, love, observe the Lord's Supper, give, pray, and evangelize.

2. *Apostolic Practices* (not commanded)--which carry only the authority of their example: holding possessions in common, laying hands on new believers, serving the Lord's Supper frequently in homes, baptizing immediately, speaking in foreign tongues as a sign to unbelievers, etc.

3. *Human Customs*--whose authority is derived from a given congregation's united agreement on the matter, which is recognized in heaven as binding on that specific congregation (Matt. 18:18-20). For this cause we should not judge another congregation by the customs of our own.

Nearly all church divisions and quarrels come from someone requiring apostolic practices or human customs (second or third level above) as though they were divine commands (first level above).

In Honduras we have been using a "Congregational Progress Chart" which lists activities ordered by Christ and His apostles for His churches. Under each activity are listed suggested studies for the corresponding theory, as well as questions which verify the necessary practical work. For the new church leader, this functionally ordered curriculum, oriented strictly toward obedience to Christ and His commands, combines the two ministries of church edification and theological education in one pastoral program. As the student works through the list of activities (the sequence is determined by his needs), he also works through all the essential elements of a traditional pastoral training curriculum.

We refer to the progress chart every two weeks or so when we meet with the student or less experienced pastor. We base all assignments on *obedience to Christ*, not to the teacher. First, we let the student explain the needs and his church's progress to the teacher; we note this on the chart. This should reveal the next logical step in obedience to Christ; we ask him what his plan is and write it down with a carbon copy, to verify his work at the next extension session; we make suggestions if needed but write them down as a formal assignment only if the student agrees. When assigning specific practical field work, deal with *one man at a time*. This establishes responsibility.

5. What is the basis of the obedience-oriented curriculum?

_____

6. What is the objective of this type of training?

_____

_____

7. According to the author, what is the cause of most church quarrels and divisions, and how can an understanding of the "three levels of authority" help us avoid these problems?

_____

_____

_____

ORGANIZE FOR SPONTANEOUS MULTIPLICATION

Build an Extension Chain

Each church should send one or two extension workers, as did Antioch (Acts 13:1-3), to raise up daughter churches. The sooner the better. It is much harder to mobilize an older church for multiplication. Any mother church can start one or more daughter churches which can in turn start more churches. This is the process we call an "extension chain." The links are not individuals but congregations.

Any chain of spiritual reproduction (in which one reaches and trains another, who does the same for another, and so on) eventually fizzles out unless it is continually re-energized by a *body* of believers indwelt by the Holy Spirit. The reproducing unit in the chain of spiritual reproduction is not the individual witness but his church. Plan your extension chains with this in mind. Each church should be a link in the chain; each witness for Christ, an arm of his church.

Take New Believers to Relatives and Friends to Witness

Develop a plan to *show* each new convert how to witness to his family and friends. The Holy Spirit flows most readily through these bonds which already exist between people. If you do not use these ties between people as bridges for the gospel, those very bonds will soon become barriers.

In Honduras we furnish simple studies for each new convert to teach to his kin and close friends. Some older Christian goes with him the first few times to show him how. We prepare the materials both for literates and illiterates (pictures only). They teach of Christ, repentance, faith, and forgiveness, leading to baptism.

Plan Field Objectives With National Leaders

Use a map of your area of responsibility, of where your national colleagues will work to plan *evangelism* (church planting) and *education* (pastoral training) objectives together.

Let the nationals take the lead in this; you simply help them to know what kind of objectives will get the job done which Christ has ordered. If you leave out the national leaders in these field plans, they will cooperate only *passively* later on.

Ask each man to sign his name on the map by the communities for which he accepts responsibility on behalf of his church. To get a group to agree on concrete plans, proceed one step at a time, praying about each decision. Keep reorienting the group to the basic demand of Christ's Great Commission; train disciples to obey His commandments.

Write out a brief outline of the field objectives agreed upon. What are the new communities you hope to reach, where are the strategic centers for extension of the work, and who are the men who accept the responsibility?

In Honduras we began our extension program working with one mother church (Olanchito). We met and divided our area of responsibility (the Aguan Valley) into nine regional areas. Our first objective was to start a daughter church in each of the nine areas, with a view toward each church reaching all the villages in its area through extension classes. The workers signed their names to the areas of a large map, where each would work. The second objective was to mobilize each daughter church to do the very same thing for her own, smaller area of responsibility. This has resulted, in 11 years, in 80 congregations, over half of which are now self-supporting, self-governing, and self-reproducing *churches*.

Be sure to plan for specific results. How many daughter churches this year? How many new converts and pastors-in-training?

The students of Honduras Extension Bible Institute plant an average of seven new churches a year, which have an average of 15 baptized adult believers after a year's time. Each congregation has from one to three pastors-in-training. We anticipate the same progress in the future in our original area of responsibility; also we are opening up entirely new areas where we will repeat the whole program. We set yearly goals in keeping with Christ's evangelistic orders, our field objectives, and our *faith*.

Note Impediments to a Church's Normal Growth and Development

Christ's "church growth" parables (Matt. 13; Mark 4:26-29; John 15:1-6) show us that churches, obediently shepherded, will grow normally quite like plants. Like all other living things which God has created, they will reproduce after their own kind, bear good fruit, yield an abundant harvest, and grow on their own (one worker plants, another waters, but God gives the growth). It is the inherent nature of the church to grow. If it doesn't, it is like corn which stops growing when only a few inches high; something has to be wrong. An obedient church in normal conditions *has* to grow: it's her very nature. If not, it was planted in the wrong field, or it needs water, weeding, pest control, or more light. When a church doesn't grow among a fairly responsive people, something is quenching the power of the Holy Spirit in the body.

There are several pitfalls to avoid:

1. Avoid Decision Rites

Do not try to confirm men's salvation with American decision-making rites (hand raising, card signing, going forward, etc.). None of them sufficiently emphasizes the need of repentance. Such decision rites are a novelty in church history. They replace baptism as God's ordained rite for confirming a new convert's faith and repentance. Baptism is changed into a graduation ceremony following a discipling course and time of probation.

Do not expect men from non-democratic societies to "decide" for Christ as individuals. Normally, a sincere decision requires much discussion (often arguing) with his closest friends and relatives. The Bible does not speak of "decisions" for Christ nor "accepting" Him; it requires life-transforming faith and repentance from sins.

2. Avoid Delaying Baptism

We dare not disobey Christ's command by refusing baptism to a sincerely repentant sinner for any reason (Acts 10:47-48). Serve him the Lord's Supper as soon as he is baptized. Teach him to do everything Christ commanded, especially to love, as our Lord and His apostles taught as most important (Acts 2:41-42; John 13:34-35).

The first few weeks of a convert's new life in Christ are most important for molding his future Christian character. An older believer can hardly be mobilized to work for Christ once he has passed his spiritual adolescence simply listening passively to sermons.

Some evangelicals require the new believer to sanctify himself outside the church before he can be baptized and become a member. The apostles baptized new repentant believers immediately, with no exceptions. Their indoctrination and perfection continued within the church under pastoral care. Do not delay obedience to Christ's commands once a man confesses his repentance and faith.

3. Avoid Missionary Subsidies

Many missionaries hesitate to teach stewardship. They corrupt their churches by giving them "easy money," discouraging the believers from giving. Supporting God's work is a privilege; a believer, rightly taught, enjoys it. Don't rob poor believers of this blessing. God multiplies their bit by His own celestial mathematics, and their church will prosper spiritually (Luke 21:1-4).

Few missions normally pay national pastors. It tends to corrupt both pastor and church, especially in poor communities. If a congregation is too poor to pay its ministers, let them serve voluntarily. Train several men to work together. Never create a church dependent on foreign aid. It creates resentment, weak churches, and missionary control.

4. Avoid Delays

Do not accept the argument, "We can't start a daughter church yet; our church is too weak; we must wait until we have a strong home base first."

No church is too young to obey Christ. As soon as a worker is available, send him. New churches raise up daughter churches more readily than old ones. If you wait for your church to get strong, it will also get hard; it is often impossible to mobilize an old church to start daughter churches.

5. Avoid Communication Breakdown

One church often starts another, which starts another, and another, to several generations. The flow of extension studies may follow the same chain. One teaches another who teaches another. The best church growth seems to occur one or two links removed from the foreign missionary; there is less dependence on his help and more reliance on the Holy Spirit. But beyond three or four links of teacher-student relationships, communication may break down and reorganization of the chain is necessary.

The teacher must have continuous, accurate reports from each church down the line. If he is not getting this feedback, he cannot teach well; the chain will break. He must detect and strengthen weak links.

6. Avoid Pressuring for Growth

We cannot *make* the church grow; we only *let* it grow. Do not push your student to convert men by human devices. Let his church grow spontaneously. A normal, obedient church simply grows as we obey our Lord. Jesus' church growth parables show this growth to be similar to that of plants and animals. All created living beings (the church included) grow and reproduce. The church is alive. She is Christ's body. We must *expect* her to grow. If we try to control this growth, we kill it. It is spiritual. All we do is obey God's commands. We plant, water, weed, shoo birds, and God gives the harvest.

8. How do "extension chains" work?

_____

_____

9. What procedure does Patterson suggest for planning field objectives?

_____

_____

_____

Planning a strategy leading to the spontaneous multiplication of churches requires much more than simply hoping the Holy Spirit will do His work. Our plans must count on the Spirit's work and then allow it to happen. Using obedience to the commands of Christ and His apostles as a yardstick for measuring progress, we can combine evangelism and training to initiate and maintain church planting momentum. Under this strategy new leadership is mobilized early. Training focuses on the developing church, not on the student. Paul/Timothy relationships are fostered between individuals and mother/daughter/granddaughter relationships between churches. Recognizing the principles of spontaneous growth, the wise missionary helps orchestrate the effort through encouragement, planning, and allowing the Holy Spirit to move as He will to guide and control the work.

SUMMARY

It is not enough simply to identify an unreached people and send someone to preach the gospel to them. The initial process of evangelization requires great sensitivity to the culture of the target group. The way the gospel message is received by a people depends on the way the messenger is perceived. In planning a comprehensive strategy, then, we should consider who can best reach an unreached group and then do what we can to mobilize that person or group for the task before undertaking E-3 evangelism ourselves. We must also be sensitive to the leading of the Spirit in an individual's life towards the evangelization of a people and should be ready to encourage his efforts from the outset.

Little is gained by maintaining a dichotomy between evangelism and the meeting of basic social needs. A balanced approach recognizes the importance of both aspects in evangelization. Strategies which incorporate meeting basic human needs through Christian community development not only create channels for expressing Christian love and concern, but may also open doors to areas of the world that are closed to conventional missions. Any pioneer mission strategy should consider a team approach which addresses physical needs as well as spiritual need among the targeted people.

Once the gospel penetrates a culture and the initial group of believers is gathered into a church, the missionaries should plan for ongoing spontaneous reproduction of churches among that people. By stressing obedience as the principle channel of discipleship, they can combine evangelism and training in raising up new congregations. Through the fostering of relationships between individuals and between churches, extension chains are developed which can sustain an ongoing church planting movement. In this way, the new church within the people group can carry on and complete the task of evangelization.

INTEGRATIVE ASSIGNMENT

In this assignment you will continue the report you started in the last chapter. You will be answering the following questions: Who should reach the targeted people group? How shall they be reached? What will be the result? The worksheets that follow are designed to help you complete the assignment.

WORKSHEET #3: THE FORCE FOR EVANGELIZATION

Who should reach them? In this section, you will try to determine who is in the best position to reach the targeted people group. Since you may have no accurate way of evaluating this question, it may be necessary to assume that an E-3 effort is required. You could also assume that your church or mission agency is called to reach this group. If you think that another group, such as a church at E-2 distance, is best suited to reach this people, incorporate into your strategy how you might go about persuading and supporting this group in their effort to evangelize the targeted people. Use the following outline as the basis for your analysis:

A. Three Forces for Evangelization

1. What is the present involvement of the national church in evangelizing this people?

2. Are there individuals within the group that have become Christians? If so, what is their potential for evangelizing their people?

3. Is there a mission agency that has targeted this group or one that, because of their emphasis and background, is uniquely suited to reach these people?

B. Difficulties in Mobilizing the Force for Evangelization

1. What hindrances may be keeping the national church from evangelizing these people? Are there walls of prejudice, lack of vision, or lack of personnel or resources?

2. If there are reached individuals within this group, what is hindering them from becoming an effective force for the evangelization of their group?

3. What are the main obstacles that a mission group attempting to target this group would need to overcome?

C. Mobilizing the Force for Evangelization

1. In your estimation, who is in the best position to reach these people? Why?

2. *Accountability*--Who will authorize the mission and bear the responsibility for it? What relationship will exist between the authorizing body, those who are sent, and any others who are involved in sending?

3. *Personnel*--Who will be sent? What qualifications or skills will they need to have or develop?

4. *Training*--What kind of preparation will the missionary personnel receive? How and where will they receive it?

5. *Leadership*--What supervisory structure will exist on the field?

6. *Support*--How will the missionaries be supported or support themselves?

WORKSHEET #4: APPROACH AND METHODS

How shall they be reached? Tactics and methods must be based on a sound knowledge of the people, so you will want to plan for adequate time to learn the language and culture. Since at this point you may have only a general knowledge of this people, your outline for approach and methods may be largely conjecture.

A. Establishing a Presence

1. How will you establish a presence among your target group? In what capacity will you go? How will you be perceived?

2. How will you go about learning the language and culture?

3. How will you identify with the people?

4. How will you demonstrate the love of Christ and the power of the gospel to them?

B. Proclaiming the Good News

1. What will precede your sharing of the gospel?

2. How and with whom will you first share the gospel?

3. To what social structures will you be paying close attention in your evangelization?

4. What role will translated Scripture play? Will you need to plan for translation?

C. Planting Churches

1. What will the church look like?

2. What elements of the culture will be expressed in worship and fellowship?

3. How will the leadership be selected and trained?

4. How will a spontaneous movement of church planting be initiated and maintained?

5. How will this church reach beyond its own cultural frontiers to other peoples?

D. Anticipated Problems

1. What will be the biggest barriers to overcome in each of the following areas?

   a. Mobilizing the force for evangelization

b. Establishing a presence among the people

c. Identifying with the people

d. Transmitting the gospel

e. Initiating and maintaining a spontaneous church planting movement

2. What opposition to evangelization can be expected?

a. Physical forces (from government, religious leaders, etc.)

b. Cultural forces (illiteracy, closedness, etc.)

c. Spiritual forces

E. Expected Helps

1. What will work in favor of evangelization?

a. Physical factors (government, economy, etc.)

b. Cultural factors (social unrest, openness, etc.)

c. Spiritual factors

2. What other factors are there which leave you optimistic about the evangelization of these people?

WORKSHEET #5: TIMETABLE AND TIMELINE

What will the result be? No strategy is complete until it projects what the results will be. One of the best ways of doing this is to create a timetable describing objectives and to measure those objectives against a timeline. Such an exercise not only helps you visualize the results, but also sets up a chart by which you can measure progress towards your goals.

In creating a timetable, list all of the objectives your strategy contains in chronological order. Next to each objective set an approximate time projection in months or years for the accomplishment of that objective. Your timeline will begin at the point of identification of a people group. It will end with the establishment of a viable church, which is evangelizing its own people and ready to carry out its own cross-cultural mission.

The following three categories of objectives are suggested as a general organization for your timetable. You should also list several specific objectives under each general category.

A. Objectives in Mobilizing the Force for Evangelization--Identifying the senders and goers, training, etc.

B. Objectives in Establishing a Presence--Arriving and settling in, learning the language, establishing relationships and roles, etc.

C. Ministry Objectives--First communication of the gospel message, first individuals or families won, first church organized, Scriptures translated, leadership training program established, first missionaries sent, etc.

After you have completed your list of objectives, graphically illustrate this timetable by drawing a timeline down the left-hand side of a sheet of paper and keying in each objective as it is supposed to happen. For example:

MOBILIZATION

0	People group is identified Force for evangelization sought
4 mos.	Sending agency agrees to target group
6 mos.	Experienced team leader found and allocated
1 yr.	Team formed with two couples and two single men Team development, schooling, church internship
3 yrs.	Team completes training and preparation

etc.

QUESTIONS FOR REFLECTION

It may seem presumptuous to predict how God might work in reaching a people group with the gospel. It is true that there is much we cannot know, but we must move forward by making plans based on what we do know, in accordance with God's will as revealed in Scripture. We can trust God to straighten our plans as we go along. Consider the wisdom found in Proverbs 16:9 and 16:3. What important principles related to strategy are contained in these verses? Write your thoughts in your journal.

CHAPTER 10

WORLD CHRISTIAN TEAMWORK

INTRODUCTION

As you study these chapters on mission strategy and work on your unreached people project, we trust that you are gaining a working knowledge of the whole mission task. We also hope that through this understanding you are becoming more and more committed to world evangelization.

Not all Christians are called or gifted to become cross-cultural missionaries. However, that does not mean that they can't be involved in evangelization. For every missionary who goes out, many people must stay behind in coordinated, active, support roles. There are no "solo" performers in mission. As in any situation where war is being waged, the success of the front line combatant depends largely upon the support he receives from the rear. An individual can be gifted and well trained for cross-cultural mission and still fail as a missionary. Because of the teamwork needed, it is just as crucial for those who remain behind to understand the missionary task as it is for those who go. "Senders" must be as committed and as actively involved as "goers." Both groups are essential to the world Christian team.

World Christian teamwork is more than just the necessary interaction between goers and senders, though. If the war is to be won, it is equally important that the front line troops know their allies and coordinate the war effort with them. During World War II, for example, the Normandy invasion for the liberation of France required the allied forces to combine and coordinate their efforts. The armies of several nations were involved, but each one knew its responsibility and was committed to come to the aid of the others. So it must be in mission. If we are to win the war, world Christian teamwork is a requirement, not an option. We must recognize that we have but one commander-in-chief, and we must be willing to coordinate our efforts across national, denominational, and mission boundaries.

World Christian Teamwork

World Christian teamwork is all-encompassing. It begins when an individual teams up with God by committing himself to God's worldwide cause. The teamwork is expressed outwardly when the person teams up with God's people in fulfilling that cause. As a sender or goer, the world Christian joins ranks with all those who claim Christ as Lord and are committed to the fulfillment of His Great Commission.

I. TEAMING UP WITH GOD

Most people who claim to be Christian recognize Christ as Savior. Relatively few recognize His authority as Lord of their lives, however, and whatever comprehension they do have of His sovereignty is usually vague and generalized. In this respect, the kingdom of God is not unlike an earthly kingdom.

In the political realm, most countries have a sovereign who is the designated head of state. Such a person is vested with power to uphold the law of the land and direct the country in the pursuit of national objectives. Citizens of that country can respond in a number of ways to the sovereign's authority, but the minimal expectation is that they will act within the boundaries of the established laws of the land. If they fulfill this minimal expectation, the governing authority is, in turn, expected to extend protection and other benefits to the society.

Many Christians have a similar view of the kingdom of God. They recognize Christ as a distant sovereign whose laws they should obey in order to receive salvation and the other benefits of being a Christian. They fulfill what they feel is a minimal commitment by going to church on a self-regimented schedule, maintaining a code of behavior, expressing loyalty to their group, etc. They are satisfied to live out their Christianity in this way and consider anything else above and beyond the call of duty.

Unfortunately, neither political nations nor the kingdom of God can function solely on the basis of a minimal commitment on the part of the citizenry. In any country the citizens must put aside self-interest in the pursuit of national objectives or in the interest of national security. Historically, the most significant national achievements have been accomplished through the voluntary, lifetime commitment of citizens to national objectives in education, health, science, industry, and other areas of national life. And in war time, the survival of a nation in many cases has depended entirely upon the willingness of great numbers of its citizens to die for the preservation of their country.

If God's worldwide purposes are to be achieved, no lesser commitment is required from the citizens of His kingdom. Thousands of Christians must be lifted from mediocrity and self-centeredness to serve in the ranks of Christ's Great Commission army. Tens of thousands are needed at the front lines and hundreds of thousands in the support lines at the rear. There is a cause much greater than ourselves which beckons with urgency. This is the hour for God's great kingdom army to assault the last strongholds of darkness.

Becoming a World Christian

"World Christians" are ordinary believers whose lives have been transformed by an extraordinary vision. As David Bryant puts it:

> World Christians are day-to-day disciples for whom Christ's global cause has become the integrating, overriding priority for all that He is for them. Like disciples should, they actively investigate all that their Master's Great Commission means. Then they act on what they learn.[1]

World Christians have captured a vision. They have seen the world as God sees it. They have thrilled at what God has done and is doing to establish His kingdom, and they fervently desire to be a small part of that kingdom program.

In the following excerpt[2] David Bryant outlines three steps to becoming a world Christian.

> By taking three steps we become World Christians. First, World Christians *catch* a world vision. They see the cause the way God sees it. They see the full scope of the Gap. Next, World Christians *keep* that world vision. They put the cause at the heart of their life in Christ. They put their life at the heart of the Gap. Then World Christians *obey* their world vision. Together they develop a strategy that makes a lasting impact on the cause, particularly at the widest end of the Gap.

> Many years ago a World Christian named John R. Mott, leader of the Student Volunteer Movement that sent out 20,000 new missionaries, outlined similar steps:

> > An enterprise which aims at the evangelization of the whole world in a generation, and contemplates the ultimate establishment of the Kingdom of Christ, requires that its leaders be Christian statesmen--men with far-seeing views, with comprehensive plans, with power of initiative, and with victorious faith.[3]

> Catch! Keep! Obey!--these are the three steps to becoming a World Christian. Let's examine them a little more closely in outline form:

> **Step One:** Catch a World Vision

> > See God's worldwide *purpose* in Christ

> > See a world full of *possibilities* through Christ

> > See a world full of *people* without Christ

> > See my world-sized *part* with Christ

---

[1]David Bryant, *In the Gap* (Madison, WI: Inter-Varsity Missions, 1979), p. 73. Used by permission.
[2]Bryant, pp. 74-76.
[3]John R. Mott, *The Evangelization of the World in This Generation* (New York: Arno Press, 1972), p. 191.

Step Two: Keep a World Vision

Be a World Christian

Join with other World Christians

Plan to obey the vision

Step Three: Obey a World Vision

Obey as you regularly *build* your vision

Obey as you *reach* out directly in love

Obey as you *give* your vision to other Christians

If you had not yet caught a world vision prior to this course, we trust that your study is helping you to do so. If you already had a world vision, our hope is that this study will add "fuel to the fire" and help you keep that vision and obey it.

Christ summed up all commitment and obedience to God in two commandments:

"You shall love the Lord your God with all your heart, and with all your mind, and with all your strength." The second is this, "You shall love your neighbor as yourself" (Mark 12:30-31).

1. What parallels can you draw between becoming a world Christian and fulfilling these commandments?

   _____

   _____

Obeying the Vision

How does one obey the vision? There are many ways, but the most powerful and direct avenue is through prayer. Through prayer, the most ordinary of Christians has the opportunity to affect the destiny of the world. Harold Lindsell describes prayer this way:

> Distance is no bar, space no barrier, to reaching the remotest place on earth. Nor is the power of prayer diminished by the distance between the person who prays and the person prayed for. Men and nations can and do have their destinies decided by God's praying people who, through intercessory prayer, wield power greater than the armed might of the nations of earth.[4]

---

[4]Harold Lindsell, *When You Pray* (Wheaton, IL: Tyndale House Publishers, 1969), pp. 52-53.

Few can go, but all can pray. Let us not be deceived into thinking that prayer is the lesser of the two roles. Strategy is certainly important, but prayer is still the most effective weapon there is for penetrating the last barriers to the gospel, for with it we pierce the darkened hearts of men and shackle the powers of Satan.

Pioneer missionary Hudson Taylor's motto for influencing men was, "Move men through prayer and prayer alone." He learned this principle as a young medical student working his way through school. Even when his absent-minded employer forgot on occasion to give him his wages, Taylor would simply commit the situation to prayer, trusting God to jolt his employer's memory. God never failed to "move" his employer through his prayers, even though at times the circumstances tested Taylor's faith to the utmost. Years later, after Hudson Taylor had founded the China Inland Mission and was concerned to see numbers of new missionaries go to China, he applied the same principle to a recruitment planning session with the mission board. One day was spent in fasting and prayer, followed by a day of discussion and planning, followed by another of fasting and prayer, and so forth. The recruitment goal of 100 that was set for that year was met exactly!

How does prayer work? In the following article[5] David Wells[6] offers an explanation of the nature of prayer which should help put a new dynamic in our prayers.

Prayer: Rebelling Against the Status Quo

David F. Wells

You will be appalled by the story I am about to relate to you. Appalled, that is, if you have any kind of social conscience.

A poor black, living on Chicago's South Side, sought to have her apartment properly heated during the frigid winter months. Despite city law on the matter, her unscrupulous landlord refused. The woman was a widow, desperately poor, and ignorant of the legal system, but she took the case to court on her own behalf.

---

[5]David F. Wells, "Prayer: Rebelling Against the Status Quo,"*Christianity Today* 23 (November 2, 1979), pp. 32-34. Used by permission.

[6]David Wells is presently Professor of Historical and Systematic Theology at Gordon-Conwell Theological Seminary in South Hamilton, Massachusetts. He has also been a professor at Trinity Evangelical Divinity School, Deerfield, Illinois. Wells is the author of numerous articles and two books.

Justice, she declared, ought to be done. It was her ill fortune, however, to appear repeatedly before the same judge who, as it turned out, was an atheist and a bigot. The only principle by which he abode was, as he put it, that "blacks should be kept in their place." The possibilities of a ruling favorable to the widow were, therefore, bleak. They became even bleaker as she realized she lacked the indispensable ingredient necessary for favorable rulings in cases like these--namely, a satisfactory bribe. Nevertheless, she persisted.

At first, the judge did not so much as even look up from reading the novel on his lap before dismissing her. But then he began to notice her. Just another black, he thought, stupid enough to think she could get justice. Then her persistence made him self-conscious. This turned to guilt and anger. Finally, raging and embarrassed, he granted her petition and enforced the law. Here was a massive victory over "the system"--at least as it functioned in his corrupted courtroom.

In putting the matter like this I have not, of course, been quite honest. For this never really happened in Chicago (as far as I know), nor is it even my "story." It is a parable told by Jesus (Luke 18:1-8) to illustrate the nature of petitionary prayer.

The parallel Jesus drew was obviously not between God and the corrupt judge, but between the widow and the petitioner. This parallel has two aspects. First , the widow refused to accept the injustice of her situation, in the same way that a Christian should refuse to resign himself or herself to the world in its fallenness. Second, despite discouragements, the widow persisted with her case as should the Christian with his or hers. The first aspect has to do with prayer's *nature* and the second with its *practice.*

I want to argue that our feeble and irregular prayer, especially in its petitionary aspect, is too frequently addressed in the wrong way. When confronting this failing, we are inclined to flagellate ourselves for our weak wills, our insipid desires, our ineffective technique, and our wandering minds. We keep thinking that somehow our *practice* is awry, and we rack our brains to see if we can discover where. I suggest that the problem lies in a misunderstanding of prayer's *nature*, and our practice will never have that widow's persistence until our outlook has her clarity.

What, then, is the nature of petitionary prayer? It is, in essence, rebellion--rebellion against the world in its fallenness, the absolute and undying refusal to accept as normal what is pervasively abnormal. It is, in this its negative aspect, the refusal of every agenda, every scheme, every interpretation that is at odds with the norm as originally established by God. As such, it is itself an expression of the unbridgeable chasm that separates good from evil, the declaration that evil is not a variation on good but its antithesis.

Or, to put it the other way around, to come to an acceptance of life "as it is," to accept it on its own terms--which means acknowledging the *inevitability* of the way it works--is to surrender a Christian view of God. This resignation to what is abnormal has within it the hidden and unrecognized assumption that the power of God to change the world, to overcome evil by good, will not be actualized.

Nothing destroys petitionary prayer (and with it, a Christian view of God) as quickly as resignation. "At all times," Jesus declared, "we should pray" and not "lose heart," thereby acquiescing to what is (Luke 18:1).

The dissipation of petitionary prayer in the presence of resignation has an interesting historical pedigree. Those religions that stress quietistic acquiescence always disparage petitionary prayer. This was true of the Stoics who claimed that such prayer showed that one was unwilling to accept the existent world as an expression of God's will. One was trying to escape from it by having it modified.

That, they said, was bad. A similar argument is found in Buddhism. And the same result, although arrived at by a different process of reasoning, is commonly encountered in our secular culture.

Secularism is that attitude that sees life as an end in itself. Life, it is thought, is severed from any relationship to God. Consequently the only norm or "given" in life, whether for meaning or for morals, is the world as it is. With this, it is argued, we must come to terms; to seek some other referent around which to structure our lives is futile and "escapist." It is not only that God, the object of petitionary prayer, has often become indistinct, but that His relationship to the world is seen in a new way. And it is a way that does not violate secular assumption. God may be "present" and "active" in the world, but it is not a presence and an activity that changes anything.

Against all of this, it must be asserted that petitionary prayer only flourishes where there is a twofold belief: first, that God's name is hallowed too irregularly, His kingdom has come too little, and His will is done too infrequently; second, that God Himself can change this situation. Petitionary prayer, therefore, is the expression of the hope that life as we meet it, on the one hand, *can* be otherwise and, on the other hand, that it *ought* to be otherwise. It is therefore impossible to seek to live in God's world on His terms, doing His work in a way that is consistent with who He is, without engaging in regular prayer.

That, I believe, is the real significance of petitionary prayer in our Lord's life. Much of His prayer life is left unexplained by the Gospel writers (e.g., Mark 1:35; Luke 5:16; 9:18; 11:1), but a pattern in the circumstances that elicited prayer is discernible.

First, petitionary prayer preceded great decisions in Jesus' life, such as the choosing of the disciples (Luke 6:12); indeed, the only possible explanation of His choice of that ragtag bunch of nonentities, boastful, ignorant, and uncomprehending as they were, was that He had prayed before choosing them. Second, He prayed when pressed beyond measure, when His day was unusually busy with many competing claims upon His energies and attention (e.g., Matt. 14:23). Third, He prayed in the great crises and turning points of His life, such as His baptism, the transfiguration, and the cross (Luke 3:21; 9:28-29). Finally, He prayed before and during unusual temptation, the most vivid occasion being Gethsemane (Matt. 26:36-45). As the "hour" of evil descended, the contrast between the way Jesus met it and the way His disciples met it is explained only by the fact that He persevered in prayer, and they slept in faintness of heart. Each of these events presented our Lord with the possibility of adopting an agenda, accepting a perspective, or pursuing a course that was other than God's. His rejection of the alternative was each time signaled by His petitionary prayer. It was His means of refusing to live in this world or to do His Father's business on any other terms than His Father's. As such, it was rebellion against the world in its perverse and fallen abnormality.

To pray declares that God and His world are at cross-purposes; to "sleep" or "faint" or "lose heart" is to act as if they are not. Why, then, do we pray so little for our local church? Is it really that our technique is bad, our wills weak, or our imaginations listless? I don't believe so. There is plenty of strong-willed and lively discussion-- which in part or in whole may be justified--about the mediocrity of the preaching, the emptiness of the worship, the superficiality of the fellowship, and the ineffectiveness of the evangelism. So, why, then, don't we pray as persistently as we talk? The answer, quite simply, is that we don't believe it will make any difference. We accept, however despairingly, that the situation is unchangeable, that what is will always be. This is not a problem about the *practice* of prayer, but rather about its *nature*. Or, more precisely, it is about the nature of God and His relationship to this world.

Unlike the widow in the parable, we find it is easy to come to terms with the unjust and fallen world around us--even when it intrudes into Christian institutions. It is not always that we are unaware of what is happening, but simply that we feel completely impotent to change anything. That impotence leads us, however unwillingly, to strike a truce with what is wrong.

In other words, we have lost our anger, both at the level of social witness and before God in prayer. Fortunately, He has not lost His; for the wrath of God is His opposition to what is wrong, the means by which truth is put forever on the throne and error forever on the scaffold. Without God's wrath, there would be no reason to live morally in the world and every reason not to. So the wrath of God, in this sense, is intimately connected with petitionary prayer that also seeks the ascendancy of truth in all instances and the corresponding banishment of evil.

The framework Jesus gave us for thinking about this was the kingdom of God. The kingdom is that sphere where the king's sovereignty is recognized. And, because of the nature of our king, that sovereignty is exercised supernaturally. In Jesus, the long-awaited "age to come" arrived; in Him and through Him, the messianic incursion into the world has happened. Being a Christian, then, is not a matter of simply having had the right religious experience but rather of starting to live in that sphere which is authentically divine. Evangelism is not successful because our technique is "right," but because this "age" breaks into the lives of sinful people. And this "age to come," which is already dawning, is not the possession of any one people or culture. God's "age," the "age" of His crucified Son, is dawning in the whole world. Our praying, therefore, should look beyond the concerns of our private lives to include the wide horizon of all human life in which God is concerned. If the gospel is universal, prayer cannot restrict itself to being local.

It is not beside the point, therefore, to see the world as a courtroom in which a "case" can still be made against what is wrong and for what is right. Our feebleness in prayer happens because we have lost sight of this, and until we regain it we will not persist in our role as litigants. But there is every reason why we should regain our vision and utilize our opportunity, for the Judge before whom we appear is neither an atheist nor corrupt, but the glorious God and Father of our Lord Jesus Christ. Do you really think, then, that He will fail to "bring about justice for His chosen ones who cry to Him night and day? Will He keep putting them off?" "I tell you," our Lord declares, "He will see that they get justice, and quickly" (Luke 18:7-8).

2. What two aspects of prayer does the author describe, and how do they relate to the mission task?

_____

_____

_____

Prayer and the Word of God are the greatest weapons the Christian has to combat the spiritual forces of darkness. The Word is a sword, and our prayers are arrows which can be launched at the enemy near and far. It has been truly said that, "God's army advances on its knees."

World Christian Lifestyle

An understanding of God's purpose and plan can bring about commitment to His cause. As that commitment grows, it is bound to have a profound effect on our lifestyle. No longer will we be satisfied with the petty self-seeking which characterizes the world and which often contaminates the church. The realization that the church is involved in a worldwide war for the souls of men will begin to make us conscious of how we are spending our time. We will want to identify with those who are on the front lines of the battles. We will want our lives and our resources to count towards victory.

No matter what our role is in the fulfillment of God's global cause, who we are and what we do will have as great an impact as what we say. In fact, what we say will be validated or invalidated by our lifestyle. In the following article[7] veteran missionary David Adeney describes an appropriate lifestyle for missionaries and others who are interested in promoting the gospel.

Lifestyle for Missionaries (and Other People)

David H. Adeney[8]
Before leaving England 45 years ago for my first seven-year term of service in China, I was greatly influenced by a man of God who had served as a missionary bishop in Africa. Before going overseas, Bishop Taylor Smith had kept a four-word motto on his desk: "As now, so then." He often reminded us that going overseas will not suddenly turn you into a saint.

What you are now will determine what kind of missionary you will be in the future. There are not two kinds of lifestyles: one for home and the other for overseas. If you are considering missionary service, adopt *now* the lifestyle you expect to follow in the coming years.

This does not mean that there will not be changes in our lifestyle throughout our lives. We should be learning more and more of what is involved in living as a true disciple of the Lord Jesus and be able to adapt to different situations.

---

[7]David H. Adeney, "Lifestyle for Missionaries (and Other People)," *His 40* (April 1980), pp. 21-24. Used by permission.

[8]After years of service in China with the China Inland Mission (now the Overseas Missionary Fellowship) working with both rural people and urban university students, David Adeney became Representative-at-Large for OMF, currently coordinating the Pray for China Fellowship. He has also worked with Inter-Varsity USA and is Vice-President of the International Fellowship of Evangelical Students.

PAUL'S LIFESTYLE

The clearest description of a missionary's lifestyle is found in Paul's message to the Ephesian elders in Acts 20.

Paul's lifestyle was a direct result of the vision he received at the beginning of his Christian life. Years later he could say, "I was not disobedient to the heavenly vision." His compelling desire was to see the Gentiles presented as an offering to God. His lifelong purpose, to preach where Christ had not been named, determined the kind of life he lived.

If I am convinced that God has a certain task for me to fulfill, my whole manner of life must contribute to that overall objective. Some of you who are at medical school know that you have had to make real changes in your lifestyle in order to qualify as a doctor. How much more willing we should be to accept changes that will fit us for service as true ambassadors for Jesus Christ.

A self-centered vision wrapped up in material things will result in a lifestyle characterized by the love of the world. But a vision of the kingdom of God--and a deep desire to serve our generation according to the purpose of God--will produce a lifestyle worthy of God's calling. You may already have begun to see some great area of need, and a conviction is growing in your mind that this is the task to which God is calling you. Your whole way of life in the coming days may be changed by this vision.

OVERCONFIDENT?

Now let us look in detail at the things which were basic in Paul's lifestyle. In Acts 20:19 he speaks of serving the Lord with all humility. In his letter to the Corinthian Christians he writes about the "meekness and gentleness of Christ."

The greatest barrier to effective missionary service is pride, which often takes very subtle and unrecognized forms.

When I arrived in China, the general director of the China Inland Mission was D. E. Hoste, an old man, a member of the Cambridge Seven. Enthusiastically I talked to him about the student work at Cambridge and our plans for an evangelistic mission.

He was interested, but I remember only one sentence of his response. "Beware," he said, "of national pride which shows itself just like a man who has been eating garlic."

I was to experience this danger. During my first term in China, much of my self-confidence had to be stripped away.

I had been active in student and young people's work and had served as missionary of the British Inter-Varsity. But now I found myself handicapped by my lack of language, working among country people, many of whom were illiterate. I would have liked to go into a university center to work with students, but God saw that I needed to go to the "university of the countryside" and learn from these simple village Christians, living in their homes and sharing in their way of life. Years later, the desire to do student work would be fulfilled, but only after the humbling experience of those early years.

I shall never forget the way in which a Chinese pastor ministered to me during a time of spiritual depression. I went to live with him in what was known as "The Spiritual Work Team." I was refreshed as he opened up the Scriptures. And I was amazed when, responding to an invitation to go and pray with him, I found him flat on his face, pouring out his soul in confession to God.

It is easy for a young worker to be judgmental and fail to appreciate the strengths of those with whom we are sent to work. I had to learn through mistakes.

I remember once telling a Chinese fellow worker that I felt there was something lacking in his message. He was deeply offended. I had failed to speak in a spirit of love and humility.

Years later, the leader of one of the IFES national movements emphasized this need for humility. "There are two kinds of missionaries who come to our country," he said. "The first comes full of ideas and plans. He asks us to help him with some new evangelistic project. In contrast, there is the missionary who comes with a much more sensitive approach to the new culture into which he is entering. He asks how he can be of help to *us*. He has something to contribute, but he does not push himself. He is ready to listen and learn."

This kind of missionary has no wish to see national Christians follow a Western pattern. He wants them to be completely identified with their own cultural and political background, as long as it does not prevent them from manifesting the life of the kingdom of God in "righteousness, peace, and joy in the Holy Spirit."

We may so easily in our methods and approach appear to be Americans or British first and Christians second. Without true humility, it is all too easy to set up Western organizations which depend upon Western leadership, even though national leaders may nominally be in control. Only Westerners with a truly humble spirit will be able to enter into the kind of partnership which is so desperately needed in the church today. There must be true equality, with each one contributing the varied gifts received from the Lord.

3. Why is pride a subtle danger which can ensnare a missionary? How can it be overcome?

   _____

   _____

   _____

SHARED SORROWS

In the same verse Paul also speaks of great conflicts and sufferings. Nothing binds people together so much as sharing in trials.

In the early days of World War II, we shared in the sorrows and dangers of our fellow believers in China. And they shared in ours. I shall always remember our Chinese fellow workers standing with us by the side of the little grave where our second child was buried, praying that as God had taken our treasure to be with Him, our hearts might be drawn closer to heaven.

When we went out with the evangelistic bands to country villages, sometimes in brigand-infested areas, we lived together in often very primitive conditions. We shared simple air-raid shelters in our garden when the Japanese bombers rained their bombs on our town.

Later, we shared the heartache of seeing some students give up their faith during the Communist revolution. Since then, our brothers and sisters in China have entered far more deeply into the fellowship of Christ's suffering.

One of the most moving experiences of my recent visit to China took place when a door opened and a white-haired man greeted me with the words, "I am Stephen." Actually he spoke in Chinese and used his Chinese name. I had not recognized him. In the 30 years since we last met, he had greatly changed. Twenty years of hard labor in prison and labor camp had left their marks on him.

I had known him as a keen young graduate dedicated to serving the Lord, especially in the field of literature. In the early years, before his books were taken away, he would translate helpful passages and send them to his friends. Later, pulling a cart and doing other rough forms of manual labor, he felt that his experience was that of Job.

As I talked and prayed with Stephen and saw the reality of his faith, I was reminded of James' words, "Behold, we call those happy who were steadfast. You have heard of the steadfastness of Job, and you have seen the purpose of the Lord, how the Lord is compassionate and merciful" (Jas. 5:11). I realized afresh that the Christian lifestyle is one which is not offended by trials and temptations. No effective work can be done without a willingness to endure hardship as a good soldier of Jesus Christ.

Hudson Taylor, speaking to his fellow workers after a year full of difficulties and dangers said, "We have put to the proof His faithfulness, His power to support in trouble and to give patience under afflictions as well as to deliver from danger. I trust we are all fully satisfied that we are God's servants sent by Him to the various places we occupy. We did not come to China because missionary work here was either safe or easy but because He had called us."

SPREADING THE WORD

In Acts 20:20-21 we see that Paul's lifestyle was characterized by untiring zeal in proclaiming the Word of God. "I did not shrink from declaring to you anything that was profitable, and teaching you in public and from house to house, testifying both to Jews and to Greeks of repentance to God and of faith in our Lord Jesus Christ." Like Christ (John 17:8), Paul could say, "I have given them the words which thou gavest me." He told the Thessalonian Christians that he had boldness to speak to them the gospel of God under much opposition.

God is still looking for men and women with this kind of boldness and zeal to proclaim His Word. But the Word of God must come to me personally with deep conviction if I am to communicate it with power and authority to others.

I discovered the power of the Word of God in my own life during a time of depression when I was strongly tempted to give up. Almost in desperation, I turned to John's Gospel and read it all through at one sitting. God spoke to me through it, and I realized again that faith comes through the hearing of the Word of Christ.

To be really effective, the messenger must be disciplined, carefully guarding his times of fellowship with God. If I am to plant churches or strengthen student groups, I must be prepared to teach the Word of God in all kinds of situations. Whether it be in leading a small Bible study group, instructing others in the ministry of teaching, or opening up the Scriptures from the pulpit, I must be known for my love of the Word of God.

MATERIAL GOODS

Another characteristic of Paul's lifestyle is found in Acts 20:33 where we read, "I coveted no one's silver or gold or apparel." He is an example in his attitude toward material things. He knew times of hardship and financial strain when he worked with his own hands to support himself and his fellow workers. At other times he was well provided for with gifts from the churches. A missionary's lifestyle may well vary according to his area of work. We must always aim to avoid a disparity between our own lifestyle and that of the people around us.

During our first term in China we lived in a simple, two-room Chinese house, at the end of the church building, with an outhouse. To us it seemed a very simple home, but to those from the countryside who lived in very primitive dwellings, it must have seemed luxurious. Later, when working with students in a large city, we shared a house with our Chinese Inter-Varsity staff coworkers. In Hong Kong our apartment was comparable to one in this country. Many of the students with whom we worked came from more luxurious homes, while others lived in tiny flats and crowded government high-rise housing estates.

The important thing was not the size of the house. What really mattered was to have a house in which our Chinese friends would always feel at home. We wanted to be an example of not coveting silver or gold, for in an economy in which inflation is rampant, it is terribly easy to become preoccupied with prices and opportunities for bargains.

Far more important than the type of home in which we live is our attitude toward the people. They want to know if we really belong to them.

YOU ARE THE MESSAGE

Like Ezekiel, the missionary's whole life is the message. The life of Christ has to shine forth from his or her life. True identification with the people will entail deep concern for every area of society and a sympathetic entering into the social, political, and economic problems together with a sharing of whatever trials and tests may come.

If the way should ever open again for me to live in China, I would want to share with the people in the house churches. I would not want to go back to the Western church buildings or to the ecclesiastical organizations of the past. I would have to learn from those who have experienced so much of what it means to suffer for the sake of Christ. I would want to contribute, under the guidance of the Holy Spirit, insights given to me from the Word of God. But I trust I would not seek to impose customs and patterns of Western Christianity which are not essential to the witness of the church which is living and serving in a communist society. I would want the believers to live as truly Chinese Christians. And I would seek to identify as closely as possible with them.

To rejoice with those who rejoice, to weep with those who weep, to learn from the experiences of God's people, and to give not only the gospel but one's own self, is surely the only way that the lifestyle of the messenger can fulfill God's purpose.

4. How does one develop humility, a willingness to endure hardship, depth in the Word, and a simple lifestyle? Is there some way that our Christian educational programs could be structured to promote the development of these qualities?

_____

_____

_____

"YOU ARE THE MESSAGE."

World Christian teamwork must begin at the individual level. It must start with individual men and women who have caught a vision for what God is doing in the world and who are willing to commit themselves wholly to be a part of His program. As such individuals grow in their commitment, they will become participants in Christ's global cause as senders and goers. They will commit themselves to join in the battle through the mighty weapon of prayer and through a consecration to a "missionary" lifestyle. They will become the message as God works through them for the accomplishment of His redemptive purpose.

II. TEAMING UP WITH GOD'S PEOPLE

Fellowship for Christians is not optional. Just as we need each other to grow in our Christian faith, so also world Christians need one another to nurture their vision and develop their commitment. Unless a church has a clear grasp of God's worldwide task, it is unlikely that a world vision will be fed through the pulpit ministry. Instead, those who have the vision must band together, build their commitment, and give expression to their vision. The vision must also be communicated to others, a challenge which is difficult and often met with subtle rejection.

Teaming Up as Senders

Finding world Christians in your congregation may be easy or difficult, depending on your circumstances. If you are taking this course with others from your own church, it may be simply a matter of arranging to meet together periodically for discussion, prayer, and encouragement. Your church may already have a missions group or committee with whom you could meet. But if you feel you are the only one in your fellowship that has caught the vision, your personal mission challenge may be to communicate that vision to others. Begin to pray that God would give you an opportunity to share with others in the church. Such an opening might come through teaching a Sunday school class or leading a weekly study group. You could use the materials in this course as your basis for teaching. Key in on individuals who show an interest and develop your relationship with them.

No matter how you go about it, once you begin getting together with other world Christians in your church or fellowship, you need to keep in mind the initial goal of your group:

To nurture a *World Christian Vision* and develop *Committment* to it.

To accomplish this goal, your group need not be large, but it must be distinctive. Remember, a world Christian, by his very definition, has made a second level, adult decision to center his life around God's global cause. In essence, your group will be a sodality, a band of believers who have made a commitment beyond that required as members of the modality. The group does not purpose to be exclusive. It serves as a channel whereby any believer within a given church or fellowship can nurture a greater commitment to God's worldwide redemptive purpose along with others of like mind. Ultimately, the group does not exist for its own ends. It should have a leavening effect on the whole body.

1. In your opinion, what is the biggest obstacle to the formation of groups dedicated to nurturing a world Christian vision in local churches and fellowships? How can this obstacle be overcome?

   _____

   _____

   _____

World Christian Cell Groups

For the sake of convenience, we will label these small bands of world Christians "world Christian cell groups." The concept of cell groups is not a new one. Christians have often used this approach in the propagation of the gospel. For example, the Full Gospel Central Church of Seoul, Korea, the largest church in the world with a membership of 500,000, has used the dynamic of cell groups for years to vastly multiply its membership and nurture the hundreds of thousands of believers who have come into the church.

The cell group concept incorporates two dynamics--nurture and multiplication. Through nurturing activities, it focuses first on building up the group. When a group grows too large to meet the care requirements of all its members adequately, it multiplies by dividing and forms two new cell groups which will then repeat the process.

Figure 10.1   TWO DYNAMICS OF CELL GROUPS

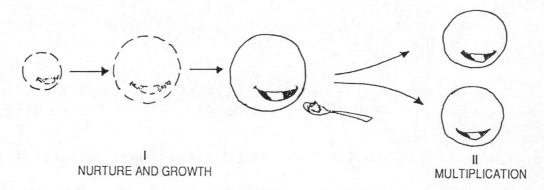

I
NURTURE AND GROWTH

II
MULTIPLICATION

World Christian cell groups can also utilize these dynamics. Through a process of nurture and growth, God will lead individuals in the group to specific roles they are to take in mission, either as those who go or those who send. As the vision for specific ministry emerges, individual senders and goers will develop partnership relationships. Commitments which may last a lifetime will be made. Sacrificial contracts will be entered into. A single cell group may eventually multiply into several groups, each committed to a specific mission.

2. What dynamic elements for multiplication do cell groups incorporate?

_____

_____

The Care and Feeding of World Christians

How does one get a world Christian cell group started? Much can be accomplished by a simple devotion to nurturing a world vision with a few other believers who may also be taking their first tentative steps towards becoming world Christians.

Support

As we have said before, world Christians are ordinary Christians. Most aren't spiritual giants, and are subject to the same temptations and weaknesses as any other Christian. There will be times they will positively glow with a world vision, particularly as they are first captured by it. At other times the vision may wane to an almost imperceptible point. Without encouragement a world Christian can be overcome by a sense of isolation, feeling that he's the only one who really cares.

World Christians often struggle with their commitment and how to actualize it. They may have told the Lord that they are willing to go, but due to lack of guidance and supportive encouragement, they make no plans to explore their commitment. Others burn with desire to go, but for one reason or another, their desire has been frustrated. Those who are meeting the challenges of preparing to go are often beset by struggles and frustration. Those who are meeting the challenges of staying and sending find themselves involved in a glamorless task, demanding great sacrifice and perseverance.

For these reasons and others, when you gather in your cell group you should gear activities toward providing encouragement and support for members' *personal* needs. Have a time of sharing and prayer. If your group is large, break up into smaller groups when you pray to encourage openness in sharing and greater participation. Make firm commitments to stand by each other. Through such sharing and prayer, a spirit of unity will be fostered which will bind the group together.

Other activities which provide encouragement are singing and sharing from God's Word. Singing can lift a troubled spirit and provide a channel for praise and adoration. Also, as one centers his life around God's global cause, a new understanding of Scripture will develop. Sharing insights with one another from God's Word will stimulate and broaden that understanding.

3. How would you schedule the first 30 minutes of a world Christian meeting to accomplish support goals?

_____

_____

_____

Inform

What is God trying to do? How is He accomplishing His purpose today? Many Christians have developed a defeatist attitude about the state of the world and God's involvement in it. The powers of darkness often seem to be overwhelming. Sometimes, indeed, there seems to be little to encourage believers. But God is at work in the world today! We need to share the evidence with each other. We are encouraged when we hear of God's working in an individual's life, within a local congregation, or among a people. Reports of a long prayed-for conversion, of the establishment or growth of a new work nearby, or of the zeal of Christians in communist lands have an uplifting and encouraging effect.

Part of each world Christian meeting should be devoted to sharing information about God's mission throughout the world. Start by sharing victories, new or old. Review what God has done in the past to open a new area to the gospel. Relate some part of a missionary biography. If a missionary is available, have him share how God is at work in the area where he is ministering. Praise God for what He's done, what He's doing, and what He's going to do.

During the meeting, also dedicate a time to sharing information which directs prayer towards current mission efforts. This can be general information about one megasphere of unreached peoples such as the Hindus, Muslims, or Chinese, or it can be narrowed to a specific unreached people. Move on to more specific prayer requests. If, as a group, you are supporting missionaries, give an update on them. If you do not know of specific pioneer mission efforts, seek written information from mission agencies. Write to missionaries and ask them to inform you for prayer. Then, on the basis of this information, spend some time in prayer for these unreached peoples and your missionaries.

4. How would you schedule the second 30 minutes of a world Christian meeting if you wanted to achieve the goal of informing the participants?

_____

_____

Plan

The last part of your meeting should be committed to planning. Do this in an attitude of open expectancy. You will need to plan for meeting times and maintenance of your group, but you will also want to incorporate into this planning much more than these routine duties. As a group, you should seek to narrow your focus to a "bite size" part of the world mission task. Begin by seeking the Holy Spirit's direction. Look at the world around you and see if there are "hidden" peoples nearby that you may be in a good position to reach. Plan to research these possibilities. If your church or group is capable of sending missionaries to a geographically distant place, research those possibilities as well. Through a process of research and prayer, narrow your focus to a specific mission task.

Once you have identified and "adopted" an unreached people group, set long-range goals for reaching them. Evaluate your resources and then begin planning how to develop those resources to the fullest. A timetable like the one you are creating for your unreached people project will help you to establish specific objectives as well as your long-range goal. Eventually you should be able to come up with a statement of purpose such as, "God willing, we will see a viable church planted among the _____ people by the year 2000."

Few cell groups will have the necessary resources to undertake a mission venture single-handedly. You will need to pool resources (personnel, training, funds, administration, etc.) with others who can share the vision and the responsibility. Such an approach takes research, planning, prayer, and persuasion. Perhaps the easiest way to team up with others is by enlisting the aid of a mission agency working in the area you have targeted. They may already have plans or resources available to help you pursue your objective, or they may welcome your initiative. You might elect to pool resources with churches in your denomination or sister groups. Another avenue is to team up with several otherwise unrelated congregations within a city or given locality.

Once your mission is launched, you will need planning times to support specific objectives. Although the tactics should be left up to the team on the field, an advocacy role must be carried out by those left behind. Efforts must be made to broaden prayer support, prepare new personnel, and send financial help. These things don't happen by themselves. They require planning.

5. How would you schedule the last part of your meeting to accomplish your planning goals?

_____

_____

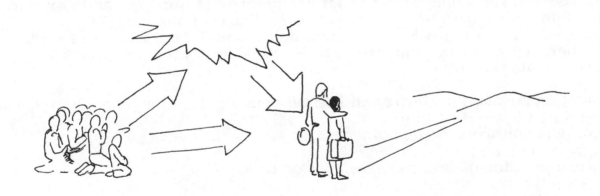

Your Mission Group and the Church

Few churches have organized groups of mission activists. In North America, it is estimated that less than 20 percent of the churches even have a missions "committee." Less than five percent have any kind of yearly organized event which emphasizes missions to the whole congregation. Among the newer churches in developing countries, a missions emphasis has been almost completely lacking.

We have suggested a way to start a group of mission activists within a congregation or fellowship. If your church already has an organized group whose focus is missions, we suggest that you *do not* establish a competing group. Work within the existing group. If their meetings are restrictive or primarily limited to business, seek permission to organize a seperate prayer and support group. With any group that you start, always inform and seek the approval of your church leadership.

This is not to say that your world Christian group could not grow into a sodality structure quite apart from the structure of one particular church. In some cases, particularly where few mission agencies are serving the churches, the formation of a new mission society may be a necessary and worthwhile goal. But whenever possible, the solid endorsement of local church leadership should be sought in the formation of the new agency.

6. Why is it important to gain the approval of church leadership in forming a group within the church?

_____

_____

Your Mission Group and Mission Societies

As we have seen, world Christian teamwork begins with individual commitment to Christ and His global cause. That commitment is nurtured and grows in fellowship with others who have made a similar commitment. We have suggested a general structure for the initiation and development of world Christian cell groups. This structure is intended to produce growth in three areas of commitment:

a. Commitment to *Christ* and His mission.

b. Commitment to *each other*.

c. Commitment to a *common mission* task.

When all three areas are well developed, in essence we will have formed a mission sodality. This sodality may be made up entirely of members from a single church congregation or may include members of various congregations. As we have already suggested, in order to carry out the mission task undertaken, it may be necessary to pool resources with others.

Earlier in our study, we noted the significant role sodality structures such as monasteries and mission societies have played in world evangelization. We trust that you've gained an appreciation for their continued use in the task of spreading the gospel. However, not every organization which claims to have mission objectives can automatically be endorsed. There are over 600 mission agencies in North America alone, each one with its own specific outlook and purpose. Before committing personnel or support to any mission agency, you should examine the organization carefully. The following questions should be considered:

a. Is the agency really accomplishing the goal of world evangelization, or is it sidetracked into "good" things which are not contributing to the stated goal?

b. Does the mission focus on the unreached and encourage churches to achieve viability, or is it perpetuating a dependency role among the churches with whom it is working?

c. Does the mission have a policy of identification and indigenization, or does it perpetuate foreign lifestyles among missionaries and alien cultural forms within the churches?

d. Does the mission use its resources efficiently, or are inordinate amounts of money expended in administration, publicity, etc.?

Don't expect to get all the answers to these and other questions simply from mission brochures. It may be necessary to do some "behind the scenes" investigation. Many missions will pass the test of a careful scrutiny on your part. Others will be stimulated by your investigation to rethink their priorities. In either case, informed senders are the key to healthy mission organizations, since nearly all missions depend on churches and individuals for their funds. Good stewards will see that their resources are well invested.

7. Why is it important that one thoroughly investigate a mission society before committing personnel or funds to them?

_____

_____

Whether or not your own strategy incorporates an existing mission, it is important to keep in mind the usefulness of mission societies and how they can serve our purposes. Briefly, good mission societies provide the following benefits:

a. They have experience and a proven record in evangelization. Historically, they have shown themselves to be a good structure for carrying out the mission of the church.

b. Missions are a specialized part of the church. They are skilled at carrying out the church's "apostolic" ministry.

c. Missions generally offer support structures which can set missionaries free for full-time ministry and long-term witness.

d. Missions usually recruit from a large pool of Christians. They are thus able to look for individuals with specific gifts and abilities and to place workers where they are most needed.

e. Missions assume responsibility for long-term goals and planning. This approach provides for continuity of the work.

f. Missions provide field supervision and home administration.

g. Missions call the church to consider her responsibility towards lost mankind and to incorporate faith and witness in a sacrificial lifestyle. This emphasis can provide an inspiring and renewing force in the church.

8. In your estimation, which of the above are the best reasons for using a mission agency? Why?

_____

_____

_____

Teaming Up as Goers

We have mentioned that world Christian cell groups intend to produce growth in three areas of commitment:

a. Commitment to *Christ* and His mission.

b. Commitment to *each other*.

c. Commitment to a *common mission* task.

In recent years, there has been a growing concern that, while mission agencies have always put a strong emphasis on the first and third areas of commitment, the second area, commitment to *each other*, has been neglected. Consequently, poor interpersonal relationships between missionaries has become a major problem in missions today. At times there is such disharmony that the cause of Christ is damaged rather than helped by the presence of the missionaries.

There is no simple explanation for this problem. Most missionaries are sent to a foreign field with a superficial knowledge of the missionaries they are to join. The expectation is that as spiritually mature people they will learn to live and work together harmoniously. This is a good theory, but in practice it often fails. Even Paul and Barnabas experienced such conflict that it split their team (Acts 15:36-40). We would do well to anticipate this kind of problem as we plan, rather than wait till it explodes on the field.

The problem is much more complex than simple "personality conflicts," although such conflicts certainly enter into the picture. Most missionaries have strong convictions and strong personalities, as well as varying levels of maturity. Unfortunately, they must often work out their differences in situations which are accompanied by a great deal of stress and which allow practically no time for developing healthy interpersonal relationships. Conflict resolution is left unattended in the pursuit of ever-demanding mission duties. To avoid possible tensions, missionaries often pursue independent ministries, thus becoming a pack of loners rather than a team which capitalizes on each member's strengths. The net effect is often a spiritually feeble group of missionaries and an ineffective mission effort.

Most missionaries are sharpened through their preparation to perform a missionary task. They are expected to be committed to Christ, to know the Bible, and to exhibit a high degree of spiritual maturity. They are prepared to preach, teach, or serve. What they are often not prepared to do, however, is deal effectively with conflict. Loving confrontation is the way to deal with conflict, and few missionary training programs include this in their curriculum.

The demonstration of love between missionaries is a far more important witness than preaching, teaching, or service. It is in this critical area of witness that Satan will most often focus his attack on the missionary task force.

9. Why is the demonstration of love more important a witness than a ministry of preaching, teaching, or service without it?

_____

_____

Creating Committed Communities

How can the problem of disharmony among missionaries be faced? Some missiologists feel that new mission structures are called for, structures which will give due emphasis to mutual commitment to one another. Charles Mellis, in his book, *Committed Communities, Fresh Streams for World Missions* (Pasadena, CA: William Carey Library, 1976), suggests that new structures are not an option. He notes that in spite of a renewed interest in missions, particularly among college students and young people, recruitment by established missions in North America is on the decline.

Mellis goes on to trace the concept of "community" throughout church history, particularly the role it has played in mission structures. He analyzes present social trends and demonstrates the effect they have had on mission recruitment. He shows that only relatively new mission sodalities which through their *structures* are emphasizing mutual commitment are enjoying surges in membership. Finally, he points to emerging models and suggests steps for the creation of "committed communities." The following is an outline of some of the principles he suggests.

Principles in Forming Committed Communities

1. "Committed people must make responsible personal *choices* in forming a true community."[9] They should know those to whom they are making a mutual commitment. We should not expect that random selection of teams will produce the kind of community hoped for.

2. "A committed community can't very well form unless committed people have some place to find each other."[10] We have already suggested that world Christian cell groups can provide such a place. Some international missions, such as Operation Mobilization and Youth With A Mission, also offer young people a "place" where they can explore their commitment with others.

3. "One crucial goal of Christian community is body-life."[11] "In the case of an intentional missionary community, the ideal situation for this kind of body-life growth is a time of learning centered on cross-cultural studies."[12] Learning to work together should ideally be part of a preparation process, not something left to be worked out on the mission field.

The implication of the committed communities approach is that mission teams should be formed largely before they are sent to the mission field. They should share a common affinity and should have spent a considerable amount of time developing relationships and mutual commitment to each other. This approach stands in stark contrast to the present practice by Western missions of sending couples or individuals into situations where neither the structure nor the emphasis encourages the development of mutually supportive relationships.

10. How might the formation of a committed community happen within a church context?

   _____

   _____

   _____

Three Models

Mellis goes on to suggest three models for the mobilization of committed communities toward mission. The first model, *community-within-mission*, is a proposal for admitting the new structures into older mission structures. The second model, *congregation/community*, suggests an initiative from a local congregation or a small group of congregations. The third or *community/*

---

[9]Charles Mellis, *Committed Communities*, Fresh Streams for World Missions (Pasadena, CA: William Carey Library, 1976), p. 106.

[10]Mellis.

[11]Mellis, p. 108.

[12]Mellis.

community model outlines an approach to sending using intentional communities as the sending base.

Community-Within-Mission Model

This first approach, while recognizing the problem of trying to pour "new wine into old wineskins" (Matt. 9:17), holds that there may be ways that new structures can be incorporated into older structures in a mutually beneficial manner. Christ's point in His illustration of the wineskins was not that the old wineskins should be discarded, but rather that both the new wine and the old wine should be preserved.

In order that the "new wine" not damage the "old wineskins," the author suggests that older missions create a new division of the mission which can accommodate the team approach with minimal threat to the existing structure. In order to minimize the threat further, he suggests that these teams be allocated to areas where the mission has not worked traditionally. This new division of the mission can be considered an "experimental" model. At worst, if the experiment does not work, it can be abandoned or jettisoned to form a new mission with its own distinctives. At best, the experimental model will pave the way for new vitality within the mission, and a gradual transition can be made to incorporate the new structural improvement throughout the mission.

11. Why do you think that a new approach might present a threat to the existing structure?

_____

_____

Congregation/Community Model

It is often easier to start something new than reform something old! Nothing is new about congregations sending missionaries to the mission field directly. But seldom have these congregations incorporated the team concept into sending. The transition from sending individuals to sending teams is much easier for congregations than it is for mission agencies. There is a vast potential inherent in local churches to send teams from their own ranks or assembled from several congregations in the same community.

Congregations which are most apt to adopt this kind of mission model are those which for any number of reasons feel uncomfortable with existing organized mission structures. Congregations who themselves are experiencing significant growth of "community consciousness" through caring/sharing groups, body-life, emphasis on spiritual gifts, or charismatic renewal are also ideal bases for the congregation/community model of mission.

This model does not necessarily circumvent mission societies. Congregation based sodalities and mission agencies can benefit from official and unofficial relationships with existing missions. The mission agencies can assist these teams through a "coaching" role and gain the benefit of helping to develop an experimental model. Eventually, older missions may come to provide an umbrella for a number of semi-autonomous congregation based mission teams. This arrangement may be particularly helpful among younger churches attempting this model in developing nations.

12. What advantages might a congregation based team gain by seeking an official or unofficial affiliation with a mission society?

_____

_____

Community/Community Model

The third model Mellis suggests is one which stems from intentional communities, that is, communities which have been formed expressly around a commitment to Christian interdependence. Many such communities have sprung up around the world in response to eroding community and family values, as a by-product of the spread of secularism. Although most of these communities are unlikely to take an active role in foreign missions, the author does suggest that the ones that do will introduce new concepts to sending.

First, they will not automatically assume that the sending community is to bear the financial responsibility for those who are sent. They are more likely to expect the team members to support themselves through employment in the country to which they go. Secondly, such communities will be helped by having already dealt with presuppositions regarding minimal lifestyle requirements. They will tend to be flexible in assuming a lower standard of living than that to which they are accustomed. Thirdly, they will be more open to changing their citizenship and taking up permanent residence in the community where they establish themselves.

13. Community based missions have played a significant role in the past. Monasteries and the Moravian mission are two examples of this kind of group. Do you think such a mission is a viable option today? Why or why not?

_____

_____

_____

_____

Figure 10.2   THREE MODELS FOR MOBILIZATION

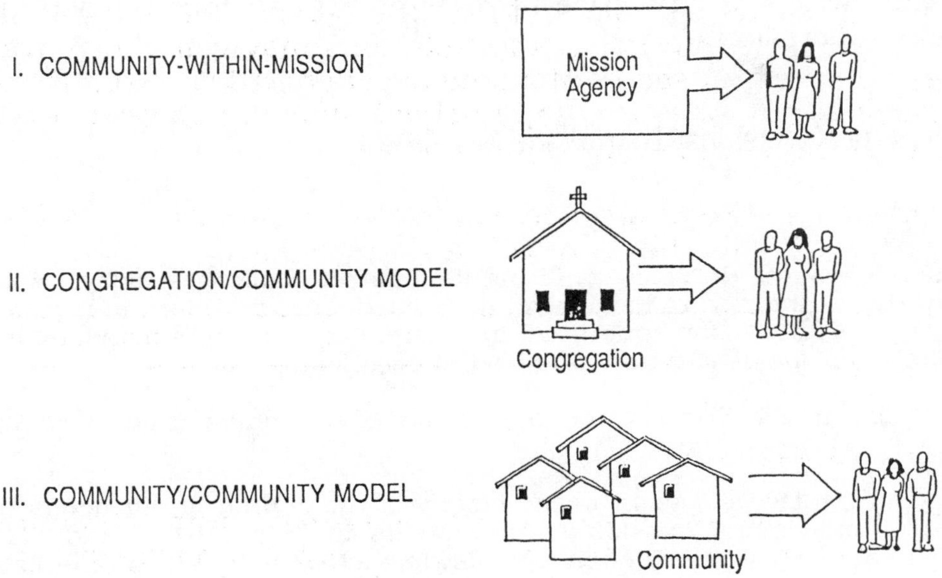

I. COMMUNITY-WITHIN-MISSION

II. CONGREGATION/COMMUNITY MODEL

Congregation

III. COMMUNITY/COMMUNITY MODEL

Community

Mellis' timely book has provided much insight into an evolving trend in mission. Mellis has not purposed to do away with old wineskins, but rather to challenge young Christians to feel free to pursue their vision in new ways. He expresses this sentiment in the closing comment of his book:

> I, like Paul, want you to be *free!* Free to commit your lives unreservedly to Jesus Christ. Free to commit yourself to one another and to create valid structures for sharing your faith with all the world's unreached peoples. And then free to *go*, risking anything and everything for our Lord.[13]

World Christian teamwork begins with an individual commitment to Christ and His global cause, but it becomes an actuality through in-depth relationships with God's people. The formation of world Christian cell groups in local congregations and fellowships becomes the means of developing those relationships at the sending base. On the front lines, a renewed commitment to Christian community and the implementation of a team approach to sending missionaries accomplish the same goal.

III.   WORLDWIDE CHRISTIAN TEAMWORK

World Christian teamwork does not stop with the formation and sending of individual ministry teams. Each group of Christians also represents a small part of the universal body of Christ, among which interdependence exists on a worldwide level. Each part of the body has its own contribution to make to world evangelization. But in order to maximize the potential of all parts, we must strive to enter much more fully into international, interdenominational, and inter-agency cooperation.

---

[13]Mellis, p. 121.

In the following article,[14] Lawrence Keyes[15] points out four needed areas of international cooperation.

The New Age of Missions: Third World Missions

Lawrence Keyes

The task of "making disciples" is facing its greatest challenges today. With over three-fourths of the world's billions yet unreached, one great need in missions is a vast new cooperative effort, prioritized in accordance with God's mandate, in order to maximize resources and minimize field duplication.

In 1978, Theodore Williams, General Secretary of the Indian Evangelical Mission, said:

> "A significant development in the history of the church in our age is the rise of indigenous missionary movements in Asia, Africa, and Latin America. . . . The winds of change blowing across Asia, Africa, and Latin America and the wind of the Holy Spirit moving upon the church in these continents indicate we are in an exciting period of mission history. . . . Third World missions have just made a beginning."[16]

No longer is Nigeria just a country that receives missionaries; it is a missionary-sending country as well. Nor is Brazil only a nation that receives North American missionaries, but a nation that sends missionaries, even to North America. In 1972, there were at least 203 Third World missionary societies which were sending out an estimated 3,404 missionaries. By 1980 there were at least 368 Third World missionary societies sending out an estimated force of 13,000 missionaries. The beginning of a new dimension in missionary involvement has come. The focus of world evangelization is turning towards the Third World. Perhaps the reported explosive growth among Third World mission-sending agencies in the '70s is a sign for the '80s, indicating that the *hour* has arrived for substantial missionary partnership.

In Scripture, God informs us concerning the normalcy of these special and strategic periods of life. One example comes from II Corinthians 6:2, where the apostle Paul describes his evangelistic message and points to a period of decision for all his hearers. "Behold, now is the acceptable time, behold now is the day of salvation." The Greek word he uses for time is *kairos*, suggesting a definite situation in life which demands a verdict. This is a critical point in one's history where decisions must be made. This "decisive moment" for salvation is now, for there is no other "day."

Elsewhere in his epistles, Paul presents further *kairos* situations. He lists additional points in time which involve activities of great importance. Even Jesus in His evangelistic preaching pointed to a specific period of decision when He said, "The time is fulfilled, and the kingdom of God is at hand; repent and believe in the

---

[14]Lawrence E. Keyes, "The New Age of Missions: A Study of Third World Missionary Societies." Dissertation, School of World Mission, Fuller Theological Seminary, 1981. Used by permission.

[15]Lawrence E. Keyes is Field Leader for O.C. Ministries in Sao Paulo, Brazil. During the past nine years he has developed a national ministry of leadership training for church growth and is continuing research into Third World mission agencies.

[16]Theodore Williams, "Bombay Consultation Papers Released," *MNS Pulse 25* (June 15, 1978), p. 2.

gospel" (Mark 1:15). As revealed in Scripture, *kairos* is part of life. It is a special period of time which forces us to focus upon priorities and challenges us to make decisions.

THE "KAIROS" OF WORLD EVANGELIZATION

One of the most demanding *kairos-type* activities mentioned in the New Testament is the phase of world evangelization. Although the word *kairos* is not specifically used, Matthew 24:14 presents an equal situation in all its fullness, for there is a specially designated time period when decisions are made--decisions concerning both those who will be sent and those who will respond to the gospel. And when this period of world witness reaches its climax, ". . . then the end shall come."

As Christians, in light of this, our faithfulness to Christ's will stirs up an inner tension. For this special phase of human history now demands of us a personal verdict: "How are we going to be involved?" It also demands a sincere decision: "Am I contributing my best towards reaching the yet unreached peoples?"

Historically, many from Western-oriented countries have effectively reached out and witnessed to a myriad of subcultures. Yet for the West to continue reaching as many "new" peoples as before with the same ability is extremely doubtful. Ninety-six percent of Western missionary personnel, it is estimated, are found presently in perfecting ministries. Only four percent are involved primarily in pioneer or frontier missions.[17]

God has raised up at least 13,018 Third World missionaries, and they are reaching additional "unreached peoples." But difficulties for these Third World agencies likewise exist. Primary needs range from financial to technical, with few solutions in sight.

What would it be like if we could supply these needs? What would happen if half our missionary monies, internationally, were invested specifically in pioneer or frontier missions? How would the Great Commission be altered if several well-trained international teams were strategically placed in the areas ripe for harvest? Serious consideration needs to be given to these questions. An honest analysis of our *own* efforts merits consideration as we enter our *kairos*. And a solid inquiry concerning our cooperative spirit, even with other Third World agencies, is necessary.

1. What is a "kairos," and why does the author feel that we are currently facing one in world evangelization?

_____

_____

THE NEW AGE OF COOPERATION

Neither the West nor the Third World is equipped to reach the yet unreached 16,750 peoples by themselves. Modern missions is beginning to involve feet and faces of all colors. The West is noted for its mission history and surplus funds. The non-West is indispensable for its valuable mentality "from below" and increased vision. Together, with cooperative relationships, we can not only "give witness to the

[17]Ralph D. Winter, "Penetrating the Last Frontiers" (Pasadena, CA: U.S. Center for World Mission, 1978), graph.

resurrection of the Lord Jesus" (Acts 4:33), but also increase our effectiveness in world evangelization.

On the basis of my personal correspondence with Third World mission leaders, at least four areas stand out as strategic for international agency cooperation. They are *education*, *information*, *finances*, and *techniques*. Each demands equal participation from *both* Western and non-Western alike, and is based primarily upon purpose or task, rather than specific theologies or experience.

Educational Cooperation

One of the first strategic areas of international cooperation must be educational. This includes both advanced courses in missions for career workers and assistance in lay education for those who have pastoral influence, whether foreign missionary or national pastor.

One example of needed educational cooperation is found within the missionary's Bible school training. Stephen J. Akangbe, President of the Evangelical Churches of West Africa, begins by saying:

> National churches need more sound Biblical graduate and post-graduate institutions and the general level training to meet the need of everybody of this generation. Seminaries, Bible Colleges, Crash programs, Theological Education by Extension, leadership courses of evangelism, Seminars and management courses, workshop and Bible study conferences are all needed. These have their places in our national churches today, for effective witnessing of the Gospel.[18]

However, it is not just any kind of theological training that is referred to here. It is biblical education which graduates students successful in church planting. Relevant contextualized courses are needed which are marked by flexibility and commitment to world evangelism. Practical training must be given so that not only does one understand God's mandate and experience the "how," but also comprehends his own gifted area, and his God-designed position in light of the task. Many churches and missions in the Third World have developed their own training programs. But much more *could* be done with cooperation.

This cooperation can be either short or long term, in seminars or mission departments. It can assist in establishing new mission courses or help to glean material from other already existing courses (i.e., the Missionary Training Course at the Institut Indjil Indonesia, Batu, Malang, Indonesia). This cooperation can work through residency or extension centers, teaching in person or by tape, through translator or in translated publications. The variations are *many*. The thrust here is that hundreds of missionaries and perhaps more lay believers throughout the missionary world could benefit from additional missiological education. And it is important to recognize, according to the latest study, that part of this assistance *can* come from non-Western sources.

---

[18]Stephen J. Akangbe, "Three Major Ways That North American Mission Agencies Can Effectively Assist National Churches in the Evangelization of Their Countries." Paper presented at the 1973 EFMA/IFMA Study Conference, Overland Park, Kansas, November 27- 30, 1973, p. 2.

2. What kinds of cooperation are needed in the area of education? How does the author suggest that this education might differ from traditional theological training?

_____

_____

_____

_____

Informational Cooperation

A second strategic area of international cooperation involves providing important researched information to active missionary-sending agencies. Information such as new governmental openings, the location of as yet unreached peoples, newly discovered population trends and societal interests, available support ministries and church growth insight, etc., is a valuable contribution to any frontier endeavor. There are several specialized information-gathering groups which contribute such pertinent trend analysis to cross-cultural societies.

Unintentionally, many research centers find their analysis gaining only limited exposure, usually assisting those agencies who lie in the same region as the researching group. To this extent the extensive research is helpful and valuable. Yet there are hundreds of additional agencies, both in the Third and Western worlds which are located outside this limited region, who are also desirous of receiving new relevant information. Could not their studied insights assist them as well? Could not a loosely structured, international research network be established whereby, no matter where the agency is located or what denomination it represents, those interested could receive pertinent insights, helpful for making future assignments and policies? Research is too painstaking a science and too expensive an art to limit its results to just a region or geographical area. The new age of missions implies international cooperation with research information.

Furthermore, our *kairos* demands *new* researched areas. One example concerns tentmaking--those cross-cultural missionaries who earn their salary in the marketplace, while planting churches in evenings and on weekends. Because of the increasing financial difficulties in missionary support, many co-laborers are choosing this alternative method. Like the apostle Paul (Acts 18:1-3; I Thess. 2:9), they support themselves in the ministry.

Since all indications point to the continued interest in missionary tentmaking worldwide,[19] why could not these study and research centers assist in providing reliable "tentmaking information"? As with other subjects, many centers could divulge key potential jobs to agency headquarters, provide information concerning the most harvestable peoples within the host country, and compile lists of existing agencies so that the tentmaker could cooperate with one or more of them while working in the country. A few research centers are doing this. Others need to begin. This related information not only helps agencies organizationally, but spiritually could help stimulate many potential tentmakers towards missionary service. International cooperation in research is crucial.

---

[19]J. Christy Wilson, Jr., *Today's Tentmakers* (Wheaton, IL: Tyndale House Publishers, 1979), p. 17.

3. Why does the author feel that new cooperation is needed in the area of research and distribution of information?

_____

_____

Financial Cooperation

A third strategic area for international cooperation in world evangelization involves financial assistance. An average of 35 percent of Third World missionaries do *not* receive their promised full salary.

Part of this problem might be resolved if lessons from the past were studied seriously, discovering how "the Karens, the Koreans, those from Oceania were able to solve this problem when wealth was not as easy to obtain as it is today."[20]

Another part of this problem could be resolved if sound financial policies were instituted within certain Third World agencies. Samuel Kim, a Korean missionary who was in Thailand for over 17 years, gives a personal testimony concerning this reality:

> There is a Korean saying, "Cha-Muc-Ku-Ku," which means "counting the fingers." Modern missionary works cannot be carried out by rough finger counting but it must be precise and scientific.

> Since 1956, my wife and I were sent out . . . to Thailand. We have suffered and become victims of these rough calculating mentalities' abstract missionary maneuvering. Nothing is really specified, including missionary housing, work budget, medical cares, transportations, children's education, etc. But the General Secretary of the board always emphasized the saying that "the Lord provides everything, just pray for the needs." We also needed the Lord's power and needed to pray in our missionary works, but administrational practice and missionary functions are certainly more precise and scientific than prayer.

> I know these kinds of mentalities of rough finger counting sort of figuring is quite common throughout the Third World missions and organizations. We have to correct these out of date methods in order to avoid jeopardy or catastrophy of the Third World mission.[21]

A third way of partially resolving the problem of unpaid salaries and deficit project spending is if additional international financial cooperation was achieved. But to spend money freely without direction or purpose is financial malpractice. Therefore, guidelines must be established for the sake of biblical stewardship.

One guideline could be that of project accounts. Within the Third World, there is a debate over the viability of foreign monies paying national salaries. Good points are expressed by both sides. Perhaps the best general policy, in light of world nationalization and missionary indigenization, is to support special missionary

---

[20]Pablo Perez, "How Can North American Mission Agencies Effectively Cooperate With and Encourage Third World Mission Sending Agencies?" Paper presented at the 1973 EFMA/IFMA Study Conference, Overland Park, Kansas, November 27-30, 1973, p. 11.

[21]Samuel Kim, "Problems of the Third World Missionaries." Paper presented to C. Peter Wagner at the School of World Mission, Fuller Theological Seminary, May 17, 1973, p. 4.

projects but allow the national churches to pay personal salaries. The basic purpose for suggesting this, of course, is to avoid the depressing problem of foreign dependence. It is demeaning for many missionaries to know that their basic existence is being influenced and determined by foreigners, not by one's own friends and Christian family. It stifles spiritual growth among national believers for there is little "stretch," little faith involved when basic mission salaries are assured from the outside and not dependent from within. The national church must be responsible to support those whom they send as missionaries and to send out no more than they can adequately support.

At times, however, it is not easy to abide by this second principle of project support. For example, on February 18, 1980, a dear brother from The Christ Church Mission in Nigeria wrote me stating:

> Since 1971, when we erected our theological school, many evangelists, Pastors, and Christian workers have been trained and sent out to plant indigenous churches within 19 states of Nigeria. Some even went to serve in the Cameroons and Ghana. The Lord Jesus is using these workers to win many souls for Himself. Many of them are working to win Muslim believers in Northern Nigeria for Christ. . . . However, some of them have returned home before completing their work and signed contract, before completing their three years. The fact is clear that lack of funds in the ministry to support these workers does not allow them to stay in the field and do a successful service to the end.[22]

What do you do in a situation like this? If you had extra funds available, the immediate tendency would be to invest in this very worthy group and help pay salaries. After all, these national missionaries are planting churches, even evangelizing Muslims in a difficult cross-cultural experience. But what would such assistance eventually do to the indigeneity of the national church? To the spirituality of those believers whose responsibility is to pray for and help support their own missionaries? Would such cooperation enhance their self-image and produce greater Christian maturity? These are some of the difficult questions which must be answered before foreign *salary* support becomes credible. However, foreign funds applied towards special time-bounded projects can enhance our *kairos* task and complement national indigeneity, as missionary history reveals.

International cooperation in financial areas can become a significant supportive force in world evangelization. Instead of exercising control over recipients, funds are used with equals towards the accomplishment of one task: the making of disciples in all ethnic peoples. Instead of being a sign of power, money becomes a symbol of cooperative trust. Generosity is expressed because of function and goal, not tradition or denomination. And although such cooperative efforts are difficult, this radical departure from past patterns is needed. While maintaining a conservative theological stance, the need now is to become financially liberal, cooperating regularly with the many rapidly developing missionary agencies "from below."

4. What dangers does the author feel lie in providing mission salaries from foreign funds? What alternative does he suggest?

_____

_____

_____

[22]Personal letter by Rev. O. M. Akpan, February 18, 1980.

Technical Assistance

The fourth strategic area of international cooperation involves technical assistance. This implies ministry from many "support groups" such as Missionary Aviation Fellowship, Medical Assistance Programs, or Missionary Services, Inc. But it goes beyond this. Many of the larger "non-support groups" can render a form of technical aid by assisting in the formation of conferences, missionary consultations, or conventions. This is what occurred with the First All Asia Mission Consultation as the Korea International Mission provided time and technical support. David Cho, president of KIM, helped plan and promote the consultation.

Also, technical assistance includes loaning office personnel (treasurer, president, founder, etc.) to other agencies in need of ideas or functional models. CLAME (Community of Latin American Evangelical Ministries), the contextualized parent organization for Latin America Mission, has shared their key personnel several times whenever other missionary agencies desire input on agency nationalization. There are *many* ways missionaries can share with one another the diversity of talents and gifts that exist in Christ's body. Each part is a significant contributory function to the whole, without which the body suffers. Thus, in the new age of missions, increased technical assistance must be part of our cooperative stance.

5. What kinds of inter-agency technical assistance does the author suggest can be provided?

CONCLUSION

The world is a global village. Missions strategy must adapt to this trend. Edward C. Pentecost, professor of missions at Dallas Theological Seminary, writes:

> The period of internationalization of missions is a period into which we are stepping. The world is shrinking. The world is becoming a world where there is exchange in spite of nationalization. The recognition of internationalization. . . . Missions must move in this direction. Both sides, those from the North American agencies and those from the Third World must take steps to build relationships. Relationships that will be built in a spirit of cooperation and demonstration of confidence and mutual recognition.[23]

By successfully cooperating together in these four suggested areas, new endeavors will be established for world missions. One example of this might be new associational organizations, such as the international network for missionary research.

Another result of our international associative partnership might be the planting of *new missionary agencies.* Whether by encouraging an already known gifted visionary to form a new work (the historical pattern) or by sensing a need and planning an effort to meet that need (the systems pattern), with counsel and cooperation from many sources new pioneer movements can be established.

---

[23]Edward C. Pentecost, "How Can North American Mission Agencies Effectively Cooperate With and Encourage Third World Mission Sending Agencies?" Paper presented at the 1973 EFMA/IFMA Study Conference, Overland Park, Kansas, November 27-30, 1973, p. 5.

Cooperation will also produce freshly *restructured agencies* as Western and non-Western societies and churches join hands in missionary partnership. On June 25, 1965, for example, after 14 years of "wandering in the wilderness" and trying to discern how to identify with Asia's millions, the century-old China Inland Mission became Overseas Missionary Fellowship, with headquarters, activity, and personnel resident in Asia.[24]   Similarly Latin America Mission spawned CLAME (Community of Latin American Evangelical Ministries) with residency in Costa Rica, and the Sudan Interior Mission's African Missionary Society became part of the Association of Evangelical Churches of West Africa. Because Third World agencies often prefer non-Western structures, meaningful, long-term cooperation can produce valuable restructured societies.

Whatever develops, we must be wise and cautious concerning the duplication of efforts. Just as cooperative endeavors assist world evangelization, too many defeat biblical stewardship.

What do you visualize for the future? What do you foresee as the task of world evangelization grows and becomes more mature? With a sizable missionary force both in the Third World and in the West, with needs and difficulties faced on both sides, with both parts of the one body under the same commander and involved in the same decision-making *kairos*, the new age of missions must be one of task-oriented cooperation. Both the Western and non-Western agencies are experienced in mission. Both are maturing and interested in preaching the Gospel of the Kingdom to the whole world. Both desire to be an effective witness to *all the nations* (peoples) before God's appointed end comes (Matt. 24:14). Therefore, let us join friendly hands and purpose in our hearts that everyone may hear before He returns. Let us accept each other as equals and cooperate together as partners. It is foolishness to think we can do the job alone. As the apostle Paul exhorts the Romans to "be devoted to one another in brotherly love" and to "give preference to one another in honor" (Rom. 12:10), so we must be exhorted to do the same in missions. By accepting God's Word as our authoritative guide, by depending upon the Holy Spirit as our energizing dynamic, and by joining hands internationally as partners, we *can* effectively disciple the nations before He returns.

6. What are your own conclusions about the article?

_____

_____

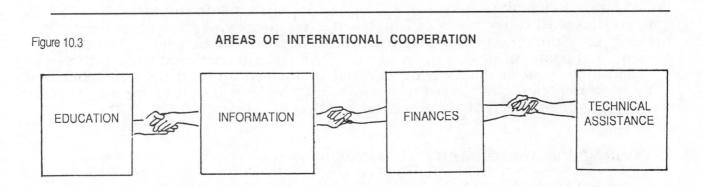

Figure 10.3   AREAS OF INTERNATIONAL COOPERATION

EDUCATION — INFORMATION — FINANCES — TECHNICAL ASSISTANCE

---

[24]Arthur F. Glasser, "The New Overseas Missionary Fellowship." Paper presented at the 1965 EFMA Retreat, Winona Lake, Indiana, October 4-7, 1965, p. 15.

International cooperation will change the way we approach the missionary task. A marked predominance of Western missions has characterized the past. It is easy to assume that this trend will continue. But since the preceding article was written, thousands of new missionaries from the young churches of the developing nations have entered the field. We must recognize what God is doing and strengthen each other's hands in the task.

Several mission agencies have taken bold initiatives towards becoming international. Others are just beginning to approach the idea. It is time for all established agencies to seek ways to foster true cooperation in the completion of Christ's Great Commission. With at least four channels of international cooperation open to us, there is no lack of opportunities.

SUMMARY

World Christian teamwork begins with a vision, a vision in which Christ rules as Lord over every nation. If a Christian captures the vision, and the vision in turn captures him, he becomes a world Christian, one who centers his life around Christ and His global cause. This commitment will have a significant effect on his lifestyle and priorities. He will no longer be satisfied with self-seeking goals. He will want his life to count towards completion of the task.

World Christians cannot thrive in isolation. They need each other for support, for sharing information, and for planning together. These activities are essential if they are to nurture the vision and allow their commitment to grow. Through world Christian cell groups, senders can team up in local congregations and fellowships. Such cell groups can also be the matrix for the formation of mission teams sent through mission agencies, through the congregation itself, or through intentional communities.

We can no longer plan missions without seriously considering active cooperation with other parts of Christ's universal body. A time of decision-making, or *kairos*, has been reached in international cooperation. Various channels of cooperation are open to us. Through international associative partnerships, new mission agencies must be formed and old ones restructured. Only as we cooperatively fan the worldwide flame of mission commitment, can we hope to see the Great Commission fulfilled in our time.

INTEGRATIVE ASSIGNMENT

1. Look again at David Bryant's three steps to becoming a world Christian. Use these three steps as your major points in outlining a short talk entitled, *Becoming a World Christian*. Support each point with Scripture.

2. Plan your first world Christian cell group meeting. List your activities and the approximate time you would give to each.

3. With which mission agency are you best acquainted? Write them a letter asking what they are doing to foster international cooperation in the equipping and sending of cross-cultural missionaries.

QUESTIONS FOR REFLECTION

Love and obedience are the two keys to discipleship. Love is the motivational factor. Obedience is the way we express love. Christ said, "If you love me, keep my commandments" (John 14:15). And what is the commandment we are to obey? John 13-15 makes it clear. Read these chapters, meditating on John 13:34-35 in particular. What implications do these verses have for the missionary task? Record your thoughts in your journal.